D1094501

MONEY

MONEY

Dian Cohen

Prentice-Hall Canada Inc., Scarborough, Ontario

Canadian Cataloguing in Publication Data

Cohen, Dian
Money

Includes index.
ISBN 0–13–599820–4 (bound) ISBN 0–13–599804–2 (pbk.)

1. Finance, Personal. I. Title.

HG179.C63 1987 332.024 C87–094063–5

Prentice-Hall Inc., Englewood Cliffs, *New Jersey*
Prentice-Hall International, Inc., *London*
Prentice-Hall of Australia, Pty., *Sydney*
Prentice-Hall of India Pvt., Ltd., *New Delhi*
Prentice-Hall of Japan, Inc., *Tokyo*
Prentice-Hall of Southeast Asia (Pte.) Ltd., *Singapore*
Editora Prentice-Hall do Brasil Ltda., *Rio de Janeiro*
Prentice-Hall Hispanoamericana, S.A., *Mexico*

Production Editor: Sharyn Rosart
Design: Cedric Hefkie
Manufacturing Buyer: Don Blair
Cover Design: Falcom Design and Communications
Composition: Q Composition Inc.

ISBN: 0–13–599820–4

Printed and bound in Canada by Gagné Printing Ltd.

1 2 3 4 5 G 91 90 89 88 87

To my mother and the memory of my father.

Contents

PART III

INVESTMENT STRATEGIES THROUGH THE TURBULENT NINETIES

Introduction

We are living through a transition. The very shape of the economy is changing. The description of who works and how we make our livings is different now from what it was twenty years ago. In another twenty years, it will be different still. That is the basic assumption underpinning this book. It has already become clear to some of us, and I think it will become increasingly clear in the next few years, that the 1950s, 1960s and early 1970s formed part of the golden age of our economic history.

But it is now history. The next few years, I believe, will continue to be unpredictable. We will need to muster all our financial skills to take advantage of opportunities as they arise, and to sidestep the potholes along the way. The pupose of this book is to tell you why, and how.

Eventually, whether two, ten, or fifteen years from now, this transition period will end. If you start now to understand what is happening to the economy and to our financial institutions, to our jobs and our lives, you are going to be in better financial shape than most other Canadians. Change is the name of the game. Your attitude to change will determine whether you make it financially or not.

The book is laid out fairly logically. Part 1, *Understanding Personal Money Mangement*, outlines where we've been economically, and how changes in the financial and economic environment affect the way we think about and deploy our financial resources.

Part 2, *Your Personal Money Management Strategy*, looks at the things we need to know about ourselves and about the financial world in order to make it easier to be flexible and adaptable in these volatile times.

Part 3, *Investment Strategies Through the Turbulent Nineties*, gets down to the nitty-gritty of investing—finally. The rationale for making you wade through half the book first is that all investing takes place in an environment, (Part 1) and within a framework, (Part 2) and isn't logical without both. So you need to understand something about the economic world around you, and you have to set up a personal financial framework before you get into the mechanics of investing.

IF I'M SO SMART, AM I RICH, TOO?

I have always wondered why people who write books about personal money management do it. I mean, you don't make fortunes out of books—at least not in Canada. So the question is, if they're so smart, are they rich enough to sit back on their assets?

I'll tell you straight out: I've made and spent a fortune. And that's really the point: I've made and spent it, and have had fun doing it, and am still here making and spending it.

Some of us want to make money more than others. I'm one of the ones who believes money can buy happiness. Let me tell you a little more about myself—without photocopying the net worth statement I send to my banker. I have a house (with a mortgage). And a country house. I take vacations from time to time. I have a few stocks, bonds, and pieces of gold. (I believe that the national symbol of the shrewd investor is the hedge.) I can afford my disability insurance premiums, so if I get sick, at least some income will be coming in. And I carry life insurance because I still have dependent children.

The financial situation I'm describing is pretty comfortable and not too worrisome. For me, that's what smart money management is all about. And that's what this book is all about.

Dian Cohen,
August, 1987

Acknowledgements

So many people contributed to the process of completing this book that a page could not possibly cover all of them.

My children, Lisa, Nina and Tamara, only rolled their eyes occasionally, and filled in often, over the years when I said I was too busy to do chores. My friends, including Max Cohen and Stephen Phizicky, never lost the faith that I would finish (although my publisher was sometimes driven to despair).

Many good souls battled mightily to keep the book on track: Chantal Boucher, Lisa Cohen, Pam Fry, Ann Gibbon, Hélène Lefebvre, Lorri Mackay, Gaby Paliotti, Walter Pike and Jan Whitford, to name a few. Iris Skeoch and Sharyn Rosart demonstrated tasteful browbeating and quiet persistence in rescheduling each time I didn't meet the deadline. Lorri Mackay worked above and beyond all reason to make sure the manuscript made sense.

I owe a debt of gratitude to CTV and Canada AM for exposing me to millions of viewers, many hundreds of whom have written to me to further my education and help me understand their needs. Eventually, I always write back.

I owe a special debt to my business partner, Pauline Couture. Not only did she put in many weekends finishing what hadn't been done by Friday afternoon, she did it with stunning good humour.

Responsibility for any errors or omissions is mine.

Part 1

Understanding Personal Money Management

CHAPTER 1

The Marquess of Queensberry is Dead

The only person who likes change is a wet baby.

—Roy Z.M. Blitzer

When you think about Canada, what pops into your head?

Waving fields of grain, mountains of yellow sulphur, huge fishing trawlers, giant toppling firs, the lunar landscape of the Northern mining towns . . . all the things that spell resource-rich, twentieth-century-belongs-to-us Canada.

But now, as we head into the 1990s, grain prices have collapsed. There are many new sulphur producing countries with cheaper labour costs. Fishing is still a way of life, but it's still not a living. Acid rain and American protectionism are decimating our forestry industry. The mining towns are struggling to continue existing.

In 1987, the fifth year of economic recovery after the severe recession of 1982, we have not yet returned to 1981 employment levels. Central Canada has mini-booms in certain manufacturing and service industries, but their prosperity sheds no warmth on the Prairies, or on the Atlantic provinces.

Canadians have spent the last few years with the growing discomfort of realizing that Sir Wilfrid Laurier's promise that this was to be *our* century didn't come off quite the way we expected it. In fact, Canada was incredibly rich during the quarter-century that spanned 1950–1975. It was the golden age of economic growth and development in this country, but we didn't appreciate it at the time.

One way of getting a perspective on where the world is headed and our place in the global economy of the twenty-first century is to look at how we got to where we are now. Several years ago, I co-wrote a book entitled *The Next Canadian Economy* in which we explored change—change in economic relationships, change in our perceptions of how things are done, change in our values and in our attitudes. I happily refer you to that text. A crucial component in developing a successful personal financial strategy is an understanding of how much we expect from the economy and from our governments.

The people who struggled through the Great Depression of the 1930s without the benefit of the social safety net we now have in place were marked forever by those times. For them, having a job and some kind of financial security in life were basic goals. They believed in staying out of debt, the work ethic, getting a good education. Their suffering made them determined to offer a better life to their children. And they did, as the Second World War turned Canada into a full-fledged industrial economy, and the global demand for our natural resource wealth allowed us to do very well for ourselves, while doing good for others.

The people who were born after World War II, the Baby Boomers, are the single most important demographic group of the century. Their outlook on life was shaped by the extraordinary prosperity and the steady growth of the period right up to the 1970s. That environment, so different from the pre-war era, led them to take security for granted. Most of our current leaders are members of this generation. Their basic assumptions and frames of reference are the product of prosperity.

Our potential for prosperity seemed endlessly promising during the Sixties. Being Canadian was the best stroke of luck a person could have at birth, or choose to aspire to as an immigrant. Although Canada has always been a trading nation, our focus on the world was an internal one—we had goods the world wanted. They came to us and that made us rich. We lived in a stable and prosperous country at a time when much of the rest of the world was awash in economic and political turmoil. It did not enter our collective consciousness that things might someday be otherwise.

The prospect of guaranteed growth moulded behaviour patterns and expectations. We could look forward to increasing incomes. We could expect to be better housed, better clothed, better fed. We could anticipate vastly improved health care services for our families. We would even have money to waste on some of the luxuries and frivolities which add spice to the getting-and-spending routine of living.

Most of the people who are now in charge of our industries, unions, educational institutions, civil service and political parties grew up during this era. From a human point of view, it's not hard to understand how seductive this vision of the world was. It provided room for everyone to dream that whatever the problem, it could and would be resolved because we could afford to throw money at it. It never taught any of us how to make tough decisions for it appeared that there were no decisions to make.

When the Club of Rome said in *Limits to Growth* that we could run out of resources and the system could collapse; when the OPEC countries quadrupled oil prices; when the Americans stopped exchanging their dollars for gold, as they had for the previous forty years, Canada decided on a go-it-alone policy. Our policy-makers assumed that we could just cut ourselves off from the inflation and recession that was rocking the rest of the world. The notion of interdependence was a heresy to people who had been told that we had a 200-year supply of energy.

Governments had to spend more and more to enable us to keep up the habits we'd acquired: subsidizing oil prices, large industrial developments, agriculture, movies and massive social programmes. Their share of Canada's Gross National Product went from thirty percent in the mid-Sixties to forty-one percent in the mid-Seventies, but they still had to borrow heavily to meet their commitments.

In some ways, Canadians continued to be shielded from harsh reality by the spectacularly high prices of our resources. Wage settlements were generous, because nobody wanted to risk stopping such profitable production in the overheated international competition. In the two-year period following the OPEC shock, the U.S. led the world out of recession, but Canada's inflation rate shot up, and the Canadian dollar went into free fall.

Although shielded from the worst of the mid-Seventies recession, we learned a new word along with the rest of the world in the recovery leading up to 1979. It was "stagflation"—a condition in which unemployment and unused production capacity increase, but inflation doesn't go down. The textbooks said it couldn't happen, and no one seemed to know how to deal with it.

Fighting inflation fueled unemployment, and vice versa. All the clichés went out the window. The supposedly primitive Arab and Third World societies started buying sophisticated power and communications systems, building fancy new plants and competing with us on our own turf. They could use our technology more cheaply and more efficiently than we could. Their people were willing to work for a great deal less. Their need for foreign exchange was so great that to get it they were often willing to dump products for prices below their own costs.

The recession that began in 1981 really took us by surprise. The Canadian economy was hit harder than any other industrialized economy, yet our inflation rate has been the slowest to come down. Now, in the sixth year of this so-called economic recovery, it is much easier to see some of the changes that have been coming for a generation; changes that involve our presumptions of how the world works.

The natural resource-based regions of the country are in a depression. The big business sector that was the focal point for job creation is no longer creating all the jobs. In fact, small business is creating virtually 100% of all net new jobs. Unions are fighting for their own survival at the same time as they continue to try for higher wages and fringe benefits for their members. Deregulation, reregulation, integration and interdependence are new concepts developed for a different economic environment.

The young people who are now entering the labour force are part of a new phenomenon—jobless growth. They understand very well that they can't assume that skills learned in their early twenties will guarantee them lifetime careers. They know they can't take security for granted. But their environment is shaped by the earlier generation of people who are just beginning to question these assumptions.

Yet another aspect of the structural changes we have been undergoing bears watching: our inability to resolve the international debt situation. Canadian banks, while significant players with a substantial stake in Third World loans that will likely never be repaid, are only a small part of the picture. Canadians are footing the bill for these non-productive loans both as shareholders of the banks, which are less profitable as they write down the loans, and as customers who are faced with higher fees as a direct result.

The bigger picture, however, is more disturbing than the domestic one, which is basically under control. As the United States has become the world's largest debtor, with Japan holding much of the outstanding debt in U.S. dollars, the dynamics of the world money markets have changed. Trade patterns are also changing, as countries move to protect their own markets and interests. The tumultuous Canada-U.S. free trade discussions in the climate of growing American protectionism have been one example of the prickly new rules of the game.

There has been a break in the continuity of how we view the world, and indeed, in how the world works. Understanding the nature of that discontinuity will show us the changes we need to make in our personal strategies for financial survival.

FINDING THE NEW RIGHT WAY

Maybe the hardest thing for most of us to grasp is that behaviour which was proper and rewarding in the past may no longer be appropriate . . . that in fact, doing things the old right way may actually penalize us in the future.

For more than four decades, Canadians have expected that their real incomes would continue to rise. As we have just seen, foreigners and Canadians alike were anxious to invest here. We had a relatively educated work force that was increasingly productive; we had lots of natural resources that commanded high and rising prices. To add to our good fortune, the external environment was benign: the U.S. economy was the engine of growth—Canada had desirable products, a productive work force, and an enviable relationship with the Americans.

While there have always been regional disparities in Canada, as any citizen of Cape Breton will tell you, there has also always been hope that the situation was improving. The resource bust of the 1980s has convinced many Canadians that unless they can diversify their regional economies much faster, they are doomed to constitute "another Canada," where unemployment rates never go down very much, and where young people have no future.

Before we go any further, let us be clear about what four decades of economic growth have meant. They have allowed us to share economic benefits across the disparate regions of the country through equalization: if one region received less, the others would chip in to ensure that the material benefits of being Canadian were more or less the same wherever you lived.

That principle of equalization applied to more than just the regions: it applied to social groups as well. Our highly developed social safety net of medicare, hospitalization, unemployment insurance, social assistance, minimum wages, and so on exists because for more than four decades our real income per person was rising. We agreed that governments should redistribute some of that income so that all Canadians would have a minimum standard of living.

Canadians can no longer take for granted that our incomes will continue to rise. Productivity growth is flagging, equalizing services across the country and among social groups is getting harder to do, and the external environment is no longer looking very friendly. Whether Canada has assured access to the American market or not, the American economy is still in serious trouble. Industry in the U.S.A. is undergoing a massive shakeout and restructuring because it has been unable to compete effectively for the past few years. American industry is getting lean and mean. Canadian industry has been restructuring too, but at nowhere near the same pace. If we can't compete with the Americans, and they can't compete with other countries, how can we expect to continue to be rich?

Canadians have benefitted enormously since the mid 1960s from free trade in automobiles with the Americans. But the U.S. auto industry is sick—American Motors has been absorbed by Chrysler, and Honda is the fourth largest manufacturer in the U.S. There may be an overcapacity in the global industry in the next decade of as many as 20 million cars.

The North American economies are increasingly service-oriented. More than two-thirds of us make our livings not by producing things, but by performing services. The United States, our traditional market for just about everything, no longer needs as much of all the good stuff that made us rich in the Fifties, Sixties and Seventies. And even in the service sector, the United States is being challenged as the engine of world economic growth. Two decades ago, nine of the top ten banks in the world were American; today, seven of the top ten are Japanese.

There is a steadily increasing world surplus of many of the agricultural commodities Canadians are most efficient at producing. Demand for our natural resources is falling as new sources of supply emerge, and as synthetic products displace natural resources in the manufacturing process. Manufacturing industries themselves are increasingly globalized, and traditional manufacturing activities are shifting to low wage countries or, if they remain here, automating and cutting jobs.

In view of all this, it does not seem like an overstatement to say that if we try to do what we did when we lived in the last economy, we are in for trouble. I said a little earlier that one of the things that had made Canadians pretty well off for four decades was our relatively highly educated work force. How well-positioned are we to compete internationally in an increasingly service-oriented economy? Here's what a recent Economic Council report said:

> We are lagging in the introduction of new technologies. Ultimately, therefore, the gains bought by technological change will be enjoyed outside our borders. This means that industrial adjustment will still take place in Canada, but it will be in response to failure, not to success.

> Consequently, the adjustment task will be made more difficult because it will be based on a dwindling supply of resources that could be used to ease the adjustment process. It is therefore vital that there be a national commitment to technological change.

That commitment has been a long time coming. One of the features of the information age is that the basis of wealth is different from what it was in the industrial age. In the industrial age, physical resources were the source of wealth; in the information age, intellectual resources are the source of wealth. There is a real question about whether we understand the importance of building and exploiting human capital.

Canadians will have to reconsider their approaches to many things. Attitudes that stood us in good stead in the past will almost certainly have to be re-examined in the new economy. Let's look at a couple of personal financial strategies that worked well in the Sixties and Seventies, but were disastrous in the Eighties.

SMART INFLATION-CONDITIONED BEHAVIOUR

In the years when the Consumer Price Index was rising faster than you could earn money, it paid to borrow to the hilt, buy anything immediately and repay the loan in cheaper dollars. Consumers, farmers and bankers who did this early in the game were winners. However, if they continued with this strategy after inflation turned to disinflation, they were in deep trouble.

In the mid-Seventies, the farming community borrowed millions to expand its operations because the Club of Rome predicted a world food shortage. Government policies had made it easy to do this, and farmers understandably assumed that food prices would keep on rising, and that their costs would be covered. It came as quite a shock when commodity prices collapsed, interest rates shot up, and they were left holding the bag with everything to lose.

In Canada, tax reform had left principal residences as the greatest tax-free investments for most individuals. Canadian house prices quadrupled between 1972 and 1976, fed by the tax exemption of an owner-occupied house, and by eight-percent-a-year inflation, which made a house a risk-free investment. Tell that to the folks who dropped their house keys on the banker's desk in Calgary in 1985 or 1986, and walked away from years of hard work with nothing to show for it. Or tell it to the bankers who are still stuck will all those unsaleable houses with bank capital tied up in them.

Alberta is a prime example of what can happen when we forget about contingencies. The oil boom, which brought long-awaited prosperity to the Prairies, was treated as though it was a sure thing with no end in sight. People staked career decisions, investments, family moves and house prices on it. And when, as was bound to happen in a cyclical industry some day or other, the boom went bust, a lot of people found themselves with aching tailbones.

What happened to Albertans is understandable. The upside is that since the industry is cyclical, there will be other booms eventually. The trick is not to get caught with your pants down.

Blind confidence in the system has done many Canadians a great disservice. Take Registered Retirement Savings Plans (RRSPs), which have been available as tax-sheltered retirement savings plans for Canadians since 1957. Very few people took advantage of RRSPs until the latter part of the 1970s. Why? Because we believed our salaries would continue to go up every year, everybody would have a pension plan at work, all of us would have jobs, and if worse came to worst, the state would step in and take care of us.

That changed in the late Seventies. The realization began to dawn on many people that nobody else was going to look after them. Faced with the potential prospect of choosing among brands of pet food, some Canadians started to contribute to RRSPs for the first time.

A FRAMEWORK FOR YOUR PERSONAL MONEY MANAGEMENT STRATEGY

If you're happy with what you're making and how you're spending it, and if you have a written guarantee that your financial life will remain uneventful, there is no point in going to all the trouble of learning about money management. It's a hassle to get your financial house in order.

But let me ask you a few questions. How much money have you made in the last five years? The average industrial earner in Canada has made more than $100,000. How much have you saved? If Canada's average worker had saved as little as five percent of his or her income over the past five years, and had invested it at the going rates of interest, that person would today have something in excess of $25,000. How much do you have?

The average Canadian can expect to earn in excess of a million dollars in his or her working lifetime (except if he or she is an average Canadian who didn't manage to get and keep a job).

The average Canadian can also expect to live 15 to 20 years beyond his or her working lifetime. How much will you have saved? Whose money will support you in retirement in the style to which you have become accustomed during your working years? Who's going to pay for your summer vacation? Can you afford your children's education? Can you afford your children, period? Do you want more control over your financial life?

The starting point for becoming a smart money manager is to understand clearly that nobody cares about you, or your education, or your money as much as you do. All your advisors want to help. Your insurance agent really wants you to have the insurance he or she recommends. Your stockbroker's recommendations are absolutely sincere. Your real estate agent does have just the house for you. All the banks and trust companies which advertise their Registered Retirement Savings Plans each year may very well believe their plan is the best on the market. The Canadian government has faith in Canada Savings Bonds.

But does your insurance agent tell you whole life insurance costs two or three times more than term? Is it clear what the difference is? Do you know that his or her commission—income—is higher if you buy one kind of insurance and not another? Do you care?

Does your real estate agent tell you that a $50,000 mortgage at even ten percent interest rates will cost you $180,000 to repay? Did you know? Do you care?

Do you know that RRSPs are just empty boxes into which you put different kinds of investments? Do you know that some plans earn six, seven, ten times more than other plans? And that that can mean the difference between getting $200 or $1200 a month in your retirement years?

Did you know that an investment in Canada Savings Bonds has, for eight of the last ten years, been a guaranteed loss of purchasing power?

It's not that anyone is lying to you. It's just that no one but you is going to make a real effort to figure out what's best for you. People who sell insurance and stocks and retirement plans and government bonds do so because it's good for them. It may be good for you. And if it is, the seller will be even happier. But the seller's primary goal is to convince you that it's good for you. Whether it is or not is for you to decide.

You need half a dozen things to be a smart money manager. First, you need some facts: you need to know where you are now, that is, what your present financial status is, in order to determine how satisfied you are with how you make, spend and save your money.

Second, you need to know where you're going: you need a definite financial plan with specific objectives.

Third, you need some financial skills—how to figure interest, how to evaluate investment options. Basically, what to do with your money to achieve your objectives.

Fourth, you need to know the tax system so you can make it work for you.

Fifth, you need to know something about political economy and politicians, so you can decide for yourself how the state of the economy and the deficits of governments may affect your earning capacity and your investments.

Sixth, you need to start now: time is the most valuable asset you have, and making decisions gets easier the more you practice.

WHERE ARE YOU NOW?

Not long ago, I listened to a hotline show on which the question of the day was: "What's wrong with our schools?" One caller's opinion was that schools didn't prepare children for meeting the financial challenges of the real world. The host's response was: "Well, is that really the purpose of schools? Isn't school really to educate us?"

We are a nation of financial morons. Our inability to gather financial information and make informed financial decisions is one reason so many people can get rich writing books about how to get rich. Nobody can teach you how to get rich. Nobody can make decisions for you. But you can learn how to gather information, evaluate it, and come to an informed decision. The way to start the process is to take a financial inventory to find out where you are now. Without this knowledge you have no benchmarks against which to measure.

Take this test:	Hardly at all	Not Often	Often	Very Often	Most of the time
1. How often do you think you'd like to manage your money better?	______	______	______	______	______

2. Do you have concrete goals for:	Yes	No
a) Spending	________	________
b) Savings	________	________
c) Accumulated wealth	________	________

If you said "no" to a, b, and c, skip over to Question 5. Otherwise, carry on with Question 3.

	Very Realistic	Realistic	Not Realistic
3. How realistic do you think your goals are for:			
a) Spending	______	______	______
b) Savings	______	______	______
c) Accumulated wealth	______	______	______

	Reached Few Goals	Reached Some Goals	Reached Most Goals
4. In the last few years, how successful have you been in reaching your goals?			
a) Spending	______	______	______
b) Savings	______	______	______
c) Accumulated wealth	______	______	______

5. Are your bills and receipts organized? Yes ______ No ______

	Yes	No	Aren't Organized
6. If you sat down with your financial records, could you quickly say how well you're doing in your:			
a) Spending	______	______	______
b) Savings	______	______	______
c) Accumulated wealth	______	______	______

	Every 12 Months	Every 6 Months	Don't have a budget
7. How often do you review your budget?	______	______	______

	Yes	No
8. Have you thought about what obstacles keep you from achieving your financial goals or improving your financial situation?	______	______

	Yes	No
9. Do you know what specific financial knowledge or skills you need regarding your:		
a) Spending	______	______
b) Savings	______	______
c) Accumulated wealth	______	______

	Yes	No
10. Do you reward yourself when you achieve one of your financial goals?	______	______

The purpose of this test is to help you analyze your present financial situation. It should help you establish your attitudes towards your own money management. Not only do you need goals, you need realistic or achievable goals. Not only do you need achievable goals, you need a certain amount of organization. If you want to manage your money better, if you want a financial plan with achievable goals but don't have one, you have to start thinking about it. Money means a lot of different things to people. For some it's love, or sex, or power. I'm not writing a psychology text here. But if you feel a great need for financial management improvement—if you don't have specific goals, or if you have them but haven't been successful in achieving them—then you have to consider that something is standing between you and your financial objectives. I can't tell you what that might be, but I can introduce you to a few ideas that might help you figure it out.

Part 2

Your Personal Money Management Strategy

CHAPTER 2

Priorities, Goals and Decision-Making Techniques: Getting Your Head Together

> The winds and the waves are always on the side of the ablest navigator.
>
> —Edward Gibbon

How much do you know about yourself, how you make decisions and where you are financially? That's really the starting point. Before you can make any kind of money management plan, you have to be honest with yourself.

There's no point in starting a six-month diet of salads and mineral water if your willpower collapses the first time a waiter waves a steak under your nose. It's the same with effective money management. Making radical resolutions is a sure recipe for failure. When you fall off the wagon, you feel worse about yourself than you did in the first place.

The first ingredient for good money management is knowledge of what makes you tick as a consumer. No matter where you are in your financial planning, you're making choices every day. Unless you're T. Boone Pickens (in which case, why are you reading this book?) you quite simply can't afford to buy everything you want to have.

Sometimes we are unreasonable. Many of us, for example, will spend days pondering brochures and comparing performance charts before we buy a car, but will buy a house because we fell in love with the little round window in the stairwell.

The truth is that managing money means knowing exactly where we stand, and having a strategy. It certainly means being wise consumers when we make big purchases. It also means being selective and having the right priorities, so that eventually, we don't have to squeeze and shave on little things.

If your financial situation is a mess, you may have to face a period of doing without things you want in order to reach your goals. You'll find it very hard to do this if you haven't set goals to keep you on the straight and narrow, and if you can't celebrate having achieved something every so often.

This process involves investing some time, which will pay off in financial control.

Get your priorities straight first. It can take years to undo the consequences of a hasty or impulsive wrong decision. Remember that up to the moment when you've handed over your cash or your plastic, you're dealing from a position of strength. At that moment, you assume the onus of proving that you haven't been given value for your money.

WILL THAT BE THE BLUE OR THE YELLOW?

All of us start with our basic needs: food, clothing and shelter. But none of us is exactly alike. We choose to satisfy our basic needs in different and individual ways. We reconcile our wants with our needs based on a framework of values, means and knowledge that we acquire from childhood on and rarely think twice about.

In our economic system, satisfying even basic needs demands a certain amount of money. True, we have a collective social contract that says no one should be allowed to die of starvation or exposure. However, this guarantees bare survival at best. Only money creates an effective demand in the marketplace.

Most of us could spend more than our paycheques in no time flat sitting at home with a mail-order catalogue or home-shopping on TV. It's amazing, really, that most of us do have enough self-discipline to resist all the siren songs of the dream merchants. We're able to resist, to some extent, because we know we have to make choices. It's not always easy to make safe, practical choices.

Sometimes, even a thoughtful choice turns out to be the wrong one, not because of the item itself, but because of the way the selection was made. For example, you may decide your family's health would benefit if they joined a health club. You may pay for a yearly membership in advance, only to find after a few visits that you're encountering more and more resistance—the life of a couch potato is more attractive than the rippling muscles of the gym floor. While you may be absolutely right about the family's need to exercise and the attractiveness of the health club, what was the point in paying for the membership if your relatives just won't go?

Getting the views of those who will be affected by the choice, and agreeing on the particulars of the choice usually leads to better decision-making. The bigger the purchase, the more this is worth remembering. Don't spring an expensive piece of equipment on a family member who hasn't been consulted in advance. You'll regret it.

WHAT'S IMPORTANT TO YOU?

We learn what's important to us throughout our lives—as children from our parents, from our friends, at school, at church or synagogue, through personal experience. These experiences become determining factors in your spending decisions. Think about it. Why do you prefer one brand over another? Why do you have a cast-iron belief that one dry cleaner gives better service than another? Why do you prefer to put your money in Canada Savings Bonds rather than buy stock?

Let me introduce you to the teenage son of a friend. The boy really wanted money to buy a particular kind of denim jacket. His father said the request was unreasonable because the son had already received a substantial contribution to his wardrobe that year. In desperation, the son pleaded, "But Dad, I have to have it! It's what all the non-conformists are wearing this year!"

If you can identify with this anecdote, give some thought to your own reactions to external pressures. Do you have to keep up with your neighbours' entertaining? Are you, like the kid who thinks of himself as a non-conformist, deluding yourself about your own attitudes?

This kind of knowledge and understanding is a self-conscious process. For a while, you may have to make an effort to think about how your friends' attitudes and actions affect your own behaviour. You'll have to think consciously about your reaction to advertising. Do you identify with strong, masculine images?

Do you see yourself as a beautiful person when you drink a certain brand of beer? Are you the type of person who prefers to melt into the background? Do you think of yourself as a loner?

These are the kinds of things that advertisers target. Having a sharp mental picture of your reactions will help you understand whether you're on automatic pilot, or whether you're thinking on your feet.

An advertising specialist told me once that he had held a beer account for which no advertising was allowed. Why? Because the drinkers of that particular brand fancied themselves as marginal, Marxists, and rebels. Any ad in a mainstream publication or on television would have made them feel betrayed. Don't ask.

"BUT I'VE ALWAYS USED MY PHONE BILLS AS BOOKMARKS . . ."

The pigeons always come home to roost. Even if you carry the maximum load of plastic, someday the bills come in and have to be paid. There are limits to how much you can actually spend. The amount of money you have at your disposal has a major influence on your spending decisions. The more money you have, the more money you're likely to spend. Good money management can bring you much closer to your "wish list" and beyond just meeting your needs. No matter how much money you have, your spending decisions will also be influenced by how knowledgeable you are about the decision-making process, and how the marketplace works.

Achieving our goals requires planning. And to do that, we have to set priorities. Each of us has personal priorities and, if we live with others, we have family priorities as well. For many people, effective money management is a financial priority. Here's how to develop a list of financial priorities.

First, list the things *you* want. You don't have to list them in order; that will come after you've made the list. The things you list can be short term (going out to dinner once a month) or long term (saving to buy a house); they can be financial goals (being able to afford your children's education); or material possessions (a colour TV).

You may find it helpful to let every member of the family complete a priorities list. It's not unusual to find that members of your family have different financial priorities. I've included a "Wish List" worksheet to help you establish the family priorities.

WISH LIST

Item	*Have to have it*	*It would be nice*	*A dream come true*

Instructions for Use

Give one to each member of the family. Write down the items in any order. Then label them necessary, desirable or luxury items. If family members are shy, encourage them with such suggestions as owning a home or a car, taking a vacation, having a computer or a bicycle, seeing a movie once a week, and so on.

After you have gone through this exercise, you'll be in a better position to make a single, common priorities list for each person's individual efforts. Schedule a family meeting to discuss the results of your efforts. If you think that sounds corny, remember that money (lack of it, actually) is one of the foremost causes of family stress and strain. Misunderstandings often stem from lack of communication. Make sure everyone is on the same wavelength, and working towards the same goals.

DO WE WANT A BMW OR EDUCATED KIDS?

Would a million dollars solve all your financial problems? Chances are your answer is yes. Yet the fact is that the average Canadian earns a million dollars over his or her working life. And most of those Canadians, whether they make $20,000 or $100,000 a year, will tell you that all that stands between them and their financial goals is just a few extra bucks. In fact, what stands between most of us and our financial goals is planning and organization.

Your lifestyle depends entirely on your priorities and your values. You and your family are the only ones who can decide what you all need at any given time. And once you've decided your priorities, you'll have to plan how to achieve them. Unless you have unlimited resources, you're part of the world of economics where you have to make choices. You'll probably have to give up things you want very much in order to afford those things you want just a little bit more.

If it's of prime importance to you and your family to live in a certain neighbourhood, you may have to cut down on savings, drive an older car, or give up a monthly meal in a nice restaurant.

If you put a high priority on education, you may have to take the bus to work in order to be able to send your children to a particular school.

If you're concerned about your family's security and believe you must allot a certain percentage of your income to savings and insurance, you may have to pass up a number of things that would give you satisfaction right now.

There is no magic recipe for success. Nobody can tell you the "right" thing to do. You and your family have to decide what your priorities are, and how you're going to go about attaining your goals.

If you discover that you need to take a hard look at your financial life, it might be a good idea to bring the household together to workout a realistic plan to get your finances on track. Lay everything on the table to expose all household expenses required, as well as how the money is being spent by each member of the household. This may require reorganizing where and how you spend your money. Keep track over a period of time so that it can be revised and updated.

UNLEARNING THE FINE ART OF DITHERING

Most of us like to dither. We lean towards one option until somebody gives us another, and then we just don't know any more. Learning to make decisions is like any other skill—it must be learned and practised over and over again until you get the hang of it.

Making decisions involves answering three questions:

1. Where am I going?
2. How shall I get there?
3. How will I know when I arrive?

Decision-making has two distinct parts: the planning stage and the implementing, or action, stage.

The planning stage has six steps:

1. You need a goal, an objective, a priority. It must be specific: "I want to buy a car," or "I want to get out of debt."

2. Set down the different ways of reaching your goal. Say, for example, your goal is to buy a car. How much money do you need to save? Will you save it all or borrow some? Two obvious courses of action are spending less or earning more. Another possibility is buying a lottery ticket and hoping to win. Set out all possible ways of getting the car.

3. List the trade-offs for each course of action. If you decide on one course of action that will get you to your goal, what else will it get you that you don't want? For example, if you decide to spend less in order to save money, you may be depriving yourself or your family of something that has become a regular expenditure. If you decide to earn more, the trade-off is that you will have fewer leisure hours, you will pay more income tax, and so on. If you choose to depend on lotteries, you may never win.

4. At this point, you should be able to look at the goal, the alternative courses of action, the trade-offs attached to the alternatives, and choose a basic course of action. In other words, decide on the alternative that best suits your purposes for reaching your goal, or re-evaluate the goal itself.

5. Develop a strategy based on the course of action you have chosen. A strategy means you must decide on the priorities and the timing of the major steps. For example, where will you cut your spending and when will you begin?
6. Make a list of checkpoints so that you can determine at regular intervals how well you are succeeding in reaching your goal.

Once you've got to the point of having measurable checkpoints, you are in a position to begin on the implementation stage. There are six steps in the implementing stage.

1. Decide who is going to do what to reach the goal. In other words, if you're involved in the process with other people, identify who's going to be responsible for what.
2. State clearly each person's responsibility. If any member of the group needs help in carrying out their new responsibilities, be prepared to give it.
3. Draw up a schedule that lets everyone know when they should be halfway or one-quarter of the way to having the money or the information they require.
4. Here's where you use your checkpoint list. At regular intervals, determine whether your planned activities are actually going to produce the chosen goal.
5. If the checkpoints indicate that your strategy is proceeding as you had planned, go to step 6. If not, take corrective action now—revise, re-think, and redesign your strategy.
6. Build in a reward system for each person involved in the strategy. Everybody likes to have a good job recognized and will perform better the more frequently they have their own good jobs recognized.

In a world where so many problems seem to be beyond individual control, it's gratifying to know that if we set up a realistic plan and put sufficient effort into it, we can control our own financial well-being.

CHAPTER 3

Getting Your Records Together

To overcome difficulties is to experience the full delight of existence.

—Arthur Schopenhauer

Don't kid yourself. Getting organized is hard. It takes patience and willpower, just like getting into shape or taking off weight. Not only is it difficult, it's boring. The reason I'm telling you this is that unless you understand that you're embarking on one of life's most difficult jobs, you're likely to stop halfway through and never get it together.

But think of it this way. From the day we're born to the day we die, records follow us. Notice that I didn't say paper. Right now I could drown in the paper that comes in the mail, or that awaits me at the bank and the tax department. But a lot of our records are in computer banks somewhere. What records? Your birth certificate. Your medical records. Your report cards from the teacher. Your SIN number, tax number, unemployment insurance number, your home ownership insurance policy, your life insurance policy, your group health form . . . need I go on?

Before you panic, remember: there is an upside to all this horror. You will be organized. You will know where all your important papers are. You will never again go to renew your mortgage and have to go back three times with the deed, the legal discharge of the balance of sale from when you first bought the house, your divorce papers and the name of the judge, and the receipt proving your taxes are paid. You'll have them all in hand the first time around.

You'll have a lot to talk about when you go to parties. You'd be surprised how few people are organized. If you are, just think of all the advice you can offer. People will search you out to listen to your expertise. Really. And think of how much easier it will be on your family and friends if it ever happens that you can't look after your own affairs.

Okay. Now make up your mind. Go back to Chapter 2 and review your priorities and goals. You can't be a good money manager without a certain amount of old-fashioned housekeeping. The way to approach this housekeeping is to begin with a longish time frame. Getting organized is a process that you will not likely accomplish in a weekend.

Get a loose-leaf binder so you can change the pages as necessary. Or, format a new disk, and make a backup. What follows in this chapter are worksheet samples that you can transfer into your binder or onto your disk. The worksheets are self-explanatory.

One final word. Put the papers themselves in a safe place—a safe deposit box, if you want, although your lawyer's safe deposit box is better. Do not, however, put the binder or disk in your safe deposit box. If you die, your box may be sealed and your family or friends may not be able to get to it. Tell someone you trust where the binder or disk is. Remember to update it when any big event happens in your life, or once a year, whichever comes first.

THE FAMILY STATISTICS

Personal Data

Family name: ______________________________

Address: ______________________________

Phone: ______________________________

	First name	Date of birth	Social Insurance No.
Husband:	________	________	________
Wife:	________	________	________
Children:	________	________	________
	________	________	________
	________	________	________
	________	________	________

Birth certificates are located: ______________________________

Citizenship papers (if any) are located: ______________________________

Date of marriage: ______________ Marriage certificate is located: ______________

Date of divorce (if applicable): ______________ Divorce papers are located: ______________

Date of military service and discharge: ______________________________

Military records are located: ______________________________

Education records & diplomas are located: ______________________________

Driver's licence numbers:

Husband: ______________

Wife: ______________

Children: ______________

____

____

____

Real Estate

Home is in the name of: ______

Date purchased: ______ Price: ______

Cash: ______

Mortgage: ______

Mortgage is held by: ______

Lender's address: ______

Mortgage will be paid off (date): ______

Homeowner's insurance policy number: ______

Amount of coverage: ______

Insurance company: ______

Address: ______

Agent's name and phone number: ______

Policy located: ______

Cost and dates of major improvements: ______

______

______

Other property owned includes:

Type and location: ______

______

______

Title, mortgage, insurance information: ______

______

______

Gross rental income: ______

Location of any pertinent documents: ______

NOTE: Capital gains are taxable from Valuation Day. For all property including publicly traded shares and securities, Valuation Day is December 31, 1971. There is a lifetime exemption of the first $100,000 of capital gains.

In 1987, one-half of any gain in value after that date is taxable; for 1988, two-thirds is taxable. Your principal residence is exempt from capital gains tax.

Automobiles

Car #1: Owned in name of: ____________________
Model, date: ____________________
Title, registration number: ____________________
Located: ____________________

Car #2: Owned in name of: ____________________
Model, date: ____________________
Title, registration number: ____________________
Located: ____________________

Car #3: Owned in name of: ____________________
Model, date: ____________________
Title, registration number: ____________________
Located: ____________________

Car insurance policies:
Policy number: ____________________
In name of: ____________________
Coverage: ____________________
Company: ____________________
Address: ____________________
Agent's name and phone number: ____________________
Location of policy: ____________________

Policy number: ____________________
In name of: ____________________
Coverage: ____________________
Company: ____________________
Address: ____________________
Agent's name and phone number: ____________________
Location of policy: ____________________

Policy number: ____________________
In name of: ____________________
Coverage: ____________________
Company: ____________________
Address: ____________________
Agent's name and phone number: ____________________
Location of policy: ____________________

Financial Records

Financial Institution: ______________________

Address: ______________________

Savings account in name of: ______________________

Account number: ______________________

Chequing account in name of: ______________________

Account number: ______________________

Name of personal manager: ______________________

Financial Institution: ______________________

Address: ______________________

Savings account in name of: ______________________

Account number: ______________________

Chequing account in name of: ______________________

Account number: ______________________

Name of personal manager: ______________________

Financial Institution: ______________________

Address: ______________________

Savings account in name of: ______________________

Account number: ______________________

Chequing account in name of: ______________________

Account number: ______________________

Name of personal manager: ______________________

Financial Institution: ______________________

Address: ______________________

Savings account in name of: ______________________

Account number: ______________________

Chequing account in name of: ______________________

Account number: ______________________

Name of personal manager: ______________________

Health Insurance

Health insurance company: ____________________

Policy number: ____________________

In name of: ____________________

Agent's name and phone number: ____________________

Plan/coverage: ____________________

Location of policy: ____________________

Health insurance company: ____________________

Policy number: ____________________

In name of: ____________________

Agent's name and phone number: ____________________

Plan/coverage: ____________________

Location of policy. ____________________

Health insurance company: ____________________

Policy number: ____________________

In name of: ____________________

Agent's name and phone number: ____________________

Plan/coverage: ____________________

Location of policy: ____________________

Income Tax Records

Tax accountant's name: ____________________

Address: ____________________

Phone: ____________________

Location of tax records: ____________________

(receipts, cancelled cheques)

Life Insurance

(Be sure to include any company life insurance benefit plans here.)

Life insurance company: ____________________

Policy number: ____________________

In name of: ____________________

Agent's name and phone number: ____________________

Plan/coverage: ____________________

Location of policy: ____________________

Life insurance company: ____________________

Policy number: ____________________

In name of: ____________________

Agent's name and phone number: ____________________

Plan/coverage: ____________________

Location of policy: ____________________

Life insurance company: ____________________

Policy number: ____________________

In name of: ____________________

Agent's name and phone number: ____________________

Plan/coverage: ____________________

Location of policy: ____________________

Life insurance company: ____________________

Policy number: ____________________

In name of: ____________________

Agent's name and phone number: ____________________

Plan/coverage: ____________________

Location of policy: ____________________

Wills

Will in name of: ______________________________

Date of will: ______________________________

Drawn up by: ______________________________
(lawyer's name)

Executor(s) ______________________________

Address: ______________________________

Phone: ______________________________

Location of original will: ______________________________

Second copy is located: ______________________________

Safe deposit box number: ______________________________

Location (bank, address): ______________________________

Key number: ______________________________

Names of persons who have access to box: ______________________________

____

____

Retirement Records

R.R.S.P. 1. ______________________________

Type (equity, self-administered, etc.): ______________________________

2. ______________________________

Type: ______________________________

Purchased from: ______________________________

Located at: ______________________________

Registered company pension plan: ______________________________

Type (money purchase, defined benefit): ______________________________

Investments

Government Savings Bonds Location: ____________________

List by serial number and denomination:

____________________ ____________________
____________________ ____________________
____________________ ____________________
____________________ ____________________
____________________ ____________________
____________________ ____________________

Stocks

Location of stocks: ____________________
____

Broker's name: ____________________
Address: ____________________
____
Phone: ____________________

List by name and current number of shares, estimated value:

____
____
____
____
____
____
____
____

Other investments (corporate bonds, mutual funds, money market funds, tax shelters)

Location: ____________________
Broker's name: ____________________
Address: ____________________
Phone: ____________________

List by type of investment along with any pertinent data:

____
____
____
____
____
____
____

Credit Accounts

Bank credit cards:

VISA
Account number: ______________________

In name of: ______________________

MASTERCARD
Account number: ______________________

In name of: ______________________

Travel and entertainment cards:

AMERICAN EXPRESS
Account number: ______________________

In name of: ______________________

DINERS CLUB
Account number: ______________________

In name of: ______________________

EN ROUTE
Account number: ______________________

In name of: ______________________

OTHER
Account number: ______________________

In name of: ______________________

Department store credit cards

Name		
1 ______	______	______
2 ______	______	______
3 ______	______	______
4 ______	______	______
5 ______	______	______
6 ______	______	______
7 ______	______	______
8 ______	______	______

Current Records

Medical receipts: ______________________________

____

Location: ______________________________

Charity receipts: ______________________________

____

____

____

Location: ______________________________

Business expenses: ______________________________

____

____

____

Location: ______________________________

Other:

BUSINESS INTERESTS

General

Full name of business: ______________________

Address: ______________________ Phone: ____________

Nature of business/type of product or service ______________________

____

Date incorporated or partnership commenced: ______________________

Provincial or Federal Charter: ______________________

Future prospects for this business: ______________________

Are any related companies vital to this business or dependent on it?:

____

Are any changes contemplated in the ownership, organization, or operation? ______________________

How was business acquired?: ______________________

Is business dependent on you for successful operation?: ____________

Are there any "key players" (names & ages)?: ______________________

____

Are they insured?: ______________________

Is anyone capable of taking over (son, wife, other)?: ____________

____

Should the company be kept or sold after your death?: ____________

Have you given any personal guarantees (bank or other)?: ____________

____

Relevant papers' location: ______________________

Employee Information

Number of full-time employees: ____ Part-time: ____________

Group life insurance: ____________ Group health insurance: ________

Pension plan: ____________ Profit-sharing plan: ____________

Deferred profit-sharing plan: ______________________

Shareholder Information

Partner or shareholder	Age	Relation to you	% of Part.	No. of Common	No. of Preferred

Valuation

Is your spouse on the payroll?: _______ For how long?: _______

Salary?: _______

Does company own life insurance on your life?: _______

On life of others?: _______

Does company owe money to you?: $_______

To members of your family?: $_______

For what amount would you sell your interest?: $_______

NOTE: Valuation Day in Canada is December 31, 1971. Capital gains made after that date are taxable. There is a lifetime exemption of the first $100 000 of capital gains.

For 1987, one-half of capital gains are taxable. For 1988, two-thirds of capital gains are taxable.

Agreements and Contracts

Buy/Sell agreements: _______

Deferred compensation agreements: _______

Partnership agreements: _______

Any other business agreements: _______

Date completed: _______

The following forms needn't worry you if your capital gains are well below $100,000. (They needn't worry you if your capital gains are above $100,000, because you are winning the fight for financial independence.)

PERSONAL INVESTMENT RECORD

Name and type of security: ______________________

Number of shares or bonds: ______________________

Bought on (date): __________ Unit price: __________

Gross price (include commission): ______________________

Valuation Day value: ______________________

Sold on (date): __________ Unit price: __________

Net price (deduct commission & taxes): ______________________

Net Gain (Loss) from Cost: ______________________

Net Gain (Loss) from Valuation Day: ______________________

Income: Dividends: __________ Interest: __________

Name and type of security: ______________________

Number of shares or bonds: ______________________

Bought on (date): __________ Unit price: __________

Gross price (include commission): ______________________

Valuation Day value: ______________________

Sold on (date): __________ Unit price: __________

Net price (deduct commission & taxes): ______________________

Net Gain (Loss) from Cost: ______________________

Net Gain (Loss) from Valuation Day: ______________________

Income: Dividends: __________ Interest: __________

N.B. The Personal Investment record and Inventory of Assets segments would work best in ledger-style format.

Inventory of Assets — December 31, 1971*

Real Property (other than principal residence)

Farm

Item: ____________________ Date acquired: ____________

How acquired: ______________ Cost when acquired: ________

V-Day value: ________________ Date disposed: ____________

Net proceeds: _______________ Gain: ________ Loss: ________

Depreciable Property

Item: ____________________ Date acquired: ____________

How acquired: ______________ Cost when acquired: ________

V-Day value: ________________ Date disposed: ____________

Net proceeds: _______________ Gain: ________ Loss: ________

Land

Item: ____________________ Date acquired: ____________

How acquired: ______________ Cost when acquired: ________

V-Day value: ________________ Date disposed: ____________

Net proceeds: _______________ Gain: ________ Loss: ________

Other

Item: ____________________ Date acquired: ____________

How acquired: ______________ Cost when acquired: ________

V-Day value: ________________ Date disposed: ____________

Net proceeds: _______________ Gain: ________ Loss: ________

*Capital Gains Tax Valuation date.

Listed Personal Property

Jewellery

Item: ________________ Date acquired: ________________

How acquired: ________________ Cost when acquired: ________________

V-Day value: ________________ Date disposed: ________________

Net proceeds: ________________ Gain: ________ Loss: ________

Art (etchings, paintings, sculpture)

Item: ________________ Date acquired: ________________

How acquired: ________________ Cost when acquired: ________________

V-Day value: ________________ Date disposed: ________________

Net proceeds: ________________ Gain: ________ Loss: ________

Rare books, folios, or manuscripts

Item: ________________ Date acquired: ________________

How acquired: ________________ Cost when acquired: ________________

V-Day value: ________________ Date disposed: ________________

Net proceeds: ________________ Gain: ________ Loss: ________

Stamp or coin collection

Item: ________________ Date acquired: ________________

How acquired: ________________ Cost when acquired: ________________

V-Day value: ________________ Date disposed: ________________

Net proceeds: ________________ Gain: ________ Loss: ________

Other

Item: ________________ Date acquired: ________________

How acquired: ________________ Cost when acquired: ________________

V-Day value: ________________ Date disposed: ________________

Net proceeds: ________________ Gain: ________ Loss: ________

Personal Use Property

Boat

Item: ____________________ Date acquired: ____________

How acquired: ____________ Cost when acquired: ________

V-Day value: ______________ Date disposed: ____________

Net proceeds: _____________ Gain: ______ Loss: ________

Cottage

Item: ____________________ Date acquired: ____________

How acquired: ____________ Cost when acquired: ________

V-Day value: ______________ Date disposed: ____________

Net proceeds: _____________ Gain: ______ Loss: ________

Antiques

Item: ____________________ Date acquired: ____________

How acquired: ____________ Cost when acquired: ________

V-Day value: ______________ Date disposed: ____________

Net proceeds: _____________ Gain: ______ Loss: ________

Other

Item: ____________________ Date acquired: ____________

How acquired: ____________ Cost when acquired: ________

V-Day value: ______________ Date disposed: ____________

Net proceeds: _____________ Gain: ______ Loss: ________

INVENTORY OF PERSONAL PROPERTY

It's a good idea to take a picture of your personal property and send it to your insurer. Include a photostat of the bill of purchase so you have proof of ownership and cost.

Living Room

Article	Date Purchased	Original Value	Replacement Cost
Sofa			
Chairs			
Lamps			
Rugs			
Tables			
Window shades			
Curtains			
Draperies			
Mirrors			
Clocks			
Radio			
Television			
Piano			
Paintings			
Stereo			
Bric-a-brac			
Other			
TOTAL:			

Dining Room

Article	Date Purchased	Original Value	Replacement Cost
Buffet			
Chairs			
Lamps			
Rugs			
Tables			
Window shades			
Curtains			
Draperies			
Mirrors			
Clocks			
Paintings			
Appliances			
China			
Glassware			
Bric-a-brac			
Linens			
Silver			
Other			
TOTAL:			

Bedroom #1

Article	Date Purchased	Original Value	Replacement Cost
Beds & Springs			
Chairs			
Bureaus			
Rugs			
Tables			
Window shades			
Curtains			
Draperies			
Mirrors			
Clocks			
Radio			
Paintings			
Toilet Articles			
Linens			
Television			
Other			
TOTAL:			

Bedroom #2

Article	Date Purchased	Original Value	Replacement Cost
Beds & Springs			
Chairs			
Bureaus			
Rugs			
Tables			
Window shades			
Curtains			
Draperies			
Mirrors			
Clocks			
Radio			
Paintings			
Toilet Articles			
Linens			
Television			
Other			
TOTAL:			

Bedroom #3

Article	Date Purchased	Original Value	Replacement Cost
Beds & Springs			
Chairs			
Bureaus			
Rugs			
Tables			
Window shades			
Curtains			
Draperies			
Mirrors			
Clocks			
Radio			
Paintings			
Toilet Articles			
Linens			
Television			
Other			
TOTAL:			

Bedroom #4

Article	Date Purchased	Original Value	Replacement Cost
Beds & Springs			
Chairs			
Bureaus			
Rugs			
Tables			
Window shades			
Curtains			
Draperies			
Mirrors			
Clocks			
Radio			
Paintings			
Toilet Articles			
Linens			
Television			
Other			
TOTAL:			

Kitchen

Article	Date Purchased	Original Value	Replacement Cost
Stove			
Refrigerator			
Tables			
Chairs			
Cabinets			
Utensils			
Cutlery			
China			
Glassware			
Dishwasher			
Appliances (list)			
Rotisserie			
Blender			
Mixer			
Radio			
Clocks			
Other			
TOTAL:			

Other Areas

Article	Date Purchased	Original Value	Replacement Cost
BATH			
HALLS			
Rugs			
Mirrors			
Paintings			
DEN			
Television			
Rugs			
Mirrors			
Books			
Typewriter			
Tape recorder			
Desks			
TOTAL:			

Article	Date Purchased	Original Value	Replacement Cost
BASEMENT			
Tools			
Mowers			
Snow blower			
Garden equip.			
Ladders			
Barbecue			
ATTIC			
GARAGE			
TOTAL:			

Article	Date Purchased	Original Value	Replacement Cost
HOBBY ITEMS			
Bicycles			
Cameras			
Golf equip.			
Ski equip.			
Boating equip.			
Power tools			
Exerciser			
TOTAL:			

Article	Date Purchased	Original Value	Replacement Cost
CLOTHING – HUSBAND			
CLOTHING – WIFE			
CLOTHING – CHILDREN			
TOTAL:			

Jewellery, Furs, Silverware, Other Valuables

Article	Date Purchased	Original Value	Replacement Cost
TOTAL:			

Miscellaneous

Article	Date Purchased	Original Value	Replacement Cost
Luggage			
Heating system			
Air conditioning			
Washer			
Dryer			
Freezer			
Vacuum cleaner			
Lawn furniture			
TOTAL:			

Summary

Living Room:	$________________
Dining Room:	________________
Bedroom 1:	________________
Bedroom 2:	________________
Bedroom 3:	________________
Bedroom 4:	________________
Kitchen:	________________
Other areas:	________________
Hobby items:	________________
Clothing:	________________
Jewellery, Furs:	________________
Miscellaneous:	________________
Total:	$________________
Present Insurance:	$________________
Additional Insurance (ordered ______ 19 ______)	$________________
Total insurance now:	$________________

Date: ________________________________

FINANCIAL ADVISORS

	Name and Address	Phone No.
Lawyer	________________________	________________
Accountant	________________________	________________
Bank Manager	________________________	________________
Other	________________________	________________

CHAPTER 4

Spending Smart

Success is not searching for you. You must do the seeking.
—Frank Tyger

In the good old days, the vast majority of Canadians worked for corporations, nine to five, Monday to Friday (except for holidays), fifty weeks a year, forty years to retirement. Our expectations for the past two generations have included steady employment and regular raises.

Now, much of the certainty that characterized our expectations is disappearing. It has been very difficult, especially since the 1980 recession, for us as parents to justify telling our teenagers to "work hard and follow the rules," when we, and particularly our children, know so many people who have always done so, but are currently without jobs.

Increasingly, Canadians are looking at the structure of work in different ways: more than a million Canadians are self-employed, partly because big business jobs are scarce, and partly because there is an appeal to being self-employed with which many Canadians can identify.

In a transitional world, such as the one in which we now live, you can see why it's more important than ever to be reasonably fluent in the language and world of money, business, and finance. No one cares about your money as much as you do.

That means you need some skills that will enable you to get work; you need to know something about pension plans and social programmes, because contributions and premiums for things like unemployment insurance are deducted from your paycheque if you work for a company, or paid by you directly if you're self-employed.

You need to know about the tax system, because paying taxes is an obligation of everyone who earns money, and because different kinds of earned income are taxed differently. And you need to know something about smart shopping and smart investing, because what you do with your money will greatly affect how you live while you're earning and when you retire.

CAN YOU READ YOUR PAYCHEQUE?

If you work for someone else, you need to know what's taken off the top before you get your paycheque, what you have no choice in spending, and what's left after you've discharged your obligations. If you're unemployed, or thinking of starting your own business, you need this knowledge even more, because it will make you think about things (like saving for retirement) that you will have to arrange for yourself.

On the following page, there's a sample of the grand-daddy of all paycheques. If you can read this one, you should manage with any other. There are two important things about paycheques. One is the purchasing power they represent. The other is that they reinforce one of life's more unpleasant realities—only part of what you earn is yours to spend. Putting it another way, the salary you are hired at is not what you have to spend. Forgetting that fact has gotten a lot of people into financial trouble, because they made a habit of spending their "gross" salary and not their "take-home" pay.

NO BANANA DIETS FOR YOUR BUDGET

All budgets, like all diets, work for a while. The problem with making them stick is that a lot of them are just too onerous or boring to continue for more than a few weeks (in the case of diets), or months (in the case of budgets).

Can you imagine living forever on a diet of cottage cheese and three slices of tomato? By the same token, a budget that compels you to keep track of every dime you spend is doomed to failure for all but a few. The same goes for any budget that gives you a constant feeling of martyrdom.

You're doing yourself a favour by managing your money sensibly—so you can do some crazy things later on, right?

The best way to ensure that your budget works is to build it into your normal routine. The analogy with dieting is accurate: if you are overweight, you have to concentrate at the beginning on acquiring new, healthy food and exercise habits. With budgets, you have to be determined to find time to keep your records in place, then stick to it.

DEPT. / SERV.	NAME OF EMPLOYEE / NOM DE L'EMPLOYÉ	SOCIAL INS. NO. (1) NO. D'ASS. SOCIALE	PERIOD ENDING MO. DA. YR. (2) MO. JR. AN. PÉRIODE AU

ACCOUNT NO. (3) NO. DE COMPTE	REGULAR (4) SALAIRE NORMAL	OVERTIME (5) SALAIRE SUPPL.	SPECIAL (6) SALAIRE SPÉCIAL	GROSS PAY (7) SALAIRE BRUT	TOTAL DEDUCT (8) TOTAL-DÉDUC.	NET PAY (9) SALAIRE NET

FED. TAX (10) IMPÔT FÉD.	PROV. TAX (11) IMPÔT PROV.	GOV. PENS. (12) RENTES.-GOUV.	PENSION FUND (13) C/RETRAITE	CHARITY (14) DONS	U.I.C. (15) ASS.-CHÔM.	BONDS (16) OBLIGATIONS	MISC. A AUTRES-A	MISC. B AUTRES-B

GROUP A & S (17) ASS. A/M	GROUP LIFE (18) ASS.-VIE.	ACC. INS. (19) ASS.-ACC.	PROV. HOSP. (20) ASS. HOSP.	MEDICARE (21) MEDICARE	ADVANCE (22) AVANCE	WKS U.I.C. (23) SEM. ASS.-CHÔM.	YEAR TO DATE BONDS OBLIGATIONS CUM.-ANNÉE	MEDICARE MEDICARE

GROSS PAY SALAIRE BRUT	FED. TAX IMPÔT FÉD.	PROV. TAX IMPÔT PROV.	GOV. PENS. RENTES.-GOUV.	PENSION FUND C/RETRAITE	CHARITY DONS	OVERTIME SALAIRE SUPPL.	QTR. TO DATE PENSION FUND C/RETRAITE CUM.-TRIM.

STATEMENT OF EARNINGS AND DEDUCTIONS

RELEVÉ–SALAIRE ET DÉDUCTIONS

1. **Social Insurance Number** Every working Canadian needs one, and can get one by applying to the nearest Employment Canada office.
2. **Period Ending** This shows the pay period—one week, two weeks, one month, and so on, ending on the date shown.
3. **Account Number** Your personal bank account number, if pay is automatically deposited with your financial institution.
4. **Regular** The full amount of pay, before deductions for the pay period.
5. **Overtime** The amount of overtime pay, if any.
6. **Special** Salary adjustments, like retroactive pay increases, if any.
7. **Gross Pay** The sum of numbers 4, 5, and 6.
8. **Total Deductions** The sum of numbers 10 through 12.
9. **Net Pay** The amount that you actually receive. In the jargon, this is your disposable income.
10. **Federal Tax** Must, by law, be deducted.
11. **Provincial Tax** If any. (Provincial tax is payable in all provinces, but shown separately in Quebec.)
12. **Government Pension Plan** This is your Canada or Quebec Pension Plan. Compulsory deduction of percentage of salary, with a specified maximum per year.
13. **Pension Fund** Company's own pension fund, to which contributions may or may not be compulsory. (Legislation affecting payroll deductions is constantly being revised. It is worth watching out for this kind of news, since it also affects your pocketbook.)
14. **Charity** Donations pledged, if any.
15. **UIC** Unemployment insurance contribution, compulsory.
16. **Bonds** Canada Savings Bonds installment payments, if any.
17. **Group A & S** Accident and sickness insurance, if any.
18. **Group Life** Life insurance contribution, if any.
19. **Accident insurance** If any.
20. **Provincial Hospital Plan** If any.
21. **Medicare** Compulsory, but shown separately only in provinces where premiums are charged.
22. **Advance** Salary advance, if any.
23. **Year to Date** Figures reflect total earnings and deductions for the various listed items relative to the date shown on the pay slip.

After you have gotten back on an even keel, you'll discover not only the joy of knowing that all your financial matters are in order, but the reality that budgeting is almost automatic.

First, find a place in your home where you can keep all your budgeting paraphernalia together. That means you need a small desk; a box, drawer, or file where you can put all the bills as they come in; a place for receipts. One of those folding fan files might be handy, if you don't have too many papers. Personally, I've had to move out of three rooms . . . but I'll get you better organized.

If you've been into a bank in the last five years, you've probably been approached to put money into one of the new tiered chequing accounts. These tiered accounts encourage you to keep a higher balance by offering better interest rates the more money you deposit. For example, you might get the bare-bones daily interest rate on the first $5,000, an extra three-quarter percent on the amount between $5,000 and $10,000, and the Treasury Bill rate on amounts above $10,000.

If you're a disciplined person who can keep the various functions of the different tiers straight in your head, this is simpler than the old-fashioned way. But if you think having lots of money in the account you use to pay your bills will only encourage you to spend it all, the old way might still be the best way for you.

To start, you can divide your take-home pay or, if you're self-employed, your drawings, between three bank accounts. Your first account will be your basic living account. Make this account one on which you can write cheques, and preferably one on which you can also get interest. Into it you will deposit your take-home paycheque or drawings.

Your second account is your own personal long-term savings account. This is the one that's going to get you out of debt, and after that, put you on the road to financial independence. Immediately take ten percent of your pay and transfer it into this account. Now forget it exists, until your next pay. The ten percent, of course, is an arbitrary number. But it's a good round number, and a good place to start. After you detail your living expenses, you may find that it has to be juggled either up or down. But try it this way first.

Your third account is another savings or non-chequing account, but this time for short-term objectives. You might want to make it a daily interest account, so you won't lose as much interest when you make withdrawals. This is the account you'll use for the consumer goods you need to save for—birthday gifts, Christmas, Hanukkah, vacation, the car you're going to need two years from now. You don't know yet how much you need to deposit into this account. So start calculating. Now is the time to list all your living expenses: rent or mortgage, food, clothing, insurance, transportation—everything on which you spend money. Set it all down and add it up. If you've been practising good money management habits, the total will be considerably less than your take-home pay minus ten percent.

OH-OH . . .

This is where a lot of budgets fail. If your expenditures outweigh your income right off the bat, go to jail, go directly to jail. Do not pass go, do not collect $200. Skip ahead to the Crash, Get-Out-of-Hot-Water Strategy.

The rest of you aren't home-free yet. The next step is to look or think back to your larger consumer spending. How much did you spend last Christmas? How much will you need for your new car? How much for your vacation? Add it all up and divide by the number of paycheques you get. This is the amount that goes into account number three.

This is only the beginning of the process. You may find that your living standard costs more than you make. This is when the juggling begins and when some serious decisions have to be made.

Mark Twain said that his family never talked about money because there was never enough of it around to make it a topic for discussion. Many people may be in the same boat. If you're one of them, you have to make some basic decisions about how you are spending your money.

Let's look more closely at that chequing account—the first of the three accounts we just talked about. If you are in the position of not having enough money to live on, you're going to have to do some serious figuring.

THE CRASH, GET-YOURSELF-OUT-OF-HOT-WATER STRATEGY

This section will take you through the actual budgeting process. Some of you may already be in trouble. You may not be able to wait six months to see results. For those of you who need an immediate tourniquet to stop the money from pouring out, here's the crash budget.

As with all emergency situations, budget hemorrhaging demands extreme short-term action.

1. Practise looking in your mirror every morning and saying, "You are not a bad person." You'll need this moral support.

2. Get out all your credit cards, bank charge cards, department store cards. Seal them in an envelope and put them away in a safe place. They will stay there until the crisis is over. Nothing, not a repayment schedule, not a consolidation loan, not a session with a financial counselor, will help you if you continue to borrow with your charge cards.

   The beginning of emergency treatment, when most people are feeling really awful, is the best time to take extreme measures. If you have to tighten your belt, do it right at the beginning when your feelings of guilt and fear of being overextended are stronger than the greed that got you into this position.

3. You'll find it easier to succeed in your austerity programme if you decide in advance what its duration is going to be. What we're doing in our financial lives is an exact analogy to a strict diet—it will have an immediate salutary effect. It will make you feel better. And after the initial panic has subsided, we can get on to dealing with the fact that in order to be financially healthy, money management is something we must practise throughout our lives.

4. If you haven't been saving money on a regular basis, you're going to begin with your next paycheque. These savings will, for the duration of your crash budget, be used for debt reduction. Open a new bank account, and deposit ten percent of your take-home paycheque. If you're in charge of the household accounts, you should also deposit ten percent of your household allowance.

5. Add up all your outstanding bills, and leave room beside them to mark down how much each outstanding account is costing you. You'll end up with something that looks like this:

Account	*Amount*	*Cost*
Mastercard	$600	18.6%
VISA	540	15.9
Eaton's	380	28.8
Texaco	150	21.0
Bank loan	800	12.0

   Your priorities for paying these off should be on the basis of how much they're costing you. Your department store, gas, and bank cards are costing you the most; therefore you should concentrate on paying them off first. This doesn't mean you can stop paying on your other outstanding bills without prior arrangements being made. You can arrange with your creditors to pay smaller amounts for a number of months. Better still, consider going to your banker and taking out a larger loan at 12% to pay off the 28% and 18% creditors. The yearly interest on $1620 at 21.6% is $351; at 12% it's $194. The saving of $157 could go toward paying down your bills.

6. Contact your creditors. You may be lucky enough to live in a community where you can get financial counselling. Ontario is well set up with consumer help offices across the province. In Quebec, the ACEFs perform much the same function. Few other provinces in Canada have such resources readily available. Unless you are prepared to declare personal bankruptcy or put yourself in the hands of the Court, you will have to do a lot of searching for sound financial advice. Your bank manager may be able to help you; otherwise, you're on your own.

That's why the next step is talking to your creditors. While it may be embarrassing, you must remember that creditors want the money that is owed them. Under normal circumstances, and certainly in today's economy, car dealers don't want the car back; trust companies and banks don't want the house back; department stores don't want the television back. They want their money; failing that, they want to know when they will get their money.

So when you go to see them, have a plan ready. Offer a new repayment schedule. Offer to pay the interest but hold off on the principal for a few months. Remember that it is in the interests of the creditor to come to some agreement with you.

If you've gotten this far, you're back on the road to financial well-being. You'll also have joined the ranks of Canadians who have come to the brink of financial disaster and stepped back, wiser, but basically unscathed.

7. Banks generally like to have your life insured if they've lent you a lot of money. If you already have a life insurance policy, give it to them. What you don't need right now is to spend more money on another premium.

If you have this kind of debt, and you're an average income earner taking home say, $500 a week, it's going to take you about a year to get out of debt. Well, nobody promised you a rose garden. But I can guarantee that if you start the crash budget this week, you'll be able to see the results within six months. I can also guarantee that if you don't do anything to get yourself out of debt, things can only get worse. The one thing financial planning does for you is give you control over your own life. Considering how little influence any individual has in altering the state of world affairs, what more can we ask?

WHAT IF I DON'T NEED A CRASH DIET?

Most Canadians aren't in serious financial difficulty. Most of us are just feeling pinched and reluctant to accept the fact that we have been getting poorer. Let me put it another way.

It used to be that, from year to year, the vast majority of us floated upward on a generally rising standard of living, without much effort on our parts. A fact of life in the 1950s and 1960s was rising productivity in the economy and fatter paycheques in our pockets. We all shared in the wealth we helped create: the economy was growing fast enough that there was a little bit more for most of us, from the top to the bottom of the income scale.

By the middle of the 1970s, it had become clear to many people that the economy just wasn't growing fast enough to give everyone that extra little morsel. Indeed, that was the beginning of the jockeying for who was going to get the extra little bit that was produced. When we, as an economy, produced five, six or seven percent more goods and services than we had the year before, (and as we did in the 1950s, 1960s, and early 1970s), the people at the bottom, in the middle, and at the top each got a share.

When the economy produces only three or two percent more than it has the year before (that's what we've been doing since 1976), the question then becomes, "Who should get the extra? The most needy? Or the most powerful?"

And when the economy produces nothing more than the year before, we're all going to get a little bit less or, if someone gets more, someone by definition is going to get less.

BASIC BUDGETS

The world is changing rapidly. What we want out of life is changing. And no matter what, money management will always be in style. The sooner we master it, the better off we'll all be. And the best way to start is with a budget. The first step in budgeting is to list your expenses.

The organized list reproduced here is one the Royal Bank has offered its clients for several years.

Income:

Take-home pay ____________

Other (gifts, dividends, and so on) ____________

Expenditures:

Regular cheques, regular amounts (could be rent or mortage, insurance, car payments.)	______
Regular cheques, varying amounts (could include phone, electricity, charge cards.)	______
Contingency (a regular percentage you set aside for the unexpected.)	______
Irregular cheque payments (could include occasional purchases, such as clothing, or intermittent insurance payments.)	______
Cash payments (whatever you pay for in cash—groceries, drug store, dry cleaning, and so on.)	______
TOTAL	______

Or, you may find it easier to use this arrangement:

Household Expenses:	Rent/mortgage	______
	Telephone	______
	Gas, oil, wood	______
	Electricity	______
	Water	______
	Other	______
Personal Expenses:	Allowance	______
	Food	______
	Clothing	______
	Hairdresser, barber	______
	Dry cleaning	______
	Other	______
Transportation:	Car registration, licence	______
	Gasoline, oil	______
	Commuter costs (tolls, bus, train, parking)	______

Insurance:	Life	________
	Auto	________
	Homeowner's	________
	Health, disability	________
Loans/Debts:	Bank loans:	
	Automobile	________
	College	________
	Other ____________________	________
	____________________	________
	Credit cards	________
	____________________	________
	____________________	________
	____________________	________
Medical:	Doctor	________
	Dentist	________
	Drugs, prescriptions	________
Education:	Tuition	________
	School supplies	________
Gifts:	Christmas, Hanukkah	________
	Anniversaries, weddings	________
	Birthdays	________
	Other	________
Contributions:	Religious	________
	Charitable	________
	Political	________
	Other	________

Entertainment:	Dinner out	________
	Baby-sitting fees	________
	Movies, plays	________
	Family vacation	________
	Clubs	________
	Sports, hobbies	________
Savings:	Savings bank	________
	Bonds	________
	Stocks	________
	Other investments	________
	________________________	________
	________________________	________
Miscellaneous:	Alimony, child support	________
	Child care	________
	Household repairs	________
	Other	________
	________________________	________
Total Monthly Expenses		________

You may prefer a system like the one above, but with an extra column for possible cutbacks. Such a table would probably change from month to month. Although it would involve some extra work, it could be an added encouragement to keep your budget up-to-date.

There are other budget arrangements you may prefer. That's fine. The purpose of the exercise is to give you an opportunity to examine each expenditure with an eye to reducing it. You may have to do this kind of budgeting for two or three months before you can come to a realistic decision. Remember that while you may be locked into certain payments today—car payments, rent payments, and so on—you can decide now not to be locked into them in the future. You can stop buying on installment plans. That way you will no longer incur those particular expenses.

SMART SPENDING IS A GOOD INVESTMENT

Actually, smart spending is better than a good investment. It's better because it's guaranteed to provide a high rate of return, and because the rate of return is tax free. You can find those kind of investments if you do some work. But the real reason smart spending is so terrific is that you don't have to know much of anything, and you don't have to do much research to get that tax-free positive rate of return.

What I'm talking about, of course, is buying in bulk. For years now, I've bought my toilet paper in bulk because I know I'm always going to need it, and because it doesn't go bad. If you buy in bulk, you can go to a wholesaler where your saving is going to be at least 25% off the retail price. At the very least, you can get a 12% to 15% discount if you shop at a discount store or a retail outlet where items are regularly used as "loss leaders" (a "loss leader" is an item a store will sell really cheap in order to get you into the store to buy the regularly priced items, which are marked up anywhere from 40%to 200% of the wholesale price). The owner of my local discount drugstore used to say that 75% of the people who buy the loss leader he has every week come in and buy something else. But then, he's out of business now.

Buying in bulk automatically guarantees you a 20% to 25%, or maybe even 35% rate of return on the money you would otherwise have spent each week at the local supermarket. If you run out of toilet paper on Saturday night, you're going to save maybe 50% of what you'd spend at the corner grocery. This return is tax free. If you're in a 25% tax bracket (and you are, if you're eating regularly), you'd have to find an investment that pays 28% to beat the 20% saving on your bulk purchase. I'm making this sound better than it really is, because I'm not taking into account that you'll have to lay the money out in lump-sums sooner than you would if you spent it in dribs and drabs, but you get the idea.

And we haven't even talked about inflation. You can add the inflation rate to your rate of return, because that's how much you've saved by buying this year instead of next.

Say you buy toilet paper (you think I'm obsessed, right?) by the case from a wholesaler, and save even 20% on your money. That's a 20% rate of return. Say inflation is 4%—the toilet paper will be 4% more expensive next year. That' another 4% to add to your return. Now you're up to 24% return. If you found an investment that paid 24%, you'd have to pay tax on it.

If you're in a 25% tax bracket, you'd have to find a guaranteed, no-risk investment paying 33% to beat the toilet paper. If you know of such an investment, please write.

Obviously, the bulk-buying bit can be extended to things other than toilet paper, such as sanitary supplies, toothpaste, peanut butter, canned goods. This is one $1000 investment that will pay big dividends.

There are a lot of ways to spend smart. One of the best is to pay off your charge accounts. There are't many creditors who charge less that 15% on outstanding balances. Some of them charge 30%. Paying off your charge card is a guaranteed, risk-free, tax-free investment of somewhere between 15% and 30%.

Here's a handy little table that tells you how much smart spending is worth:

	If Your Tax Bracket Is:			
	20%	30%	40%	50%
And you save this much a year in smarter spending:	That is the same as if you had this much money in the bank.			
$ 100	$ 125	$ 143	$ 167	$ 200
$ 200	$ 250	$ 286	$ 334	$ 400
$ 300	$ 375	$ 429	$ 501	$ 600
$ 400	$ 500	$ 572	$ 668	$ 800
$ 500	$ 625	$ 715	$ 835	$1000
$1000	$1250	$1430	$1670	$2000

NOTE: The recent tax reform has given us only three tax brackets at the federal level. However, you must calculate your provincial tax as well, so one of these categories should apply (in general) to your situation, at least for illustrative purposes.

The Shop and Save Calendar

At certain times of the year, different items are traditionally on sale. If you watch and wait for these sales, you can save a lot. The Shop and Save Calendar is a general guide to when you might expect to find certain types of goods on sale.

JANUARY

Bicycles
Blankets
Books
China
Christmas items
Furs
Home applicances
Furniture
Jewellery
Linens
Lingerie
Sportswear
Stereos
Toys
Winter Clothes

FEBRUARY

Bedding
Cars (used)
China
Curtains
Furniture
Radios
Men's shirts
Silverware
Toys

MARCH

- Hosiery
- Luggage
- Skates
- Ski equipment
- Spring clothing
- Washers, driers

APRIL

- Dresses
- Housecoats
- Infants' wear
- Stoves
- Washers, driers
- Women's and children's coats.

MAY

- Blankets
- Handbags
- Linens
- Lingerie
- Rugs, carpets
- Tires
- Towels
- TV sets

JUNE

- Building materials
- Dresses
- Frozen foods
- Furniture
- Housecoats
- Summer clothes and fabrics
- TV sets

JULY

- Bathing suits
- Children's clothes
- Handbags
- Home appliances
- Lingerie
- Radios
- Rugs, carpets
- Men's shirts
- Shoes
- Sportswear and equipment
- Stereos
- Summer clothes and fabrics

AUGUST

- Air conditioners
- Bathing suits
- Bedding
- Bicycles
- Camping equipment
- Carriages
- Cars (new)
- Furs
- Gardening equipment
- Hardware
- Furniture
- Men's clothes
- Paint
- School clothes

SEPTEMBER

- Batteries and mufflers
- Bicycles
- Children's clothes
- China
- Dishes
- Lamps

OCTOBER

- Bicycles
- Fishing equipment
- Hosiery
- School clothes
- Silver

NOVEMBER

- Bicycles
- Blankets
- Cars (used)
- Children's clothing
- Dresses
- Men's clothes
- Stoves
- Shoes

DECEMBER

- Cars (used)
- Party items
- Shoes
- Women's and children's coats

SO TELL ME ALL ABOUT YOURSELF . . .

It's always a better idea to be earning interest on your money than to be paying it. Nevertheless, there are sometimes good reasons to borrow money. Just keep in mind that whatever you want to buy with borrowed money, the item must be worth not just its price tag, but the cost of borrowing as well. Borrowing has been around for a long time and many thousands, perhaps even millions, of words have been written about the pros and cons thereof.

Nevertheless, misinformation and misunderstanding still abound. What follows are answers to the most-asked questions about credit.

Q. How do I get credit?

A. The most important thing for a credit grantor to know is that your basic intentions are to repay any money borrowed. The credit grantor will evaluate you on the basis of your performance as a bill-payer, your financial ability to repay loans, and the assets you already own that may, in a pinch, be used to repay borrowed funds.

Credit grantors have different standards, but basically all of them will want to know whether you have a job, how much you make, where you bank, what you own. They'll also probably run a check on you at the local credit rating agency. When you fill in a loan or credit application form, you are giving blanket permission for the credit grantor to check out all these details.

Q. How do I know if I have a credit rating?

A. Anyone who uses credit gets a credit file opened at the local agency. If you've never used credit, but have been slow at paying utility bills, for example, you may also have a credit file. Even if you never intend to use credit, you may want to consider getting a credit file opened. One of the simple things that is almost impossible to do without a credit card is renting a car. Also, establishing a credit rating before you need it makes it infinitely easier to get credit when you do need it. To find out whether you have a credit file, phone your nearest credit rating bureau. They're in the yellow pages.

Q. How do I get a credit rating if I don't have one?

A. Open a bank account. That will give you a financial identity. Apply for a bank card *in your own name.* This is particularly important for women who may marry and take their husband's surname, or who may not always work. If you're not working, you probably can't get credit. If you have a credit card because of your husband's credit rating and something happens to him or to your relationship with him, *you* will not have an independent credit file. Your best bet is to get credit when you're single and working, and to keep your single name for legal purposes—i.e., your credit cards. If you're married and working, be sure to use your own personal name—Judy Miller, not Mrs. William Fraser.

Use your bank card and pay it off in full within the interest-free period. That will help establish your financial responsibility.

You can apply for a small loan and repay it according to the terms you and your banker agree on. It will cost you a bit in interest, but your credit rating will be established.

Q. What happens to my credit rating if I quit my job?

A. Unless you apply for new credit, probably nothing. Your employment status was established when you applied for credit. Unless you tell a credit grantor that your employment status has changed, your previous status remains.

Q. What happens to my credit rating if I marry?

A. Nothing, unless you precipitate a change. If you notify your credit grantors of your name change, you risk having your own personal credit file closed, and your credit experience will become part of your husband's. As I said before, even if you choose to take your husband's name for social purposes, you are legally entitled to keep your maiden name for legal purposes and in Quebec, you are obliged to keep it.

Q. What happens to my credit rating if I become separated, divorced or widowed?

A. If you have maintained your own independent rating, nothing. If you have credit cards because your husband ordered them for you, you will find them rescinded. You will then have to establish a credit file in your own name. If you have been out of the workforce and intend to remain out, it is likely that you won't be able to do so.

Q. What do I do if I'm turned down?

A. The first thing to do is to try to find out why. Start with the loan officer at the institution that turned you down. You should be able to get a reason. Either it is a legitimate reason or it is not. If it's legitimate—you don't meet the credit requirements of the credit grantor—you will have to improve your own performance or apply elsewhere. If you want credit from that particular grantor, ask for advice on how better to qualify (make more money, pay your bills on time, and so on). Remember that credit grantors evaluate applicants themselves. You may very well get credit if you apply elsewhere. If the reason is not legitimate—for example, for credit file says you haven't paid a bill and you have—then you have to try to get your credit file changed.

Q. How do I know what's in my credit file?

A. You are legally entitled to see your personal credit file at your local credit bureau. Phone your credit bureau and make an appointment to see your file. If you find that the information on it is not correct, it is your responsibility to show that it's wrong. This may be the best reason there is to keep receipted bills and cancelled cheques. Credit bureaus in general are anxious to have accurate information on file. Once you've brought proof of incorrect information to the attention of the bureau, you should have no trouble having it amended. (You can then go back to the credit grantor who turned you down and ask them to check your credit file again.) If you have trouble with the credit bureau, you can complain to your provincial consumer protection agency.

It's probably a good idea to check your credit file every now and then. And you should be aware of what may, and what may not, be included in your credit file in your province. For example, in Prince Edward Island, Ontario and British Columbia, no information about your race, colour or politics can be included. In Manitoba, information about race, politics, religion or health is not permitted. Your local Human Rights Commission can fill you in on the details in your province.

KNOW YOUR LIMIT

There are no hard and fast rules about what your credit limit should be. You alone must decide how much debt you can comfortably carry.

No matter what level of debt you decide you can live comfortably with and pay off, the key to success is to plan for it and build it into your budget. Before you move any new purchase from discretionary spending over to the fixed expenses side of your budget as a loan to be repaid, you must be sure you can afford the repayments.

Over the years, budget counsellors and personal money advisors have come up with several different guidelines for setting a limit for successful debt management. None of these guidelines includes the mortgage on your home. So, excluding your mortgage, one guideline is that your debt should not be greater than 15 or 20% of your take-home pay.

Another guideline suggests that you should not owe more than 30% of your discretionary income, that is, the income that remains after you've paid your taxes, your basic food, housing (rent or mortgage installment payments), and other absolute essentials.

A third guideline says your total debt should be able to be repaid within 18 months with 10% of your monthly take-home pay.

A fourth guideline says that if you can't afford to save at least 5% of your take-home pay each and every payday, you can't afford to borrow at all.

Obviously, there's no one right guideline for everyone. Don't be misled into thinking you can carry a prescribed percentage of debt because an expert said so. Do some hard calculations yourself to arrive at the discretionary funds you have available before you commit yourself to an increased debt load, and check your situation against these warning signs.

If even one or two of the following warning signs applies to you, it's time to embark on a plan to put your finances in order.

- you're behind in your payments and regularly receive delinquent notices.
- you pay only the minimum on your charge cards and department store accounts. You are never out of debt.
- you aren't sure how much you owe.
- you tend not to open any piece of mail that you think is a bill.
- you take cash advances on your charge cards to pay for ordinary expenses such as rent or food.

SHOPPING FOR MONEY

A lot of different kinds of institutions sell money. We're used to talking about "borrowed money", "taking out a loan", "charging it", "buying on credit." It's important to remember that what you're doing in all these cases is buying the right to use someone else's money. The price you pay depends on how much competition there is for the money, and how much you're paying for the services of the seller.

Before you make the decision to borrow, however, remember: borrowing and debt management is one area where a family consensus makes money management more effective.

Furthermore, you must know your own borrowing habits.

If you do decide to borrow, you might find the following Shopping Guide For Money, which describes the different sources of funds, useful in making your decision.

1. Relatives and friends

Pluses: Freely negotiable interest rate (often zero); freely negotiable repayment schedule (often indefinite).

Minuses: The lack of discipline in repaying, at a specified interest rate. May lead you to sloppy credit habits. Your relatives and friends may also attach strings to the loan.

2. Chartered banks

Pluses: Several types of cash loans available. Therefore you can choose the loan most advantageous to your purposes. One of the cheapest sources of cash loans, although interest rate varies. Relatively simple. You fill out an application, have an interview with a credit officer, wait a short time for a credit check and an answer from the bank.

Minuses: Bank may sell the asset if the loan falls delinquent, in which case you may find unpleasant persons haunting your premises.

Types of Loans

Demand Loan Principal amount to be repaid on demand at the lender's option. Interest rate tied to prime rate. Repayment may be lump sum or monthly payments.

Personal Installment Loan Principal and interest to be repaid in scheduled monthly installments over a specified period of time at a fixed interest rate.

Collateral Loan Same terms as personal installment loan, except because you have deposited with the bank some asset to back your pledge to repay the loan, the interest charged may be at a lower rate.

Mortgage Loan Long-term loan for purposes of buying a home. The property is put up as collateral; interest rate is renegotiable at specific times.

3. Credit Unions/Caisses Populaires

Pluses: Interest rates are competitive.

Minuses: Co-op may limit amount you may borrow; you have to be a member.

4. Savings Banks/Trust Companies

Pluses: Interest rates are competitive.

Minuses: May not be available to all potential borrowers.

5. Life Insurance Companies

Pluses: No repayment necessary. Simple to get—just fill out an application, you won't be refused. If your policy is an older one—issued before the mid-1970s inflation, interest rates will usually be lower than current rates, sometimes significantly lower.

Minuses: You must own a life insurance policy with a cash surrender value. Loan limited to 95 percent of cash surrender value. You reduce your family's insurance protection by the amount of the loan.

6. Consumer Loan Companies

Pluses: Relatively easy to get.

Minuses: Interest rates relatively high.

7. Bank/Credit Card Advances

Pluses: Immediate small loan upon presentation of credit card anywhere that it is accepted.

Minuses: Interest rates relatively high and payable from time cash advanced.

8. Pawnbrokers

Pluses: Can get cash on pledge of a valuable asset that's small enough to store in the pawnshop.

Minuses: You will be limited to a small fraction of the value of your asset.

9. Loansharks

Pluses: None.

Minuses: Interest rates often as high as 3000 %. Your life or physical well-being is often put up as collateral against repayment of the loan.

PAYING THE PIPER

Fifteen out of every one hundred of all Canadians get into financial trouble. Between one and two of those people cannot come to terms with their creditors. For this group, there are two choices. They may either declare bankruptcy or formally request the guidance of the (provincial) Court. Provincial laws regarding the "orderly payment of debt" vary. All provide for the Court to decide on a sum of money to be taken from the family income (depending on salary, number of dependents, and so on) and be deposited with the Court to be paid to creditors. Check with the Supreme Court office in your province (in Quebec, the Superior Court) for the procedure in your area.

While most families in financial trouble wish to repay their debts, many Court-appointed trustees believe the orderly payment of debt arrangements are onerous and inhumane. They say the process goes on for many years (the average is four) during which money is extremely tight, and that it is far less debilitating to a family to declare bankruptcy cleanly and quickly, in order to begin life again.

Bankruptcy is under the jurisdiction of the federal department of Consumer and Corporate Affairs. In order to declare bankruptcy, an individual must owe more than $1000, be unable to meet payments and not have enough property to repay the debts. A trustee in bankruptcy will prepare forms, after which all claims are frozen and all assets (except for basic furniture) are sold to repay creditors.

After about one year, the bankrupt person is released by the Court from all debts, with certain exceptions—child support, alimony, fines imposed by a court, and so on. Information about your bankruptcy will be entered on your credit files, although it will not remain there forever. Usually after five or six years the bankruptcy will not be reported. Check with your local authorities.

Regardless of whether or not your credit files carry information about your bankruptcy, the last thing in the world you'd want to do is over extend yourself on credit. Once out of debt, one must constantly be on guard against falling into that trap again. The best way of doing that is to keep an up-to-date record of your debt load, and to buy nothing on credit without first determining whether or not the debt is manageable.

CHAPTER 5

A Home of One's Own

When schemes are laid in advance, it is surprising how often the circumstances fit in with them.

—William Osler

Canada is a nation of homeowners. It is also a nation of high quality housing. We rank second only to the U.S. in providing basic equipment, such as toilets, hot water and such. We are tied with the U.S. for lowest "occupation density" (people in Canada are considered crowded if they don't have more than one room per person). And we rank first in the world with an average of more than five rooms per dwelling.

Well, you have to live somewhere. The question is should you rent or should you buy? And it really is a question. Most Canadians think that renting is inferior to buying, that paying rent is a pure waste of money, and that you only rent until you put together the down payment. Not necessarily so. Take a look at the following graph. It shows the cost of home ownership, the consumer price index, and apartment rents over the last 10 years. It also shows that there are good times and bad times to buy a home.

You can see that people who rented were far better off financially than people who owned during the high interest rate period since the 1980s began. So, having dispelled one of the great myths of our time—you should aspire to home ownership no matter what—let's take the high road to a sound decision. That means considering the pros and cons.

Let's start with what you probably know: there are no capital gains taxes on owner-occupied homes. That means anything you make on the sale of your home will be clear profit. That's a big plus, especially if the value of your home appreciates. That's one

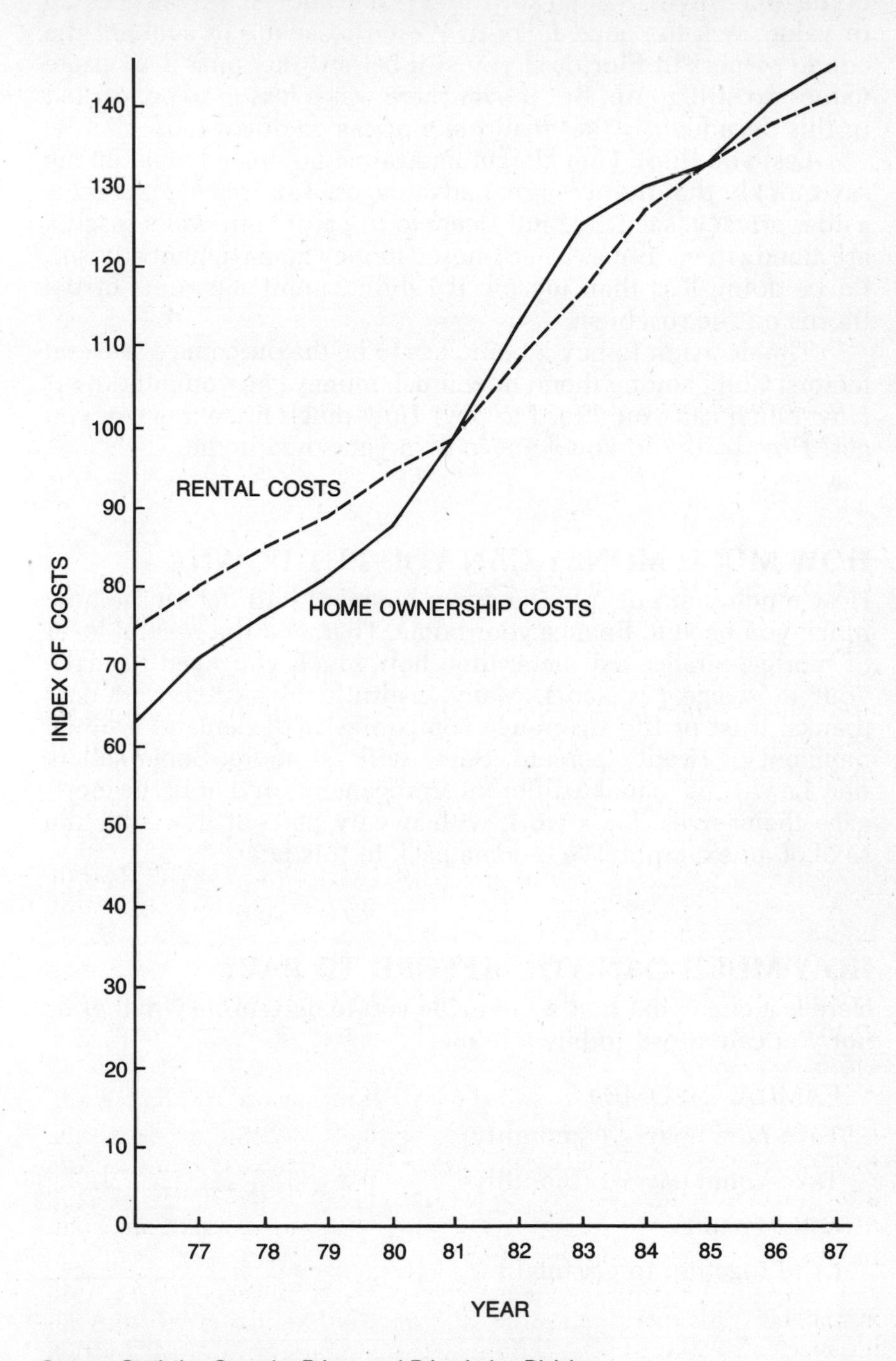

Source: Statistics Canada, Prices and Price Index Division

of the other myths which surround real estate—it always goes up in value. Ask the good folks in Western Canada or some of the condo owners in Florida if you still believe that one. Real estate values do still go up. But if ever there was a lesson to be learned in this decade, it is that real estate prices go down too.

Lest you think I am altogether against buying a home, let me say quickly that there are real advantages. Tax-free capital gains aside, privacy, security, and freedom to paint your walls fuschia are among them. But as a hard-nosed money management advisor, I'd be doing less than my job if I didn't point out some of the thorns on the rosebush.

The decision to buy a home has to be the outcome of several factors. Chief among them: how much money can you put down? How much can you afford to pay? How much financing can you get? How badly do you want to own your own home?

HOW MUCH MONEY CAN YOU PUT DOWN?

How much you put into the down payment will determine how much you need to finance your home. That, and the general level of mortgage rates will determine how much you need to make your mortgage payments. Many institutional mortgage lenders (banks, trust or life insurance companies) will demand a down payment of twenty percent. Some will ask more. Some sellers may be willing to make different arrangements and hold the mortgage themselves. Let's work with twenty percent down for the sake of an example. We'll come back to this later.

HOW MUCH CAN YOU AFFORD TO PAY?

Here is a check list that will enable you to determine whether or not you can afford to buy a home:

1. FAMILY INCOME

Take-home pay - 1 (monthly)	$__________
Take-home pay - 2 (monthly)	__________
Other income	__________
(*Add* together to get total.)	$__________

2. FAMILY EXPENSES
(other than rent or housing costs)

Savings (monthly)	$________
Food	________
Clothing	________
Installment payments	________
Education	________
Insurance	________
Transportation	________
Entertainment	________
Other	________
(*Add* together to get total.)	$________

3. HOUSING BUDGET

Income, from 1. above	$________
Expenses, from 2. above	________
(*Subtract* to get maximum available for housing.)	$________

4. HOUSING EXPENSES IF YOU BUY

Price	$________
Maximum down payment you can make, plus closing costs	________
(*Subtract* to get mortgage needed)	________
Estimated housing expenses	
Mortgage payment (monthly)	$________
Maintenance	________
Heating, utilities	________
Insurance	________
Real estate taxes	________
Other	________
(*Add* to get total housing expenses)	$________

5. BUDGET CHECK

Maximum amount available for housing, from 3. above	$__________
Housing expenses if you buy, from 4. above	$__________
House would be *within* budget by	$__________
House would *exceed* budget by	$__________

I'm going to fill in the check list for an imaginary family. Harry and Alice make $4500 a month between them. Their expenses, other than their rent, come to $3000 a month. So the maximum they have available for housing is $1500 a month.

They have savings of $20,000. That means the maximum they can pay for a house (because of the 20% down payment) is $100,000.

Say they find something for $95,000. They have to finance $75,000. At the time of writing (I put that in to make the point that there's no way anyone can forecast interest rates), the cheapest mortgage available is just under 10%. A 20-year mortgage at 10% on $75,000 means a monthly mortgage payment of $713.75. That is not the end of their home ownership costs. Maintenance is minimally $100 a month. Heating and utilities are easily $100 a month. Insurance might be $80 a month. Real estate taxes vary widely, but let's say $200 a month. TOTAL: $1193.75.

There's no question that Harry and Alice can afford a $95,000 home. Notice that I didn't tell you about the real estate industry's rule of thumb. The rule of thumb is that you can afford a house that costs up to 2 1/2 times your annual gross income. So Harry and Alice could afford a home costing $135,000, according to real estate mavens. I personally think going for a home this expensive in relation to their income is dangerous.

First, they'll have to save another $7000 for the down payment. Then, they'll need to finance $108,000. At 10%, their monthly mortgage payments become $1027. Even if their maintenance, heating, and insurance costs remain the same as in the less expensive house, the likelihood is that their real estate taxes will be higher. This couple is now facing monthly home ownership expenses of over $1500. Not only does this not fit our ownership check list, but what happens to Harry and Alice should one of them leave their job? What happens if interest rates rise? They simply have no leeway to manoeuvre. Quite frankly, I'm inclined to be conservative and not have to eat beans every night in order to live in my own home, and not have to sell my home at bargain basement prices because I lose my job.

IS HOME OWNERSHIP FOR YOU?

Before we get into any more nitty-gritty, let's establish whether you're a homeowner type. That means making sure you have a homeowner's temperament.

- Do you enjoy (and are you handy at) puttering around the house, improving the property, and so on? If you don't or are not, can you afford to hire help?
- Do you enjoy the sense of stability, roots, neighbourhood and community involvement which home ownership could provide?
- Are you likely to live in the same place at least four or five years?

If you figure you *can* afford a home and are the homeowner type, it's now time to look at the specifics.

1. Location You'll want to be near all the amenities, such as transportation, shopping, recreation facilities, community centres, and schools. The quality of the potential home environment should be compatible with your own particular lifestyle and values. But it's wise to know what appeals to other people when you decide to sell. The neighbourhood is an important consideration, and often colours the decision of the purchaser. Look hard at the neighbourhood in which you are considering purchasing a home. Is there a high density of houses, condos, or apartments? Is it a transient one, or do residents stay there for years? How aesthetic is it? Is there lots of green space, or is it in the middle of a busy shopping area? Which do you prefer?

Are the educational facilities of an acceptable standard for your children? Are they near enough? If not, is there adequate transportation? Like it or not, neighbours will be an important part of your decision. Will you be compatible with your neighbours?

Are there people of the same age and socio-economic level as you? Are there children to play with your own? It's better to be excruciatingly honest with yourself and your family by answering these questions *before* you move rather than after. And be sure you don't buy the most expensive home in the neighbourhood. The resale value of your home is influenced by the average price, not the highest or the lowest. You are better off with a cheap house in an expensive neighbourhood than vice versa.

2. Space If you have a family, will each child need a separate bedroom? Are you planning on having more children? Will some of your offspring be leaving home soon? The home may be required to accommodate your professional needs, since in this day of computer technology, it's the place where many people set up an office. If you are in this situation, does the housing provide you with an adequate workspace? Don't forget the fun side of home-owning. How much and what kind of space will you need to entertain?

3. Type Do you want an old house, or a new one? Older homes are often cheaper, but they may need more repairs. Are you good at handiwork, or would you have to spend a lot in hired maintenance? Many buyers limit themselves to new homes, convinced that the newer the property, the less worry. But age may have little to do with potential problems. Many older homes were built to last. Problems with new homes are always possible, and the price is no guarantee that you've bought a trouble-free home. Older areas also have mature shrubs and trees that provide a certain ambience that newer communities will not achieve for many years.

4. Condition When you tour the prospective house, new or old, investigate it with an eagle eye. Believe it or not, the average Canadian spends less than an hour examining a house before buying it. Take along a notebook to record your observations, both good and bad. Start outside, checking the condition of the grounds, the lawn, and so forth. Then move on to the foundation of the house. Is it solid? Is drainage up to scratch? How is the exterior of the house? Will it need a new paint job or brick-pointing in the near future?

Now go inside. How's the plumbing? Check all the taps, toilets, and water pipes. Are there any water spots on the ceiling to suggest a leak somewhere?

Also investigate the electrical and heating systems. How old are they? You don't want to move into a house in which the wiring system is a hazard to your family. Also inspect the number of electrical outlets available. Check whether the doors and windows open easily. Check on potential money savers or losers. Is the house well insulated? Are the windows properly set up to protect against heat loss? Look at the floors. Are they level? You don't want floors that resemble ski slopes. Your inspection should also include the basement, staircases—in other words, every last corner of the house.

If you don't do this yourself, hire a professional. Home inspectors are usually architects or consulting engineers. They'll charge you $200 to $300 and will give you a written report. You can make your offer to purchase conditional on such an inspection. You can contact the Consumers' Association of Canada for a helpful home inspection check list.

5. Legalities You'll have to sign an offer to purchase, a binding contract involving both buyer and seller. It specifies the price you have bid on the house, as well as everything you want the former owner to provide—like leaving certain appliances and fixtures behind for you, or taking care of any repairs or problems you have identified. Remember the early 1980s when many unfortunate homeowners insulated their home with urea-formaldehyde foam? It was later found to be linked to a variety of health problems. In many cases, the removal of the foam by the vendor was stipulated in the offer to purchase.

As an extra precaution, ask an independent lawyer or notary to check it. In fact, get one to check the entire transaction—it's likely to be the most serious you'll ever make. He or she will ensure that the seller is legally cleared to sell the property. And, of course, he or she will scrutinize the fine print of the contract to ensure you're not signing anything you shouldn't. You might also want to get some pointers from a banker in the area you're moving to. He or she will likely have a specialized knowledge of the local housing market. And it's a good idea to make your offer to purchase conditional on that home inspection.

6. Choosing a Mortgage Most homeowners don't pay cash for a home; the world of financing is beset with its own peculiar brand of jargon. *Mortgage* is simply another word for a loan that applies exclusively to houses. *Amortization* is the repayment period drawn out for you by the lending institution. The repayments are usually blended monthly installments of the capital and interest. A mortgage is repaid over several years and allows the lender to seize the house if the borrower doesn't pay up.

An *open mortgage* is one which allows the borrower to pay off the loan whenever he or she wants. A *closed mortgage* is one which allows the borrower to pay off the loan with no penalty, only at the end of the specified term. The *term* is the length of time the loan is in effect. On the last day of the term, the entire balance of the loan becomes due. It must either be paid off or be renegotiated.

It used to be that long-term mortgages with a fixed rate were the most popular. But fluctuating interest rates have prompted a whole smorgasbord of offerings from banks, trust companies, and even the seller of the home. Short-term mortgages are now commonplace, lasting between six months and five years. Seven- and ten-year mortgages are making a comeback, but won't really catch on until interest rates start going up again. The shorter-term mortgages are more flexible than 30-year mortgages (which are no longer available in Canada), but you've got to take more chances. You have to choose from either a short one and hope that interest rates drop, or a longer one and hope they don't—at least not while you're locked into yours.

The six month mortgage is the cheapest; the five, seven, or ten year the most expensive. There is usually a two-point spread between the lowest and highest interest rate. The most common mortgage is amortized over 20 or 25 years, but renegotiable at the end of the term you've chosen.

Variable rate mortgages can be arranged in such a way that the monthly payment remains the same for a fixed period (one or two years), while the interest rate floats in accordance with the prime rate of interest charged by banks. Many lenders will require a 15% down payment. At the end of the stipulated period, the lender and borrower will review the mortgage and the lending environment. Most variable rate mortgages are "open." That is, the borrower is allowed to pay off any amount of the mortgage without penalty.

Short-term and variable rate mortgages make sense in all circumstances except for rapidly rising rates. First, either rate is usually only about a half percent above the prime rate; second, most variable rate or short-term mortgages are "open". If interest rates begin rising, you can always renegotiate a fixed rate mortgage.

BIG DOWN PAYMENT OR SMALL?

There are two schools of thought about whether you should put down the most you can afford or the least you have to. On the side of putting down the most money you can afford is the fact that you will pay the least amount of interest to the mortgage lender. Look at the following table.

Even if you put down $50,000 on a $100,000 home, you still pay more than $60,000 in interest over 20 years. But if you put down only $20,000, your interest payments rise to over $100,000.

$100,000 home
(20-year amortization, 10% interest)

	$50,000 down 50,000 mortgage		$20,000 down 80,000 mortgage	
	Principal repaid	Interest paid	Principal repaid	Interest paid
After 5 years	$ 5,200	$23,350	$ 8,320	$ 37,360
After 10 years	13,700	43,400	21,920	69,440
After 15 years	27,500	58,150	44,000	93,040
After 20 years	50,000	64,200	80,000	102,720

On the side of putting down as little as possible is the fact that many people prefer to take over a mortgage when buying a home. Having a large mortgage with a low interest rate on your home when you go to sell it is a plus. To my mind, this is not a great reason. There are two valid reasons for putting down a small down payment: either you don't have more to put down and have found a house you can afford, or you have something better to do with your money.

LONG REPAYMENT PERIOD, OR SHORT?

For a long time, conventional wisdom advocated taking the longest amortization period you could get for your mortgage, on the grounds that your monthly payments would be low. However, as interest rates stayed high, people began to notice how much they were paying in interest.

It has now become smart to pay off your mortgage quickly. Here's a table that gives you some comparative numbers.

$50,000 mortgage
(20-year amortization, 10% interest)

Description	Frequency and amount of payment	Total interest paid	Mortgage paid off (years)
traditional	$475.84/month	$64,202	20 years
weekly payment based on 1/4 monthly payment	$118.96/week	$55,160	17 years
10% of original principal repaid on anniversary date ($5000)	$475.84/month	$17,790	7 years, 4 months

TIPS FOR FIRST-TIME HOME BUYERS

- Put down as much of a down payment as you possibly can. The lower the mortgage, the less interest you're going to pay. Since interest costs are not deductible for tax purposes in an owner-occupied home, you are paying both principal and interest in after-tax dollars. Say a couple has a 10% mortgage and $10,000 in a savings account. If they're earning 8% on the savings and are in the 40% tax bracket, more than $300 of their savings interest will be taxed away. Their net return on their savings after taxes is less than 5%. They would be better off taking the $10,000 out of savings and lowering their mortgage loan, which is costing them 10%.
- Shop around for best mortgage interest rates (they do vary).
- Shop around for the life insurance option on a mortgage. Many mortgage lenders offer a life insurance option that will pay off your mortgage should you die. The option is worth considering, but the cost of the premium can vary by as much as 400%. There are two things to consider when you look at insurance. First, does the coverage begin the day the funds are advanced, or on the day your formal offer to buy the house is accepted? If your offer to buy is conditional on getting financing and you get the financing, then it becomes an irrevocable contract.

  You may want to remember the case of a couple who were driving down to the lawyer's office to close the deal. There was an accident, and the husband was killed. Because their insurance coverage was effective from the date the offer was accepted, the widow got a debt-free house without ever making a mortgage payment.
- Check on repayment privileges. Can you pay without penalty? Can you repay in full? If there are penalties, what are they? With some trust companies, if you take a five year mortgage from them, it is closed for five years. That means you cannot repay it without paying *all* the interest. Beware of taking out a mortgage that will lock you in with heavy repayment penalties.

RENTING

After considering all of the above arguments for and against buying a home, you may decide that renting is for you at this time. If this is the case, many of the same considerations apply.

Just as you want to get value for your money when buying a house, you'll want the same for a rented unit. So the cardinal thing is to sign a satisfactory lease. It's a legally binding document, so be sure you're getting what you want.

Another seemingly obvious pointer is that before you sign a lease, you should *read it*! It's all too easy for an affable landlord to present you with a so-called "standard form" lease and ask you to sign it. You have every right to ask for some time alone to study it carefully. If it's too maze-like, get a lawyer or a knowledgeable friend to decipher it for you. Don't get done in by fine print.

For instance, don't assume the landlord's burdens. Your lease should not make you responsible for all repairs. You should be liable only for damage you cause. You should also ensure that the lease allows you to sublet, which may not seem likely when you first move in, but could well happen due to unexpected circumstances. You'll also want a signed copy of the lease for your own safekeeping, one identical to the landlord's copy.

If you're required to make a deposit, make sure you get a receipt. That way, you can apply it to the last month's rent instead of asking for it back. The rule mentioned earlier about making a careful inspection of a house before you buy also applies to rental accommodation. Check heating, electricity, plumbing, windows, doors, and especially fire hazards, smoke detectors, and escape routes.

A LITTLE PHILOSOPHY FOR THE FUTURE

While it undoubtedly won't be your first consideration in buying or renting, it won't hurt you to put into the decision-making pot a little information about the changing nature of Canadian society.

It has been clear for years that the population is aging rapidly. Right now, one out of every eleven Canadians is over 65. By the turn of the century, it will be one out of eight. Average life expectancy for women is over 80; for men, over 75. Similarly, one out of every three marriages ends in divorce. And the average age of divorcees is creeping up. As women divorce later in life, they tend not to remarry. Hence, there are greater numbers of single households or households which include only one parent. The three and four bedroom Canadian dream is becoming too big.

According to census figures, forty percent of new household formations are no longer child-oriented. With more two-income, no children families, not only is the three and four bedroom home too much house, the suburban bungalow is becoming an anachronism.

Condominiums, cooperatives and rental accommodation are all in demand, and single family Victorian houses with 11-foot ceilings and six bedrooms are being converted to multi-unit buildings that house three or four smaller family units.

Societies adapt to their own needs. Alternative housing is continually developing. New York, Chicago and Toronto are already experimenting with a tri-layered mix in low rises—stores on the first floor, offices on the second and third, housing on the top two or three. We may continue to be a nation of homeowners, but the nature of the housing is bound to change.

CHAPTER 6

Insuring Yourself: Life Insurance

Diane Keaton: I can't imagine anything worse than death.

Woody Allen: Oh, I don't know. Have you ever spent an hour with a life insurance salesman?

—*Love and Death*, 1975

Life insurance isn't fun. Most people rank thinking about death way down there with scrubbing the toilet. But it's just as unavoidable.

We tend to be passive about life insurance. Very few of us will undertake comparison shopping. Rather, we tend to wait until some enterprising agent knocks on the door, or telephones, to sign on the dotted line. This may be understandable, but it's hardly intelligent.

The first step in really understanding life insurance is to figure out whether you really need it. There is only one overriding reason to buy life insurance—to provide an income for your dependents if you're not around to provide for them. Some people buy life insurance as an investment. Personally, I think that's a lousy reason because, while very safe, it doesn't usually provide a great return. Others buy life insurance to make provisions for paying off their debts in case of death. This is fine, but it remains only a small part of the reason for buying.

WHO NEEDS LIFE INSURANCE?

If you have young children, you definitely need life insurance, unless you're rich (in which case you don't need this book). The younger the children, the more insurance you need. That's because it will take them longer to reach a position where they'll be able to support themselves.

If you're the sole income-earner in the family and you have dependants, you need insurance. More and more households can expect two or more incomes, but there are also a lot more single-parent families than there used to be. If you're living on two incomes and you have dependants, both people need life insurance.

If you don't have dependants, you may or may not want to have life insurance. If you're living with somebody who would be financially hard up if you died, then you may want insurance whether or not that person is a dependant. You may, for example, be a single person living with a parent with very little income and increasing needs. Life insurance could help provide for that person if you die first. If none of these conditions apply, spend the money on yourself or invest it for something you really want while you're alive.

Children don't need life insurance. They don't have incomes to replace, and it's highly unlikely you depend on them for yours unless you have a child movie star. If you have insurance on your child's life, you'd be really smart to cancel it and take out some more on your own.

HOW DO YOU DETERMINE HOW MUCH LIFE INSURANCE YOU NEED?

Don't take your insurance broker or agent's word for it. Work it out for yourself. The statistics show that most people who do carry life insurance don't carry enough. But it's also true that many new and creative policies are now available, and if you find the right person to handle your account, you may be able to get a much bigger bang for your buck.

As with everything else these days, it's hard to get good service. Some life insurance salespeople will ask you how much you need. Others will tell you it's five times your income or some other arbitrary formula. In fact, you'll need to do a fairly detailed analysis of your personal situation to determine exactly how much you need.

If you die before your time—and who doesn't?—how much income would your family need to carry on without you? Start by figuring out your current monthly expenses, and multiply them by 12 to get an annual figure. Then, using a realistic interest rate, calculate how much capital you'd have to invest to generate that much income.

Say you live on $3,000 a month, or $36,000 a year. At 10%, you'd have to invest $360,000 to generate that income, and more if you take taxes into account (I recommend you do). You're going to need more than $360,000 anyway if you have any lump sum payments to meet, such as mortgages, education for the children, or other debts.

WHAT YOUR HEIRS CAN EXPECT FROM THE GOVERNMENT

If you contribute or have contributed to the Canada or Quebec Pension Plans, your surviving spouse or your children may be eligible for a government pension. This will vary according to a number of factors, and according to which plan it is.

Remember that many government offices won't go out of their way to notify people that they're eligible for money. It's worth researching beforehand what your heirs may be entitled to, and leaving clear instructions about how to claim it.

Many rules and regulations have been changed over the last ten years to accommodate the growing number of common-law marriages and unorthodox family units. They are also not widely known. People who have to claim survivor benefits should be aware of that.

SHOULD YOU RENT OR BUY?

There are two basic kinds of life insurance: term and whole life.

Term insurance is the simplest, the cheapest, and it may be all you'll ever need. Think of it as renting your protection. At the end of the lease, or term, your protection ceases, and your rent, or premium, will go up.

Term insurance is most often sold for periods of one, five, or ten years, to age 65, or to age 100. Usually, you can renew as each term comes up. To take out the first policy, you'll need to prove you're in good health, and some policies require additional proof at each renewal. Premiums go up at each renewal, and some policies guarantee by how much. The renewal-type policies generally end at age 65 or 70, except for the policies to age 100.

Most term policies allow you to change your term insurance over to some form of permanent insurance without having to prove you're in good health. This clause is known as a "conversion feature." Make sure that any term policy you buy has it. Without it, there's no way, if your health breaks down, that you can convert your policy to permanent life insurance.

The following charts will give you an idea of the premiums for one-year, five-year, and ten-year renewable and convertible term. The charts only show the first 20 years of rates, but the policies continue to age 75, and the premiums (not shown) will show substantial increases. The rates are based on a survey of 30 companies. The criteria I used, and the ones you should use when you're comparison-shopping for insurance, are:

1. Is evidence of health required on renewal?
2. Are renewal premiums guaranteed, or were they contingent upon interest rates?
3. If it becomes necessary to convert, is there a good selection of alternative plans?

The rates I'm showing you are real market rates, but they're not the cheapest. I looked for the best value for the desirable mix of benefits. Life insurance is never cheap, but shopping around is worth it. I found differences of as much as $250.00 in premiums for one year for the same plan from different companies.

Certainly, term insurance is cheap and provides maximum protection when most needed, especially during the child-raising period. Now mortality tables tell us that we have an excellent chance of becoming very senior citizens, and that the life of a term policy rarely goes beyond age 70 or 75. At age 60, when most people are contemplating retirement, the cost of maintaining protection gets prohibitive, and the protection will cease in the not too distant future.

Term insurance to age 100 sounds like a wonderful idea, especially for those who are starting a family later in life. However, for most people, the premiums are high when compared with the rates in the charts you've just seen. To give you an idea:

Term to Age 100 — $250,000 Protection

Age 40

Female		*Male*	
Non-smoker	Smoker	Non-smoker	Smoker
$880	$1402.50	$1107.50	$1770

However, since many people's responsibilities don't obligingly melt away at their 65th birthday, it might be a good idea to add some permanence to your portfolio, not for investment purposes, not for pension income, but simply as a means of guaranteeing income to surviving family members.

$250,000 Term Insurance: Female, Age 40

	1 Year Renewable & Convertible Non-smoker		1 Year Renewable & Convertible Smoker		5 Year Renewable & Convertible Non-smoker		5 Year Renewable & Convertible Smoker		10 Year Renewable & Convertible Non-smoker		10 Year Renewable & Convertible Smoker	
Years	Annual Premium	Cumulative Premium	Annual Premium	Cumulative Premium	Annual Premium	Cumulative Premium	Annual Premium	Cumulative Premium	Annual Premium	Cumulative Premium	Annual Premium	Cumulative Premium
1	$222.50		$415.00		$307.50		$490.00		$377.50		$627.50	
2	252.50		487.50		307.50		490.00		377.50		627.50	
3	285.00		570.00		307.50		490.00		377.50		627.50	
4	320.00		662.50		307.50		490.00		377.50		627.50	
5	362.50		770.00		307.50		490.00		377.50		627.50	
		$1442.50		$2905.00		$1537.50		$2450.00		$1887.50		$3137.50
6	$297.50 *		$610.00		$420.00		$705.00		$377.50		$627.50	
7	337.50		717.50		420.00		705.00		377.50		627.50	
8	387.50		842.50		420.00		705.00		377.50		627.50	
9	445.00		992.50		420.00		705.00		377.50		627.50	
10	510.00		$1157.50		420.00		705.00		377.50		627.50	
		$3420.00		$7225.00		$3637.50		$5975.00		$3775.00		$6275.00
11	$412.50		$ 910.00		$610.00		$977.50		$787.50		$1457.50	
12	480.00		1070.00		610.00		977.50		787.50		1457.50	
13	555.00		1252.50		610.00		977.50		787.50		1457.50	
14	640.00		1455.00		610.00		977.50		787.50		1457.50	
15	747.50		1692.50		610.00		977.50		787.50		1457.50	
		$6255.00		$13605.00		$6687.50		$10862.50		$7712.50		$13562.50
16	$ 880.00		$1982.50		$905.00		$1582.50		$787.50		$1457.50	
17	1040.00		2322.50		905.00		1582.50		787.50		1457.50	
18	1225.00		2705.00		905.00		1582.50		787.50		1457.50	
19	1432.50		3127.50		905.00		1582.50		787.50		1457.50	
20	1675.00		3560.00		905.00		1582.50		787.50		1457.50	
20		$12507.50		$27302.50		$11212.50		$18775.00		$11650.00		$20850.00

$250,000 Term Insurance: Male, Age 40

	1 Year Renewable & Convertible				5 Year Renewable & Convertible				10 Year Renewable & Convertible			
	Non-smoker		Smoker		Non-smoker		Smoker		Non-smoker		Smoker	
Years	*Annual* Premium	*Cumulative* Premium	*Annual* Premium	*Cumulative* Premium	*Annual* Premium	*Cumulative* Premium	*Annual* Premium	*Cumulative* Premium	*Annual* Premium	*Cumulative* Premium	*Annual* Premium	*Cumulative* Premium
1	$260.00		$520.00		$420.00		$705.00		$480.00		$895.00	
2	297.50		610.00		420.00		705.00		480.00		895.00	
3	340.00		717.50		420.00		705.00		480.00		895.00	
4	387.50		835.00		420.00		705.00		480.00		895.00	
5	440.00		975.00		420.00		705.00		480.00		895.00	
		$1725.00		$3657.50		$2100.00		$3525.00		$2400.00		$4475.00
6	$357.50 *		$777.50		$610.00		$977.50		$480.00		$895.00	
7	415.00		920.00		610.00		977.50		480.00		895.00	
8	482.50		1082.50		610.00		977.50		480.00		895.00	
9	557.50		1265.00		610.00		977.50		480.00		895.00	
10	642.50		1467.50		610.00		977.50		480.00		895.00	
		$4180.00		$9170.00		$5150.00		$8412.50		$4800.00		$8950.00
11	$492.50		$1097.50		$905.00		$1582.50		$1070.00		$1882.50	
12	582.50		1290.00		905.00		1582.50		1070.00		1882.50	
13	687.50		1527.50		905.00		1582.50		1070.00		1882.50	
14	825.00		1817.50		905.00		1582.50		1070.00		1882.50	
15	982.50		2152.50		905.00		1582.50		1070.00		1882.50	
		$7750.00		$17055.00		$9675.00		$16325.00		$10150.00		$18362.50
16	$1160.00		$2517.50		$1317.50		$2482.50		$1070.00		$1882.50	
17	1362.50		2882.50		1317.50		2482.50		1070.00		1882.50	
18	1590.00		3270.00		1317.50		2482.50		1070.00		1882.50	
19	1847.50		3690.00		1317.50		2482.50		1070.00		1882.50	
20	2152.50		4162.50		1317.50		2482.50		1070.00		1882.50	
20		$15862.50		$33577.50		$16262.50		$28737.50		$15500.00		$27775.00

* *Every five years, if you qualify, you can pay a re-entry fee and renew at a lower annual premium.*

WHOLE LIFE

Think of term insurance as protection in case of premature death. We all have to die sometime, and even if you're thinking of dying old, you still might want the protection for whatever reason (for example, if you're unlucky enough to have several marriages to your credit). Kidding aside, there are sometimes good reasons for buying whole life insurance, or for buying your protection instead of renting it.

The reason whole life insurance is more expensive than term is that you're averaging the premium over your whole life. When you're young, you're paying much more than you would for term insurance. But when you're older, you're getting a much better deal than you would for the same term insurance protection. Simply put, the excess premium becomes a cash reserve against higher costs at a later date. If you cancel the policy, this reserve becomes available either as a cash surrender value, or in the form of a paid-up policy.

A paid-up policy is one where no further premiums are required and might be equal to or less than the original face value of the plan. Insurance has become much more complex in recent years, but if your policy provides cash value, and/or paid-up life insurance as part of its structure, it should be classified as a whole-life contract.

It may be useful to examine the premiums, or price for insurance, and see how future benefits are created. There are three elements which enter into the calculation of a premium:

1. the rate of mortality, or how many people will die at a given age, in a given time, within a given group (people who live in poor neighbourhoods die younger than people in rich ones, for example).
2. the interest rate.
3. the company's expenses, which they call the loading factor and include commissions, administration and taxes, in good company up there with death.

The loading factor goes up if the policy owner wants a piece of the company's profits when they're available. This kind of policy is called a participating policy because you get a dividend, usually based on the company's interest earnings. So the dividends will vary with interest rates and the competence of the company's investment managers.

The premium paying period is supposed to stretch over the life of the policy, that is, to age 100. But it can be shortened if you pay a higher amount for fewer years. This is known as a limited life plan. Premiums can be guaranteed for the life of the plan, or adjusted every five or ten years. The adjusted rate depends on changing factors such as the ones we have just seen.

Dozens of life insurance companies want your business. There are lots of plans to choose from. All of the plans are variations of term, whole life, or a combination. Your choice depends on your needs and what you're trying to accomplish with the amount of money you're prepared to spend on premiums.

If you have family responsibilities, it makes sense to buy the most protection you can for your premium dollar. That means term. But you do have to think about the future, once your immediate obligations no longer exist. The question then is, will there still be an obligation, a debt, or a responsibility? If so, will you have saved enough to meet your obligations? This is where looking beyond term insurance may be appropriate.

For years, insurance companies offered standard whole life products that made them a lot of money. It wasn't until the smaller, more aggressive companies started making huge inroads into the whole life market that the big players started to move, innovating and mixing new products to suit the more sophisticated consumer.

Adjustable life, for example, is term insurance to age 100 with premiums payable for a limited number of years. It has cash values and paid-up life insurance, so it's a variation of the whole life contract. Here's what a 40-year-old with a $250,000 adjustable life policy could expect:

1. a premium-paying period of 25 years.
2. at the end of 25 years, a paid-up policy of $250,000.
3. in the event of death before age 75, the paid-in premiums are returned in addition to the $250,000 face value of the policy.
4. at the end of the premium-paying period, if the policy is no longer required, it can be terminated and a cash withdrawal of $101,250 could be made (more, if kept longer).
5. a guaranteed increase is available without evidence of health.

For the first four years, the increase can be five percent of the initial amount of protection, increasing the policy by $50,000 in total if each option is taken. The premiums would increase, but so would the benefits.

Adjustable Life — $250,000 Protection

Age 40, Annual Premium

Female		*Male*	
Non-smoker	Smoker	Non-smoker	Smoker
$1117.50	$1625.50	$1582.50	$2425.50

If you're comparing rates with the previous chart, keep in mind that this plan goes to age 100, while the others are to age 70 or 75. This adjustable life premium finishes in 25 years, those in the previous chart in 35 years.

There's an interesting variation on whole life which is composed of a basic amount of participating (with dividends) whole life and an enhancement feature. Added together, the two elements make up the amount of insurance purchased. Each year, the dividends are used to buy one year of term insurance equal to the enhancement feature. Any excess dividends buy additional paid-up whole life insurance. As the total of this additional paid-up whole life increases, less of the enhancement is needed. If interest rates follow projections, the policy should be paid up by the 20th year. Here's what this means to our 40-year-olds:

Female

Non-smoker $250,000 Protection		*Smoker* $250,000 Protection	
Composed of	$ 53,191 basic	Composed of	$ 69,444 basic
	196,809 enhanced		180,556 enhanced
Total	$250,000	Total	$250,000
Premium	1,361	Premium	1,832

Non-smoker:

* Estimated date policy is self-completing — 20 years.

* Estimated cash value — 20 years:
$39,019
54,070 at age 65

Smoker:

* Estimated date policy is self-completing — 18 years.

* Estimated cash value — 18 years:
$40,606
61,118 at age 65

* Contingent upon dividend performance so that results may be higher or lower than anticipated.

Male

Non-smoker $250,000 Protection		*Smoker* $250,000 Protection	
Composed of	$ 67,568 basic	Composed of	$ 86,207 basic
	182,432 enhanced		163,793 enhanced
Total	$250,000	Total	$250,000
Premium	1,777	Premium	2,372

Non-smoker	Smoker
* Estimated date policy is self-completing — 20 years.	* Estimated date policy is self-completing — 19 years.
* Estimated cash value — 20 years: $49,213; 67,805 at age 65	* Estimated cash value — 19 years: $55,729; 79,869 at age 65

* Contingent upon dividend performance so that results may be higher or lower than anticipated. In other words, since the dividends are not guaranteed, paid-up status could be delayed and cash values would also be affected. Premiums, though, will remain level as long as required.

One of the most versatile of the whole life contracts is known as the "universal life plan." It could be classified as one-stop shopping, combining life insurance and investment in a single policy. While I don't think of life insurance as a smart investment in most cases, the following example has been chosen to illustrate an interesting combination of benefits.

Coverage:

1. Protection to remain level throughout the life of the policy.
2. Increasing protection: equal to the face value of the policy plus cash value.
3. Increasing protection: equal to the face value of the policy plus a return of the premiums paid to the date of death.

Premium:

You decide on the premium period—obviously the longer the cheaper. If you choose to pay a policy for life in 20 years, to age 65, there is a minimum and a maximum premium. In the first year the amount paid will fall between these limits. From the second year on, the client can pay any amount within these limits. If only the minimum is paid on a regular basis, the policy becomes a term plan. If the maximum premium is paid, it becomes a limited life policy. Premiums can be skipped as long as there is sufficient cash value to cover mortality, expenses, and rider costs.

What happens, then, to the premium?

When it is received, the provincial premium tax is deducted. The rest of the premium is deposited into the cash value account, where it can be invested in:

a) a daily interest account

b) a five year interest account, or

c) an equity fund

It's also possible to invest in a mix of two of the above options. I chose the equity account, which presumes a 12 percent rate of return for the life of the plan (if this sounds optimistic, read the chapter on mutual funds). I also took the whole life plan and cash value option in the event of premature death. The investment options all carry minimum guarantees. From the cash value account, expense charges are withdrawn covering sales costs, setup and administration costs, and mortality expenses. The cost of insurance is also withdrawn as well as any policy riders that are a part of the plan.

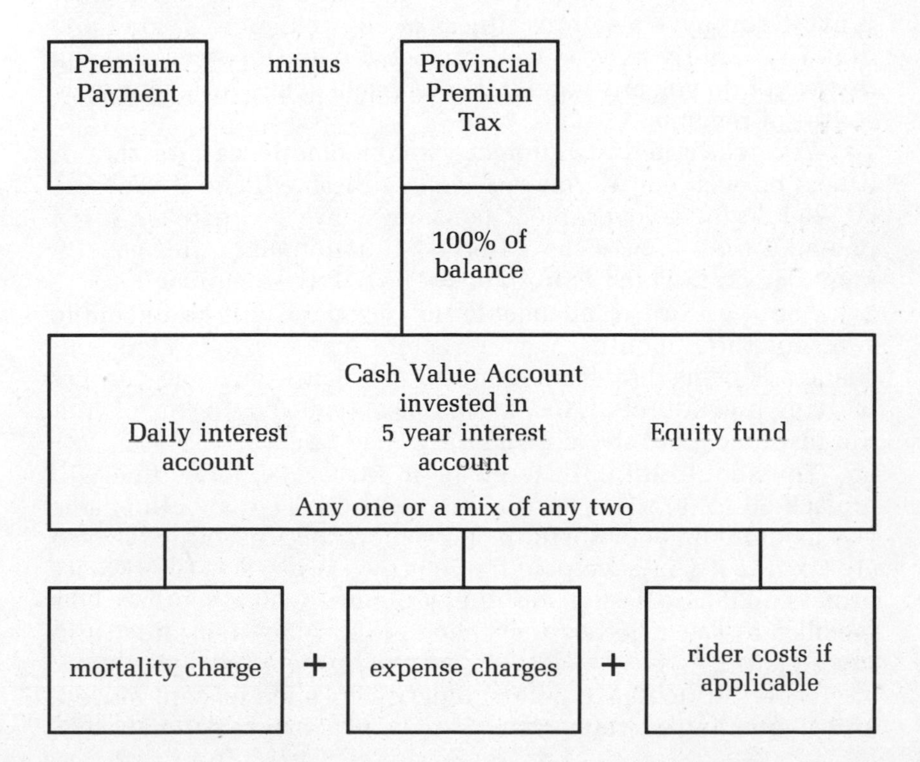

As long as there is enough cash value in the account to cover the charges, withdrawals or loans can be made, or you can use the money to cover premiums.

All life insurance decisions are long term. If you decide to surrender the policy, make loans or withdrawals from it, you will likely incur charges.

On each anniversary, you'll get a comprehensive annual statement showing all transactions, deductions, costs, premiums received, and the investment return credited. It will also show current cash values, loans, and withdrawals, as well as any pertinent information relating to the policy.

Remember that the death benefit includes the face value plus the cash value of the policy. Cash values are not guaranteed. Because you'll pay surrender charges if you cash the plan in during the first 14 years, there is a difference between the cash value and the surrender value over this period. After 14 years, you'll get the whole cash value back.

DISABILITY INSURANCE

What if you have a serious illness or an accident and you don't die? Your family may be well protected with life insurance, but that won't do you any good if you're disabled and lose your main source of revenue.

You really need to protect your income in case of serious illness or accident. If you're seriously disabled, you'll probably be eligible for a government pension. However, there's a lot of potential trouble between a normal situation and a full government pension, which is unlikely to be overly generous.

About a third of all people now aged 35 will be unable to work for three months or more before they're 65. In fact, your chances of being disabled are three times higher than your chances of dying prematurely. This doesn't mean you should cancel your life insurance, but those aren't very good odds.

You should think in terms of an insurance policy that will replace 50 to 60% of your pre-tax earnings. That should enable you to maintain your spending power, because disability benefits are tax-free if you have paid for your own insurance. Check with professional associations or other groups of which you may be a member to see whether they have group plans that are worth investigating.

Look for insurance that cannot be cancelled (except by you) and is guaranteed renewable. It not only guarantees that your disability contract is renewable; it freezes the premium at the original level for as long as you keep the insurance. It is most important to buy a policy that covers all types of disabilities.

If you want to be covered to age 65, it will cost a lot more than benefits for a limited period of say, five years. You can also reduce the cost of the premiums considerably by putting in a longer waiting period and a shorter benefit period. The longer the period during which the insurance company would have to pay benefits, and the shorter the waiting period before they start, the higher the premium will be.

Your occupation is a factor in determining the length of the benefit period and the waiting period. The factors vary from one company to another. Some companies have made the startling discovery that professional women are not the "weaker" sex and have reduced their premiums for women to the level charged for men. All "non-professionals" have trouble getting the same level or kind of coverage as professionals, and within the "non-professional" category, women are still charged more than men.

If you become disabled, you will be dependent on the quality of service from your insurance company. One tell-tale sign of a service attitude is the way your policy is delivered. If the person who made the commission on selling you the policy can't be bothered bringing it to you and explaining it to you in person, what kind of service will you get when there's no money to be made on dealing with you, such as when you file a claim? Choose your representative and your company carefully, and make sure you have read all the fine print in your policy before signing up.

One crucial element of your policy is its definition of disability. Don't hear only what you want to hear (that you'll get paid if you're off work due to an illness or an accident). As far back as 1928, the definition used often specified that you would be considered totally disabled if, due to sickness or injury, you were unable to perform the normal duties of your regular occupation and were not employed in any other occupation. It could also limit the use of this definition to the first 24 months of the policy, after which disability would be redefined.

Today, this definition is undergoing a facelift, with some companies taking a more liberal attitude. For example, you may be allowed to have a paying job in an occupation other than the one you had without losing any of your disability benefits. For the moment, this broader definition is not used throughout the insurance industry, nor does it apply to all occupations. It may be part of the policy itself, or sometimes it may be considered an additional benefit with an extra premium attached to it.

In order to qualify for disability income you must be under the care of a doctor and be prepared to provide proof from time to time as it is required. Pre-existing conditions, (illnesses or injuries you already had before you took out the policy) may be covered if they are disclosed by you, not misrepresented and not excluded by the insurance company.

It is *most important*:

a) to mention the circumstances associated with the pre-existing condition

b) that they be written into your application

c) that you understand in advance how your pre-existing condition might affect an eventual claim

d) that you go over your policy with your insurance representative and obtain detailed, careful explanations of the policy you are about to or have purchased

e) that you find out about any exclusions and why they exist.

Your ability to earn money is probably your greatest asset. Don't leave it unprotected because you didn't know or understand what you bought, or worse still because "it couldn't happen to me."

Rates, occupational classifications, benefit periods and waiting periods can all differ among companies. To add to the confusion, some companies offer riders, that is, extra clauses which can:

a) index your plan to the cost of living

b) allow you to buy additional coverage without evidence of health

c) start benefits from the first day for sickness or accident

d) extend coverage for either sickness or accident over your lifetime.

You can be eligible for rehabilitation training. Presumptive disability—speech, hearing, sight, hands, feet and recurrent disability can all be included as part of your policy.

If you are eligible for disability benefits under an employer plan, or government plan—pension, workmen's compensation, unemployment insurance, and so on—then the amount of disability insurance you want to purchase can be reduced or integrated with your other coverage. There is no way you can receive more through disability than you can by working, but there is one bright spot: if you are paying for the coverage yourself, the benefits will be tax-free.

It's not hard to find several companies willing to provide

maximum coverage, nor is it difficult to fulfill the medical requirements. But it is possible to purchase income policies in many different ways, and listing all of them available in the marketplace is not possible in this book. However, we are providing a comparative table of examples to give you an idea of what to expect.

Occupational Category	*Benefit Period*	*Benefit Starting Date*
1. Selected professionals and some white collar positions with no manual duties, such as lawyer, engineer, doctor.	2 or 5 years or to age 65, sickness or accident.	After 31, 61, 91, 121, or 181 days.
Example: Lawyer, age 40, male or female	Benefit to age 65. requires $3000/mth	To start after 31 days for sickness or accident.
Smoker: $1604.90/year Non-smoker: $1527.20/year		
2. Professional, technical and managerial positions, such as systems analyst, commercial artist, business owner.	2 or 5 years or to age 65, sickness or accident	After 31, 61, 91, 121 or 181 days
Example: Systems analyst, age 35, male or female	Benefit to age 65 Requires $3000/mth	To start after 31 days for sickness or accident
Smoker: $1783.10/year Non-smoker: $1696.44/year		
3. Persons doing light manual work, non-supervisory clerical office positions, such as secretary, computer operator.	2 or 5 years or to age 65, sickness or accident	After 31, 61, 91, 121 or 181 days
Examples: Secretary, age 33, female	Benefit to age 65 Requires $1000/mth	To start after 31 days for sickness or accident
Smoker: $890.60/year Non-smoker: $848.57/year		

Occupational Category	*Benefit Period*	*Benefit Starting Date*
Printer, age 33, male	Benefit to age 65 Requires $1000/mth	To start after 31 days for sickness or accident
Smoker: $599.60/year Non-smoker: $572.12/year		
4. Persons holding factory or blue collar positions, such as hair stylist, sales clerk, painter, TV repairer.	2 or 5 years	121 or 181 days
Examples: Hair stylist, age 33, female	Benefit for 5 years Requires $1000/mth	To start after 121 days
Smoker: $578.70/year Non-smoker: $552.26/year		
TV repair, age 33, male	Benefit for 5 years Requires $1000/mth	To start after 121 days
Smoker: $418.40/year Non-smoker: $399.98/year		

Since the amount of income you can apply for is based on how much you earn, the following two definitions are important for those considering disability policies:

1. *Earned Income*

   If you're self-employed, this means gross earnings minus operating, overhead and other business expenses before taxes. For those taking a draw in lieu of salary, it's gross earnings minus expenses before taxes. For those on salary, it's gross salary including commissions before income tax deductions.

2. *Unearned Income*

   This is income you'll continue to receive even if you can't work: dividends, interest, investment income, rental income after expenses, and pensions are examples.

When earned and unearned income are added together, they give your total annual income. However, only earned income can be replaced by benefits under an income insurance policy.

STRATEGIC PLANNING IF YOU ARE A SMALL BUSINESS PARTNER

A potential problem which has received little attention is the possibility of a business partner suffering a lengthy disability. How long should he or she be carried? How big a financial burden would be placed on the working partner(s)? At what point should there be an offer to buy out the disabled associate? From where would the funds come to activate the sale and transfer of interests?

The solution to these questions could lie in the purchase of disability buy-out insurance, which would provide the necessary dollars for the transfer of ownership interest when lengthy disability removes an owner. A written agreement would set out the terms of the buy-out providing for the purchase of the disabled's interest in the event of accident or sickness. A time would be established that would elapse before the buy-out would become effective. A clear definition of what would constitute total disability is a necessity. The insurable value of the business would be established by an acceptable formula and the funding of this sum could be accomplished by a single lump sum, a down payment, plus monthly installments or solely by monthly payments.

CHAPTER 7

Insuring Your Possessions

My riches consist not in the extent of my possessions, but in the fewness of my wants.

—J. Brotherton

HOUSEHOLD INSURANCE

If you own your home, your mortgage lender will insist that you have insurance to protect at least the outstanding balance on your mortgage. But your home is probably your biggest asset, and it's even more vital to you that your hard-earned investment be protected.

Home insurance covers both the building and its contents (we'll get to tenants in a moment), as well as personal liability. Remember that basic or standard form policies cover named perils actually listed in the policy. If these include fire, lightning, wind, hailstorms, smoke, explosion, riot or "civil commotion," falling objects, damage from aircraft, vandalism, theft, loss of property moved from the premises, you may not be protected if your pipes burst while you're away in the winter. You may be insured against damages caused by the weight of snow on your roof in winter, but not against damages caused by melting snow. You may find you're not covered for damages if your waterbed leaks, or that your satellite dish isn't covered under your policy.

Most people carry broad policies that insure their houses against all risks and the contents against specific dangers. The phrase "all risks" usually covers all the things you'll find in a standard form policy, plus things like water damage from burst pipes, plumbing, heating or air conditioning, collapse of the building, damage from the weight of ice and snow, damage to your electrical appliances caused by a sudden surge of power, and so on.

While all risks should mean everything that is *not* specifically included in the policy, you may find some specific exclusions such as floods, earthquakes, and sewer backups. If you want to be insured against these things, you may have to pay a higher premium and request specific coverage.

Your belongings, or the contents of your home, however, may not be covered in the same way as the building. They are likely only to be covered for the dangers actually mentioned in the policy, such as fire, smoke, explosion, falling objects, and theft.

You can get comprehensive policies which insure both your building and its contents from all risks, with possibly a few specific exceptions listed in the policy. If your home is a condominium, the policy will take that into account, and only your personal property will be insured. The policy will include any additions and improvements you've made to your condo.

HOW MUCH HOME INSURANCE DO YOU NEED?

You probably don't need to insure your house for its full market value, for the simple reason that if it burned to the ground, you'd still have the land on which to rebuild another one. However, the replacement costs for some beautiful old houses may be higher than the market value. Or alternatively, if you have put a big down payment on your house, insuring the outstanding mortgage will probably not be enough to cover the cost of replacing it.

Determining replacement costs isn't easy—it's usually done by professional appraisers. They base their estimates on both replacement costs and depreciated value. You can also get estimates of construction costs per square metre by calling a general contractor.

Another important point to remember: the part of your policy that insures your belongings may be for replacement costs or for actual cash value, and that can make a huge difference. If you have a perfectly good television set that is ten years old, its cash value is likely to be a fraction of the cost of a new television. To determine how much coverage you'll need for a replacement cost policy, you'll need to know how much it would cost you to replace each item at current retail prices. A replacement cost rider can be added at a nominal cost.

If you have actual cash value coverage, you will need to be able to supply your insurer with dates of purchase so that current value can be determined, taking use and depreciation into account.

The most common calculation of the value of personal belongings is roughly 60% of the insured value of your house. So if your house is insured for $100,000, its contents would automatically be insured for $60,000. Some companies are changing to a 70% standard coverage rate. You can't buy less coverage than this, but you can pay for extra coverage if you feel that your belongings are worth more than the standard amount.

Both homeowners and tenants should make a list of their possessions and estimate their value. You'll probably receive a special booklet or list from your insurer to help you do this. Each item should be listed with its date of purchase and its price. If you have a professional appraisal of value, it should be recorded with the date. Describe each item as graphically as possible. Include age, brand name, size, model number, serial number, and any other relevant information. List account numbers for all your credit cards, patterns and place settings for silverware, and china and so on.

One good way of jogging your memory is to take pictures or videotape every room so that you have a visual record of what you own. Another easy way is to go through each room with a tape recorder, describing all the contents as you go. Nobody likes taking the time to do this, but people who have been robbed of their possessions are grateful to have this kind of reminder. A good record is unlikely to be contested. Leave a copy with your insurance agent, or in your safety deposit box.

Remember that very valuable possessions such as art, jewellery, furs, silverware, and documents are often covered to a limited amount by standard household insurance. For example, there is often a $2000 limit on furs, jewellery, and watches; between $500 and $3000 for documents (manuscripts, passports, airline tickets, securities, etc.); usually about $5000 for silverware, and a couple of hundred dollars for cash, stamps, and the like.

It may be worth it to buy greater coverage on these items by listing them separately. Insurance companies call these specifically scheduled items. Professional appraisals of valuables may be required and all of this can become quite costly. Sometimes, such as in the case of valuable but rarely consulted documents, or jewellery that is seldom worn, it may be much more cost-effective to keep things in a safety deposit box rather than paying appraisers and insurance companies. This is also true of items that have great sentimental value and cannot be replaced at any price.

The personal liability side of your home insurance is meant to cover you if someone decides to sue you; for example, after slipping on your front steps. This kind of insurance can be quite broad, even covering you for actions taken by your unmarried children still at home for which you may be sued.

The standard home insurance coverage is about $500,000, but doubling it to a million dollars may cost as little as $5 a year in premiums. Very few people are ever sued under this section of their policies (that's why it's so cheap), yet no one should be without this protection. Claims have been rising.

WHAT ELSE DO YOU NEED TO KNOW?

The personal liability side of your policy, unlike the rest of the policy, usually doesn't have a deductible. Your policy's provisions on whether you have to pay for the first $200, $500, or $1000 of damages to your home or belongings will significantly affect your premiums. There may be a 20% difference between the cost of a $500 deductible and a $1000 deductible.

Premiums will also vary considerably based on the statistical risk of your neighbourhood or city. Some of the factors that are included in determining risk are crime rate, fire protection, and the materials used in house construction. The insurance company's individual experiences in a given area, their cash requirements, and their portfolio risk mix may also be considerations.

Unlike your automobile insurance, your home insurance won't necessarily become more expensive if you make a claim. But if you make several claims over a short period of time, coverage will be hard to obtain and your premiums will go up. Some companies give preferential rates for newer homes, or for older homes that have been completely renovated with new wiring and plumbing. Older people, who tend to spend more time at home, may be considered a better risk. You can also get a lower premium if you prove you have good security habits by installing smoke detectors, dead-bolt locks, or a central station burglar alarm. Of course, if you never make a claim, you'll be considered a good risk, and you may be able to negotiate a discounted premium.

Most policies provide inflation protection. You should review your coverage each year, whether or not it is indexed to inflation, to make sure it still reflects your personal needs. If you live with someone, it's a good idea to have both names on the policy. Otherwise, the person whose name isn't on it may have trouble getting re-imbursed for losses or damages. Check to see that the insurance company has a formal policy on recognizing common-law relationships. Some have set a standard of three years, or one year if the couple has a child. Unless you meet these criteria, you may not be covered.

As with so many other financial products, home insurance should be purchased from an agent or broker you can trust. Some of the large companies have their own agents. Brokers are independents who should be able to give you a good comparison shopping tour. Ask your friends and family what kind of experiences they've had, and try to find the most reliable broker who'll take your interests to heart. Choose your broker with as much care as you do your other professionals, such as doctors or lawyers.

Because automobile insurance claims are a higher percentage of insurance premiums than household insurance claims, companies may pressure their salespeople to get your household policy as well as your car insurance. Beware of a hard sell. Make sure the policy's fine print says what you want it to say, remembering that this coverage costs something, and bargain basement insurance probably cuts corners somewhere.

WHAT TO DO IF YOU ARE ROBBED

Call the police. The chances are slim that your property can be recovered, but you'll need a police report to prove your loss to your insurance company, bank, and possibly Revenue Canada.

You should immediately notify your bank and any of your credit card issuers. Thieves use chequebooks and credit cards at once after stealing them, and a few hours' delay gives them the chance to make a lot of purchases. You may have limited liability on cheques written by a thief or transactions put through on your credit card, but if the imitation of your signature is good, you may have some trouble proving the forgery.

AUTOMOBILE INSURANCE

Canada has a patchwork system of automobile insurance. Some provinces have public auto insurance (Manitoba, Saskatchewan, British Columbia) and the others have private auto insurance. Quebec has a combination system where you purchase part of your coverage from the provincial board and part from a private insurer.

All drivers must have bodily injury liability insurance. This will pay for a lawyer to defend you against lawsuits by victims of car accidents, and pay the judgement if you lose. You must also have personal injury liability insurance. If you have substantial assets or earning power, you'll need at least $500,000 coverage per accident. You may need to pay extra for uninsured motorist coverage. It can be expensive, but it can save you a lot of grief if you are injured by a hit-and-run driver, or by someone who can't pay a judgement.

Collision and comprehensive coverage on your own car may be a waste of money if your car is more than five years old. The insurer will pay you no more than its market value if it is stolen or totalled. For a newer car, you can save on collision premiums by increasing the deductible. With a $500 deductible instead of a $100 deductible, you can cut your collision premiums by more than 40%. The basic principle here is that you should never risk more than you can afford to lose. But you should also avoid paying to insure what you can afford to risk.

Brand-new cars depreciate 30% the minute they're driven off the lot. If you wreck your car two weeks after you buy it, you'll only get 70% of what you paid for it. Recently, the Royal Bank filled this market gap with a car loan that insures the 30% value, guaranteeing you the full value of your new car for the first year. Insurance companies will also offer this, for a higher cost. The Royal Bank initiative will probably lead to some changes in this area as insurers feel the pressure to compete.

Some insurance companies offer premium reductions for anti-theft devices or alarms. Here again, payments often fall far short of the full replacement value. It might be smart to buy extra coverage.

Some policies pay part of the cost of a rental car while you're waiting for the insurance settlement. The rental car payments provided by your policy may terminate before your car is repaired. That's why it's probably not a bad idea to purchase a little-known rider which provides very cheaply for much better rental coverage if your car is stolen, or if it's in for repairs of theft damage.

Many owners of upscale German cars have experienced repeated break-ins to steal their valuable stereos. You can now purchase a cheap plastic front to disguise your expensive sound system. While your automobile policy probably won't cover the cost of expensive items stolen from your car (designer clothing, golf clubs, and so on), you can probably recover these costs from your home insurance policy, as long as you can prove that the doors were locked at the time of the theft. You can also buy stereo systems that slide out, so you can take them with you. And there are kits that will convert your existing stereo to a removable system.

EXCESS LIABILITY INSURANCE

If you are ever found responsible for an accident in which the victims suffered financial losses, you could be eternally grateful for excess liability insurance which supplements the protection you already have under your home and automobile insurance. A judgement against you could lay claim to your future income for many years.

Excess liability coverage is only available to those who already have substantial primary coverage. The best policies cover almost everything, except business-related activities. For example, excess liability could protect you from lawsuits for libel, slander, invasion of privacy, malicious prosecution, wrongful eviction, defamation of character, or discrimination. Some policies may cover you for bodily injury or property damage resulting from the use of reasonable force to protect persons or property. A good policy also pays for most of your legal defense. Make sure everybody in your household who is related to you by blood, marriage or adoption, including children away at school, is covered under your liability insurance.

OTHER INSURANCE CONSIDERATIONS

Travel insurance is something everyone should consider. Even the shortest stay in a hospital outside your home province can be expensive. Notice that I said home province. Since Medicare and hospitalization are provincial responsibilities, coverage is not identical from province to province. You may find yourself out-of-pocket even though we are all led to believe that we will be reimbursed for out-of-province medical expenses. It's not necessarily so. And it's particularly not so if you incur expenses outside the country.

There are four aspects to travel insurance you'll want to look at: having an accident; illness or death; lost or damaged baggage; and something that gets in the way of your using the ticket you've purchased. You can buy any or all of these, individually or together.

Travel Insurance Compared

	Premium[1]			
Company	*Medical*	*Baggage*	*Trip Cancellation*	*Package*[2]
Travelers	52.50	51.60	100.00	148.00
Voyageur	48.00	79.00	80.00	160.00
Mutual of Canada	43.00	52.00	74.00	124.00

[1] Family of four, 21 day vacation, $1 million medical and health, $2000 baggage, $2000 trip cancellation.

[2] Plans include the same medical, baggage and trip cancellation coverage, plus flight, common carrier and accidental death and dismemberment insurance. Voyageur provides this only with a charter tour.

CHAPTER 8

Strategies to Reduce Taxes

There is only one way to kill capitalism—by taxes, taxes and more taxes.

—Karl Marx

He who knows how to suffer everything can dare everything.

—Vauvenargues

Tax systems around the world are being reformed. The reason is simple. Every government in the world needs more money to service social, economic, and political programmes put in place decades ago when national economies were growing faster and a decade of inflation had not distorted what we believed to be a reasonable, feasible, equitable, and efficient use of taxpayers' money.

But the world has changed, attitudes have changed and, most of all, the way the world works has changed. Our tax system was designed (I use the word loosely) to raise revenue to do what the private sector couldn't (or wouldn't) do. Originally, it was to pay for World War I. Gradually over the years, the tax system has been pushed, pulled, and redesigned to pay for more and more, and even to change the behaviour of taxpayers—we have incentives to invest in Canadian stocks, films, gas and oil exploration, research and development, and so on.

To many minds, the negative aspects of our system far outweigh the positive. Apart from a lot of ballyhooing, there are harmful side effects to this discontent. People, discouraged by the manoeuvres of the taxman every April, opt to leave the legitimate economy. They cope with the system by moonlighting, working "under the table", doing whatever they can to avoid declaring their income. To the detriment of the economy, they succeed, chalking up billions of undeclared dollars every year.

One of the biggest changes that occurred during the decade of inflation is that a lot of people lost their bearings. It was hard, with prices going up every day, to figure out what was a legitimate price. Those of us who grew up in the 1940s and 1950s couldn't imagine paying $6 a pound for steak, or $100,000 for a house. Those of us who entered the work force during the 1960s and 1970s had never known a world where prices didn't go up every day.

We had to learn how to cope with inflation—it took some of us longer than others. Much of the wisdom we had learned, like "save for a rainy day", turned out to be not so wise. The savers of the world got stuck with negative real interest rates and taxable nominal rates. In Canada in 1974, for example, Canada Savings Bonds were issued at 10%. But the inflation rate was also 10%, so in terms of purchasing power, the interest rate was zero. That was bad enough. Interest income is taxable, so if you owned CSBs and your marginal tax rate was 40%, you had to pay 40% of your nominal 10% interest to the taxman. You hadn't made any real income, but you had to pay real dollars in taxes.

We all learned to cope in our own way. Some of us learned to be borrowers, because we were paying back with cheaper dollars. Some of us learned to stop saving. Some of us decided that we couldn't trust our elected leaders to lead us out of the inflation fog, because they didn't know any more than we did. Some of us walked away from the tax system.

Walking away from the tax system didn't originate in the 1970s. During wars, there is always a black market—goods are bought and sold illegally, money is made outside the reporting system. What was new was the pervasiveness of the walking away, and the acceptance of it. The black market gave away to the underground economy. The underground economy is now interchangeable with the informal, or even the parallel, economy. Not too much approbation or disapproval in those words.

Estimates about the size of the underground, informal, or parallel economy range from 10% to 25% of the reported economy. Every time a government raises taxes and estimates how much additional revenue will come from the tax hike, reality comes up short of that number. That's one reason why governments need more money. There are others.

Look at the staggering amount of debt that has been accumulated around the world. Interestingly, ordinary people have caught on faster than big business or governments. As long ago as the early 1980s, individual consumers stopped buying on credit and started getting their own houses in order. It took big business and governments longer to recognize that the debt they had accumulated was going to be very hard to pay back.

All the while, technological improvements to the production and distribution process were gathering steam. The deep recession of the early 1980s put many people out of work, and many businesses folded.

New means of delivering goods and services, combined with the need to reduce the debt meant that big business had to begin a streamlining process that has not yet stabilized. Inflation, the recession, accumulated debt, the technological revolution, the need to hold market share of an increasingly competitive international market, and the need to maintain social programmes encouraged governments all over the world to keep on raising taxes.

I remember the outrage my daughter felt when she got her first paycheque. She was hired at $4.20 an hour; she worked a 42-hour week; she expected $176. What she got was $156. When she got a raise to $5.00 a hour, her deductions went from $20 a week to $45 a week.

The shock never really subsides as you realize just how much of the money you earn is not yours at all. Think about it. With over 25% of your annual income lopped off in taxes, you are, in effect, working for over one quarter of the year without earning a cent. And that's only income taxes. Counting sales taxes, excise taxes, property and school taxes, customs duties, water taxes, and others, families pay 40%, and in some cases 50%, of their gross income in taxes.

You may be interested in some Canadian specifics. At the federal level, Canada spends about $30 billion more than it takes in every year. The majority of the provinces spend several billion dollars more than they take in. If we could collectively agree to raise taxes to cover deficits, or agree to cut spending to meet revenues, the likelihood is that no one would care much about tax reform. Since we cannot agree, governments are looking to change the structure of the tax system with the idea that maybe they can solve the problem posed by the deficits.

JUMPING ON THE BANDWAGON

There have been many times and many places where people and governments have struggled with a flawed tax system. Canada underwent a massive reform only 16 years ago. We continue to "improve" the system every year—in 1986, 300 pages of amendments were added to the *Income Tax Act*. In 1987, yet another phase of tax reform was begun.

The U.S., the U.K., and a variety of European countries have patched and bandaged their leaky tax systems, all trying to cope with insufficient revenue to cover excessive government spending. Tax reform, late 1980s style, differs from earlier tax reform in two specific ways. In 1971 (more correctly, in the 1960s when the discussions were going on), we were convinced that the Canadian economy would boom forever and that our only problem would be redistributing income. We believed that governments solved problems, whether economic, social, or regional. We don't believe either myth any more, at least not those of us who remember the Glace Bay heavy water plant, the Come-By-Chance oil refinery, the Maislin bailout, scientific research tax credits, Via Rail subsidies, and the unemployment insurance system.

The unending flow of money down the drain in the guise of government incentives, industry bailouts, social bribery, and tax boondoggles has convinced many Canadians that direct government intervention doesn't always, or ever, bring expected results.

Tax philosophers around the world seem to have tired of taxing income. The new fashion is to tax consumption. In other words, tax what we take out of the economy when we spend, as opposed to taxing what we put into the economy, that is, our incomes.

In Canada, personal income tax brings in half of all tax revenues. The corollary to the new philosophy is that when you depend so heavily on one tax, people notice and try to get out of paying it (this really narrows the tax base). Therefore, governments might collect taxes more easily by collecting in bits and pieces.

Not to be entirely cynical about the current rush, or crawl, to tax reform, the present tax system is jerry-built. The parts of it we can understand show many inequities and distortions. For example, income is always taxable, but losses are not always deductible. So why should people take risks? Many hidden taxes such as sales tax on business inputs and payroll taxes reduce political accountability.

Why reform the tax system now? Aside from deficit reduction, we need a system that encourages flexibility and helps Canadians adapt to economic change. The U.S. tax reform of 1986, which was unexpected, put pressure on Canada, which was intensified when our other trading partners started following the American example.

Lower tax rates and economic efficiency are replacing government orchestrating. In the U.K., corporate tax rates went down to 35%; they got rid of fast depreciation deductions; they lowered income tax by increasing their Value-Added Tax (VAT). France, West Germany, and Australia are all going in the same direction. Japan is considering VAT and lowering personal income taxes in 1988.

The U.S. tax reform cut maximum personal taxes from 50% to 28%. Corporate tax rates were cut from 46% to 34%. Special deductions, and accelerated depreciation tax shelters are gone. It is unclear what the fallout will be. The winners among personal taxpayers will be the low income and high income taxpayers who didn't use tax shelters. In the corporate sector, winners will be the services sector—retailers, high tech, and those for whom fixed capital is not a big factor. The losers will be the high income taxpayers who have made extensive use of tax shelters and, on the corporate side, those with heavy capital investments.

Despite our seething, we do get some of our tax dollars back, though many will argue that it is an inefficient system. We receive "free" medical care and hospitalization if we're ill, an unemployment insurance cheque if we're out of work, a pension cheque when we retire, grants and loans if we want to study. Roads and garbage collection come out of our taxes as do public libraries and parks.

One thing you can count on is that we will continue to see tax reform. You can also count on this tax reform not being the last. There is no such thing as a tax system that everyone loves. With each tax reform, we redistribute our displeasure with it. That means you have to make the existing system work to your advantage, and keep up in your reading of the latest developments at all levels of government.

TAX PLANNING

The basic purpose of tax planning is to ensure that taxable income is taxed in a year in which your tax burden is lightest. At the same time, you want to use the tax laws to ensure that you will have the most money possible to spend, and that your investing decisions will yield the highest possible return. The starting point is the object of our collective displeasure—the Canadian tax system itself.

The *Income Tax Act* is the key piece of legislation in the federal money-raising process. With it, Ottawa collects taxes on behalf of the federal government, as well as the government of the province in which you live. Quebec is the only province to collect its own income taxes.

In theory, at least, the tax system attempts to promote a democratic and fair distribution of wealth. Our system is known as a progressive, or graduated, system, meaning that low income earners pay little or no tax. This does not always work, of course, and often the highest income earners legitimately avoid paying lots of taxes because they have learned to shelter their incomes from the taxman.

Canada's income tax system is partially indexed to the rate of inflation. (It was fully indexed to the rate of inflation between 1974 and 1985.) Indexing to the rate of inflation means that the government recognizes that inflation cuts into our purchasing power. For example, say you get a 5% raise and prices are going up 5% a year. Basically, your wage increases will just cover the inflation, and you will have nothing extra to spend. But because you have 5% more income, your taxes will push you into a higher tax bracket, and you'll end up paying more tax with no more disposable income.

Until 1985, the government took this into account and changed the tax brackets every year so we wouldn't pay more tax due to inflation. Faced with a staggering budgetary deficit, the federal government announced that it would index the tax systems only after the first three percentage points of inflation. Now if you get a 5% raise and the inflation rate is also 5%, the tax bracket will be widened to cover only 2% of the inflation.

AT THE MARGIN

The percentage of tax you pay on your last dollars of income is called your marginal tax rate. If you're in a 30% marginal tax bracket, for instance, then 30 cents of each of the last dollars you earn go to the government.

Knowing this may help you to make better investment and spending decisions. For instance, if you're in a 30% bracket and your 15-year-old wants you to buy him a $140 leather bomber jacket, you'll be able to give him an algebra lesson as well as an answer.

> "Sure thing, Skip, but do you know that in order to fork over that $140 I have to earn more than $200?"
>
> "That so, Dad? How come?"
>
> "Well, son, it's because I have to have 30% ready for the taxman. Seventy percent is all I have left. Now if $140 represents 70%, how much would 100% be?"

The answer of course is $200, of which 30%, or $60, has gone to Ottawa.

"But Dad, you said you'd need to earn more than $200."

"Yes, son. That's because we have provincial sales tax to pay, too. . . ."

WHERE DO I START?

In tax planning terms, the best place to start is with the tax rates in your province, and the tax rates and tax brackets that apply to you. The tax reform of June 1987 reorganized the system so that, as of 1988, there are only three tax brackets at the federal level. They are:

Taxable Income	*Federal Marginal Tax Rate*
Up to $27,500	17%
$27,501 – $55,000	26%
$55,001 and over	29%

Residents of all provinces except Quebec pay combined Federal and Provincial taxes, but at the time of writing, the provinces haven't said what they're doing (if anything) with their present provincial tax rates. Touche Ross has put out a good little book called *Your Guide to Canadian Personal Tax Reform* (Prentice-Hall Canada) and until the provinces announce their intentions, your best bet is to assume a provincial tax rate of 50% of the federal rate.

Almost all big chartered accounting firms put out pamphlets on how to reduce your taxes. Most of them also include worksheets for estimating your income and income tax. Look in the Yellow Pages to find one.

Taxable Income	*Combined Federal/Provincial Marginal Tax Rate*
Up to $27,500	approx. 26%
$27,501 – $55,000	approx. 39%
$55,001 and over	approx. 44%

Another big tax reform change is that many deductions and exemptions that had been available to us for years have been converted to tax credits or eliminated entirely.

The basic approaches to tax planning have long been called the three Ds—deduct, defer, and divide. Deducting means taking advantage of every single deduction and exemption that is legally available to you. Deferring simply means that the tax laws allow you to earn money in one year and, for tax purposes, to defer the recognition of that money until another year. This kind of flexibility has been curtailed; nevertheless, it allows you to plan when it's advantageous for you to pay income taxes—you don't always have to pay them in the year you earn the money. Dividing refers to splitting your income among other members of your family so that you can reduce the taxes the whole family pays.

DEDUCTIONS AND EXEMPTIONS 1987 STYLE

The following deductions and exemptions will apply to your 1987 tax return:

- The first $1000 of eligible investment income is tax free in 1987, but is eliminated in 1988 and onward, and will not be replaced by a different kind of deduction.
- The first $100,000 of capital gains are tax deductible. In 1987 half of all the rest are tax deductible, but the tax on the rest goes up to 66 2/3% in 1988, and 75% in 1989.
- The first $1000 of pension income is tax free for 1987. Your Old Age Security payment and Canada/Quebec Pension Plan payment aren't eligible, but you can make them eligible by putting them into your RRSP. The retirement income from your RRSP is eligible.
- Don't forget to check whether you're eligible for a child tax credit. Everyone who gets family allowance payments is entitled to at least a look. The credit works in two ways. First, it reduces any taxes payable, and second, if you still have a credit, you get it back as an actual cash refund.
- Many of the deductions that have been described are transferable between you and your spouse. Say you or your spouse has an income that is too low to take advantage of some specific eligible deduction, such as the dividend tax credit. In such a case, you may use the deduction on your own tax return. The eligible deductions that are transferable are:
  - — $1000 investment income deduction;
  - — $1000 pension income deduction;

— disabled persons' deduction (also transferable from a child);
— Over 64 years of age deduction;
— $50 a month education deduction (also transferable from a child);
— Dividend tax credit.

- There are many kinds of medical expenses that qualify as tax deductions. Eligible expenses over three percent of your net income are deductible.

 You must figure out which of a two-income couple should claim the deduction in order to get the largest tax saving. On the side of having the lower income earner claim medical expenses is the fact that it is easier to have three percent of a lower net income than a higher one. But, on the side of having the higher income earner make the claim is the possibility that the tax bracket will be lowered sufficiently to enable an even greater tax saving. The only way you can be sure is to calculate both ways.

 Eligible medical expenses include:
 — Premiums paid to non-government medical and hospitalization plans;
 — Dental treatment, excluding regular checkups;
 — Eyeglasses, contact lenses;
 — Hearing aids;
 — Wheelchairs;
 — Nursing care for bed- or wheelchair-ridden people;
 — Artificial limbs.

 Medical expenses are transferable between spouses and dependent children. Remember not to claim medical expenses which have already been paid back to you by Medicare or private insurance.

- Cash outlays. A great many expenses are considered by the income tax department to be tax deductible. For example, any expense incurred in the pursuit of earning income is a deductible expense. This includes investment counselling fees and portfolio management fees. If you borrow money to use for trying to earn income, the interest you pay on the borrowed funds is tax deductible. Notice that I said "trying to earn income." You don't necessarily have to make a profit. You only need to have a reasonable expectation of making a profit. If you have a reasonable expectation of making a profit, use this tax department interpretation to make a lot of your credit purchases tax deductible. You don't need to wish the government would pass more lenient tax laws. By re-arranging your borrowing habits, you can buy your car on credit and make ordinarily ineligible interest payments tax deductible.

Here's one way. Suppose you're in the habit of buying Canada Savings Bonds each year, or of regularly buying investment assets. Suppose, too, you're just about to take out an instalment loan to buy a car. By arranging your affairs this way, you will incur interest expenses that are not tax deductible. Tax strategy consists of borrowing the money to buy your CSBs or other investments, and using your cash to buy the car.

You can also re-arrange your affairs to make your mortgage interest tax deductible. This is especially easy if you already have investments that are fully paid for. But it can be done even if your investments are not paid for.

If you have investments that are fully paid for, all you have to do is sell them and pay down part of your mortgage with the proceeds. Then you can remortgage your property and, with the money you get from the mortgage lender, repurchase your investments. The mortgage interest on that amount of money is now related to your investments, and as such is tax deductible. You don't necessarily have to get the money to repurchase the investments from your mortgage lender, although mortgage rates are a percent or two lower than personal loan rates. You could simply borrow the money from the bank and get a preferential rate by leaving your investments there as security.

If you don't already have the paid-for investments available to make your mortgage interest immediately deductible, there's no time like the present to start accumulating the investments. It may seen like an eternity to say that within five years you could have a substantial amount of cash, but I guarantee you that unless you make a decision now to save, the five years will pass and you'll still be wishing the government would pass a law making mortgage interest tax deductible.

Suppose you have a mortgage of $40,000 and no investments, but each year you put money into a Registered Retirement Savings Plan. It doesn't matter how much you put into your RRSP, but let's assume it's $3000. The trick is to stop putting cash into your RRSP. Borrow the money for your RRSP. With your $3000 cash, buy some other income-earning investment and leave it at the bank as security for your RRSP loan. If you do this, it is likely that the bank won't make you repay the principal amount of the loan; you'll only have to pay the interest.

Say you do this for five years. At the end of that time, you'll have $15,000 in your RRSP; a $15,000 loan, and $15,000 of income-earning securities. Now you sell the securities and, on the renegotiating date for your mortgage, you pay off $15,000 of your mortgage. Then you immediately take out another $15,000 on your mortgage and, with the proceeds, pay off your bank loan. The mortgage interest on the $15,000 now relates to having borrowed the money for your RRSP and, as such, becomes tax deductible.

These tactics are perfectly legitimate, but since the government is entitled to question everything on your tax return, you'd be well advised to keep careful records of all the transactions so you can justify them should anyone ask.

Certain kinds of interest are only the first of the cash outlays the government says are a deductible expense. Others are:

- Your union or professional dues which are deductible from your taxable income.
- Your tuition fees. You can divide your income with other family members, and there is a way of getting your children's tuition fees paid with tax-free dollars. See **Dividing** on page 132.
- Safety deposit box charges and safekeeping fees.
- Child care expenses.
- Moving expenses. If you move 40 kilometres (20 miles) closer to your employment, your moving expenses are tax deductible, including any commission you pay to a real estate agent if you sell your home.
- Charitable donations—up to 20% of your total income. If you donate more than that, it can be split between two years. The charity of your choice must be registered as a charity or as an amateur athletic association.
- Political contributions are deductible to some extent. You're allowed a tax credit against your federal tax payable to a maximum of $500.

No one ever said understanding tax laws is a rose garden, and in the case of political contributions, just about every province has a different ruling. Here a handy little table. Remember that you must have an official receipt or you won't get a credit.

Political Contributions

Given to Whom	*Tax Credit Available*
Federal — Ottawa; any registered political party	• Up to $100 — 75% of contribution • $100-$550 — $75 plus 50% of what's over $100 • $550-$1150 — $300 plus 1/3 of what's over $550 • over $1150 — $500
Provincial political parties in B.C., Ontario, Manitoba, Nova Scotia, New Brunswick, Yukon	Tax credit is calculated in a similar way for federal purposes, but the credit is deducted from the provincial tax payable.
Alberta	Maximum credit $750, calculated on a sliding scale similar to the federal calculation.
Quebec	Tax credit is 50% of first $280 contributed; maximum credit $140.

DEDUCTIONS AND EXEMPTIONS—1988 STYLE

A great many deductions and exemptions have been eliminated or converted to tax credits from 1988 on to whenever the government decides to change things again. (If your kid is malleable, or you're thinking about a career change, I think every tax reform opens up 10,000 or so new jobs in accountancy or law).

Here's what's available in 1988, and what, at the end of 1987 (which is when I'm writing this) they tell us is available in 1989.

- The basic personal exemption is now a tax credit. Personal exemptions are deducted from your gross income to get your taxable income. The more money you make and the higher your tax bracket, the more valuable your tax exemption. A tax credit is an equalizer—it reduces taxes payable to the same degree for all taxpayers.
- By the same token, the married and the equivalent-to-married exemption is turned into a tax credit from 1988 onward. The equivalent-to-married credit can be claimed only for a child under 18, or disabled dependent, or a parent or grandparent.
- Exemptions for dependents become credits, except for dependents over 18, who disappear as either a tax credit or exemp-

tion. (The new, back to basics government philosophy is, "Get out and work, kid").

- The age 65 + and disability exemptions both become tax credits in 1988, and remain transferable to a spouse, as is now the case. The disability credit can be transferred to a supporting parent or grandparent, but the amount transferred will be reduced on your net income over $6000.

N.B. BEFUDDLED ALERT

You are not even half-way through this chapter, and you must be saying something akin to "What *is* all this stuff?" What I really want to emphasize is simply that in a rapidly changing economy, the rules are going to change regularly—that's the significance of the first chapter of the book. The Marquess of Queensberry was the sponsor of the Queensberry rules, the rules which governed, in 1867, the gentlemanly art of boxing. Those rules, including "no hitting below the belt" and "no hitting a man when he's down" filtered through society over the years and emerged as the general etiquette of fair play.

The bottom line today is that new rules are being forged for a new era. You have to be on your toes, first to know what rules you're playing the life game by, and second, not to be taken too much off guard by an unanticipated change.

Here is a table from the Touche Ross *Your Guide to Canadian Personal Tax Reform* that outlines the other deduction-to-credit conversions:

Deduction	*Current Treatment*	*Proposed 1988 Federal Credit*
Pension Income	Eligible income up to $1000. Unused portion transferable to spouse.	17% of eligible income, maximum $170. Unused credit transferable to spouse.
Tuition Fees	Deductible by student; not transferable.	17% for post-secondary fees; up to $600. Transferable to spouse or supporting parent or grandparent.
Education	$50 deduction for each month in full-time attendance; transferable.	$10 credit for each month in full-time attendance; transferable as part of the $600 limit for tuition fees.
Medical Expenses	Deduction for uninsured medical expenses in excess of 3% of net income.	Credit of 17% for uninsured medical expenses in excess of 3% of net income.
CPP/QPP and UI Premiums (employee share)	Deductible	Credit at 17%.

Note in all this that fees for private schools aren't eligible for a tax credit, although the education credit is transferable to a spouse, parent or grandparent.

Note too, that if you make a good enough living that the credits are going to be less valuable to you than the deductions, you should try to push discretionary medical expenses into 1987 if they are going to be more than 3% of your net income. That means marking down fees for the orthodontist or surgeon if you know you have to do something, but can decide when to do it.

DEFERRING INCOME

"It pays to pay later," is one of the cardinal rules of tax planning. If you can defer paying a tax dollar, it's money in your pocket. And despite Ottawa's increasing niggardliness, there are still opportunities to defer taxes.

There are two basic groupings of tax deferrals. The first group of shelters allows you to deduct from your other income part or all of the actual cost of the investment. This group consists of deferred income plans. The second group of shelters allows you to "write off" against your other income a variety of tax losses. This doesn't necessarily mean the investment actually loses money, although it may. It does mean that special tax rules allow you to claim investment-related expenses now against potential earning sometime in the future.

The most widely known tax deferrment in Canada is a Registered Retirement Savings Plan. These plans came into existence in 1957, when the government decided to encourage people to save for retirement. Basically, what Ottawa has said is that if you put aside a certain amount of money for your retirement, it will agree not to recognize that money for tax purposes until you start taking it out to spend. In other words, the money in a registered plan is sheltered from taxes, and remains sheltered as long as it's in the plan.

It's important to realize that all the government has provided is a tax shelter—basically an empty box into which you can put earned income and defer paying tax on it. It's just as important to realize that not all retirement plans are the same. If you are considering an RRSP, or have one, and aren't sure what kind of return it's giving you or what kind of income you're likely to have when you retire, please study the section on retirement savings plans, in Chapter 9. Deferred Profit Sharing Plans are similar to RRSPs. Whereas RRSPs are designed to provide incentives to individuals to save for retirement, DPSPs are designed to provide incentives to employers to set up pension plans for employees. The employer's contribution is tax deductible, and the income in the DPSP is tax-deferred until it is withdrawn by the employee. Maximum yearly contribution: $3500 or 20% of earned income, whichever comes first. The proposed pension reform will increase the dollar amount to $7750 by 1990, although the limit will be reduced to 18% of remuneration.

Registered Pension Plans (RPPs) allow both employer and employee to contribute to the employee's pension fund at work and to deduct the contribution from taxable income. Maximum contribution for 1987: $7000, rising to $15,500 by 1995. You will need to understand more about your pension at work, if you have one. There have always been important differences between money purchase and defined benefit plans. Those differences are even more important since tax and pension reform. Chapter 9 details some of the things you have to know.

Contributions to both RRSPs and DPSPs will be reduced according to a formula that is complicated enough that as of 1988, the government will tell you exactly how much you can contribute to your RRSP.

PENSION REFORM

New legislation was enacted to deal with your pension plan at work, effective January 1, 1987. The legislation that deals with your RRSP was introduced in May 1985, amended twice since then, and may take effect at the beginning of 1988. The new legislation provides for RRSP contributions not exceeding 18 percent of your earnings, as long as you have no other pension plan, to be phased in as follows:

Year	*RRSP Maximum Contribution*	*RPP Maximum Contribution*
1987	$ 7,500	$ 7,000
1988	7,500	7,000
1989	8,500	10,500
1990	10,500	11,500
1991	11,500	12,500
1992	12,500	13,500
1993	13,500	14,500
1994	14,500	15,500
1995	15,500	indexed

In addition, beginning in 1988, you will be able to carry forward any unused contributions for up to seven years.

If you do have another pension plan to which you contribute or to which your employer contributes, your contribution to your own RRSP is somewhat more constrained. You may still contribute to an RRSP, but you'll have to look up the regulations each year in order to determine what applies to you.

There are also some specific kinds of income that can be put into your RRSP without affecting your basic contribution.

- Old Age Security
- Canada or Quebec Pension
- RRSP refund received on death of spouse
- Deferred profit sharing plan

In addition to these specific kinds of income, two other kinds of income can be rolled into your RRSP at least until 1990. They are:

- Retiring allowance
- Registered pension plan benefits

If you're going to do any of these things, there is a maze to go through. First, if you're older than 64, remember that you're allowed a deduction from taxable income of the first $1000 of pension income (a tax credit beginning in 1988). Second, to complicate things, the tax department says that income from your Old Age Security, Canada or Quebec Pension, or retiring allowance doesn't qualify for the pension exemption. Third, to make these ineligible kinds of income eligible for the $1000 pension deduction, pay them into your RRSP. Then, if you buy an annuity with the proceeds of your RRSP, the amounts received from the annuity are eligible to be included in the $1000 pension deduction. Fourth, you will have to calculate the alternate minimum tax, including your lump sum retiring payments.

I know this sounds complicated, but if you go through it one step at a time, you'll see how to do it. And to exempt $1000 from your taxable income, it's worth it.

One other word about RRSPs, at least as they relate to tax deferrals. Most of us who have the RRSP habit have become accustomed to waiting until the last moment to put our savings into an RRSP. The reason is that most of the advertising and hard sell about RRSPs is done in January and February because contributions made during the first sixty days of the new year qualify for deduction in the previous year. We lose a valuable opportunity to make money by such behaviour. The earlier in the year we contribute to our RRSP, the more money is accumulated behind the tax shelter.

Look at the experience of Jan Jones and Tom Smith. Both can contribute $5500 to an RRSP. Both are in a 50% tax bracket. Jan Jones made her 1986 RRSP contribution on March 1, 1987. Tom Smith made his RRSP contribution on January 1, 1986.

'Here's what that 14-month difference meant to each of them:

Jan Jones	*Tom Smith*
$5000 earning 10% for 14 months = interest income of $583.30	$5000 earning 10% for 14 months = interest income of $583.30
Tax payable on non-sheltered income of $583.30 = $291.65	Tax payable on sheltered income of $583.30 = $0.00

It really pays to make your RRSP contribution early. This is particularly so in 1987. Tax rates in 1987 are higher than they will be in 1988. So, the more deductions you can make in 1987, the more tax money you will save. Make the biggest contribution you are allowed.

OTHER TAX SHELTERS

Tax savings arise through what are called tax losses, which may or may not be real money losses. Obviously the best kind of tax loss is one that is not a real money loss. Your options here involve investments in a variety of enterprises: farming, oil, gas and mining exploration, real estate, films, and videotapes. Provincial governments also offer tax shelters.

In each case, expenses incurred—whether to build up inventory on a farm, or to drill for oil, gas or some mineral, or, in the case of real estate, for depreciation or mortgage interest—are either wholly or partially deductible from your other income before taxes are incurred.

Because your ability to claim a capital gains exemption will be restricted after 1987, it's important that you consider taking some capital gains in 1987. Beginning in 1988, your capital gains exemption claim is restricted by your investment losses, calculated on a cumulative basis.

The fact that Ottawa is ill-disposed towards tax shelters suggests that the real winners in this game are people who actually make a good investment as well a a tax savings. There are those who are so furious with the government that they'll put money into any venture if it means Ottawa won't get as much tax revenue. But, as rational investors and tax planners, we have to write off such people as incurable grouches who don't have the good sense to realize that they are spiting themselves even more than they are spiting Ottawa if they throw their money away on a bad investment. They may as well pay their taxes—Ottawa has more experience than anyone in the field of bad investing.

If you think any of these tax shelters are investments from which you can benefit, your next task is to find a specific investment. Your accountant and stockbroker are starting points. You, however, will have to do the basic legwork to ensure the investment has a good chance of succeeding. And of course, the final decision to plunk down your money is yours. It is, after all your money. You have to take the ultimate responsibility in looking after it. It's hard. But if you do it, you're going to have a lot more of it to look after. (And it'll look after you, too.)

DIVIDING

Ottawa doesn't look kindly on the concept of income-splitting. The reason is obvious. One person making $30,000 will pay more tax to the government than two people jointly making $30,000. Nevertheless, it is possible for some of us to share our incomes, for tax purposes, with our families.

What income-splitting involves is steering clear of what are called attribution rules. The May 1985 budget tightened many income-splitting techniques, but there are still some that can minimize the tax burden for your family unit.

You may set up a trust to lend money to a child who will be 18 when the first income is received. The recipient of the loan can invest the money, and investment income would be taxed in the borrower's hands, not yours. Again, an example: John Burwash lives in Burnaby, British Columbia. He's the sole income earner and has a taxable income of $20,000. He also has $5,000 income from investments. He's paying $7,174 in taxes. He decides to lend his child the money he has invested.

She takes the money and invests it in the same things he had invested in. John's taxable income changes. It goes up because he can no longer claim his child as an exemption. But it goes down because he no longer has the money he lent his child. His taxes are now $5,902. His child's net income is $5,000 of investment income, but her own exemptions amount to $4,180, plus the $1,000 investment income deduction, so her taxable income is nil. The tax saving for this family is $1,272.

If you're interested in this income-splitting technique, be sure that the income is not going to be received by the child until the year he or she turns 18. Remember as well that every three years, tax has to be paid on all interest accrued by invested funds. This strategy will work with a child who is turning 15 in a given year, but not with a younger child. On the other hand, if you lend money to a child who invests it to earn a capital gain, the "attribution" rules do not apply to capital gains, no matter what the age of the child.

You may also consider a registered education savings plan. These plans, offered by investment houses and trust companies, allow you to make contributions to an educational trust. Income on the contributions will accumulate on a tax-deferred basis until it is used by the beneficiary to help pay formal school fees and living expenses. At that time the money is taxable in the child's hands. Be careful with these plans: if your child decides not to attend college or university, or if the plan can't be transferred to someone whose schooling you wish to subsidize, all you'll get back is your original contribution without interest.

If both you and your spouse work outside the home, there are still other ways of re-arranging the family finances so that the lower-income earner does the investing, and the investment income is taxable at the lowest marginal rate possible. One way is for the higher income earner to pay all living expenses. This leaves the lower income earner to invest all of his/her income.

Another way is to pay the lower income earner a salary for performing duties for your business, and deduct that salary from your income. As of 1980, you may do this even with an unincorporated business. The salary will be taxed in your spouse's hands. You may also pay your children who work in your unincorporated business, and their salaries are deductible from your income. But do not think that you have the freedom to pay your 10-year-old child $40,000 for raking leaves in front of the business property; salaries paid to spouses and children for work done in the family business must be reasonable.

One future income-splitting possibility: a high-income earning spouse can set up a Registered Retirement Savings Plan for the lower or non-earning spouse. The whole idea is that in retirement, you and your spouse will each have an income and possibly a lower marginal tax rate. In addition, both you and your spouse will be able to use the $1000 pension deduction or credit at age 65. And remember, even if you're older than 71, if your spouse isn't, you can continue to contribute to the spousal plan.

One thing to remember about spousal RRSPs is that the attribution rules do apply; any funds withdrawn within three years of contribution are included in the contributor's taxable income. On the positive side, a spousal RRSP can be quite useful for a young couple planning to have kids in the future, with one of the couple staying home for a few years. After three years the plan can be collapsed and the money withdrawn at a relatively lower tax rate.

SUMMARY

Most of us work very hard for our money, so our money should work hard for us. It cannot do so if we give away a large part of it in taxes.

One of the most important lessons to learn about investing is that you should always look at your income in after-tax terms. The general rule is that every additional dollar of taxable income you make will be taxed at your marginal rate. So it is your marginal tax rate that determines the tax you will have to pay on every dollar of taxable income you receive beyond your present income.

A number of important rules determine the timing and amount of taxable income from an investment:

1. How much of the income will be taxable?
2. When will the income be taxable?
3. Can your investment costs be written off?
4. How secure is your investment?

Measure each of your investments against these four rules and compare the results. The following counsel might be added:

1. Being able to choose when to pay taxes is as important as how much you earn on an investment.
2. Never pre-pay taxes unless you are obliged to by law.
3. There is an advantage to earning income in an economic sense that is not income in a tax sense.
4. There is little benefit to earning interest and paying tax on it if you do not need the investment income now.

WHAT TO DO IF THE TAXMAN CALLETH

Question: Under what circumstances would the choice between an impacted wisdom tooth, a migraine headache and something else elicit one of the first two?

Answer: When the "something else" is a tax audit.

The vast majority of Canada's taxpayers—all those working for wages or salaries whose tax is deducted in the payroll office—are almost immune from having a tax audit: there's just no way, really, that they can cheat (euphemistically, be creative) with their taxes.

But for a relatively small group of taxpayers—the self-employed, the athletes, the business executives, farmers, fishermen, corporations and trusts—creativity is the name of the game. These are people who have some flexibility in deciding what is an expense and what is taxable income. And these are the people who are continually investigated by a core group at Revenue Canada.

Revenue Canada employs more than 10,000 people on a full-time basis, and almost another 10,000 at tax time, in addition to several computers, to squeeze as much tax money as possible out of the system. The computers are especially important. They churn out the names of all taxpayers who aren't on a regular salary. Then they "score" each tax return on a number of points that indicate its potential for yielding additional tax. The returns that "fail" this test are destined for audit by the district audit staff.

But that's not all. The department likes to identify groups of taxpayers who are likely to report less income than they really receive. These people may be found in any industry. The department also picks out industries for special consideration each year. The fishing industry, waiters and waitresses, and real estate investors have been among the chosen people.

If you're a taxpayer not on a regular salary, and therefore vulnerable to an audit, it pays to know the process.

Point one: there are two kinds of audit—the office audit and the field audit. Pray, if you get a call from the taxman, that he asks you to come to his office. That usually means there are some small points to clear up—details of income, expenses, and transactions that can be dealt with in a short interview.

A field audit means he's coming to see you. Like the man who came to dinner, you can never be sure how long he's going to stay. This is the point at which you may have to prove every expense you've claimed. And if you can't, you can be sure that the tax man isn't going to take your word for it. That's the point at which you may be re-assessed or even penalized.

Point two: That is not the end of the story. Any taxpayer can appeal a reassessment. The first step in such appeal is to get in touch with your district office to discuss it. If, after such discussion, you still disagree with the assessment, you have 90 days to file a notice of objection. Send it by registered mail to the Deputy Minister of Revenue Canada, Taxation. This objection starts the wheels of an independent review. You and/or your tax advisor can plead your case to an appeals officer in the district office. Or, you can appeal immediately to the more senior Tax Court of Canada.

According to Revenue Canada, four out of five taxpayers leave a review at the district level, happy. The other guy takes his case up through the system, where the odds seem to be a little better than 50-50 that his appeal will be won.

Point three: The single most successful way to avoid a lousy outcome of a tax audit is to keep impeccable records. If you can verify every single expense with a voucher, the odds skyrocket that you will not be reassessed or accused of tax evasion. In dealing with the taxman, one must always remember that it is beyond the realm of reality to think you can get away with paying no taxes ever. If your goal is to pay no more than the law demands, a quiet philosophical approach and detailed expense vouchers are the keys to success.

DATES TO REMEMBER

Circle these dates in your calendar so you'll remember to comply with the rules for filing or paying your taxes.

15th of every month — employers send in employees' tax deducted at source the month before.

Last day of March, June, September and December — If you're self-employed, send in your income tax installment.

Last day of February — Last day to send out your employees' tax return information.

Last day of April — Individual income tax returns due.

Last day of December — Income tax payments due from fishermen and farmers.

If you want to file an objection to a tax assessment, you must do it within 90 days of receiving the assessment.

CHAPTER 9

Planning for the Good Life When You Retire

> A priest, a minister, and a rabbi were discussing the beginning of life. The priest said, "Life begins at the moment of conception." The minister said, "No, life begins at birth." The rabbi said, "You're both wrong. Life begins when children leave home and the dog dies."
>
> Anonymous

You've got lots of time to think about retirement planning, right? You're only 25, 35, 45, 55, right? You've got a company pension, right? The Canada or Quebec Pension Plan will look after you, right? Well, at least there's Old Age Security for everyone, right?

What's right is that even today, before the baby boomers get really old, almost half of all Canada's poor people are over 65. Even today, only about half of all working Canadians work for organizations that have pension plans. Even today, women, who make less than men and who live longer on average, have a one-in-three chance of being poor in their old age.

By 2010 or thereabouts, one of every three of us will be in our 60s or older. That's twice as many old people who will have to be supported by a much depleted work force. The population is aging so rapidly, that even with scheduled increases in contribution rates, the plans have to pay out more money than they receive. Look at the demographics again. Fewer young contributors to the plans have been born since the early 1960s, while more baby boomers (born between 1946 and 1964) will eventually retire and drain the reserves. That's the reason for so much pension reform lately, and it's the reason that as long ago as the late 1950s, the government created Registered Retirement Savings Plans.

Maybe you're the one out of every two Canadians who works for a company with a pension plan. Good stuff. Do you know how it works, who manages it, how well it's doing, and what you can realistically expect to get when you leave the work force? If you don't, pick up the phone and make an appointment with your human resources or personnel officer.

WHAT YOU WOULD GET IF YOU RETIRED TODAY?

Old Age Security (OAS): This is the foundation of the pension system and all Canadians who reach the age of 65 and satisfy certain residency requirements qualify. It is paid by the federal government from general tax revenues and is indexed quarterly to the Consumer Price Index. The pension provides for a maximum of about $3,600 per year for each individual.

Guaranteed Income Supplement (GIS): In 1967, the federal government introduced this programme to supplement the OAS programme. Using an income-tested, non-contributory benefit formula which takes into account any other income received by pensioners, the federal government offers a maximum annual payment of just over $4,200 to each individual whose spouse receives neither a pension nor the Spouse's Allowance, and about $6,500 a couple to those retired people who qualify.

GIS is indexed to the Consumer Price Index and is adjusted every quarter. Don't think the government wants you to supplement your income with a little work: for $2 of extra income earned, GIS drops by $1. That's an effective tax rate of fifty percent.

Provincial Pension Benefits: Alberta, British Columbia, Manitoba, Ontario, and Saskatchewan have plans that guarantee minimum incomes by providing small pension supplements to residents over age 65. This provides pensioners with a guaranteed annual income. Check it out if you live in one of the named provinces and need the money.

When you add it all together, you can count on an annual pension income of up to about $8000 for each individual and $13,500 per couple. But you can't really count on more than that, because of the tax-back effect if you go out and earn a few dollars. For example, in Ontario, the provincial pension benefit is called GAINS. But if you qualify for GIS and GAINS, and then you go out and work, you are docked dollar for dollar. That's an effective tax rate of one hundred percent.

Canada Pension Plan (CPP): Together with the Quebec Pension Plan (QPP), the CPP began operating on January 1, 1966, and covers virtually all employed and self-employed persons in Canada. Contributions and benefits are based on earnings, and almost every employee resident in Canada between the ages of 18 and 70 contributes 1.9 percent of earnings, with their employers contributing another 1.9 percent. Self-employed individuals are required to contribute the full 3.8 percent of their earnings.

Not all of your earnings are eligible. For 1987, the Year's Maximum Pensionable Earnings (YMPE) is $25,900. There is also a basic exemption of $2,500. So the maximum contribution for an employee is $445 ($23,400 x 1.9%) with an equal amount contributed by the employer. If you're self-employed, you contribute both halves, or about $890.

You can collect CPP/QPP retirement pension benefits from age 60, and for as long as you live. The benefits are based on 25% of earnings up to YMPE each year, averaged over the whole period during which contributions have been made to the plans. Since 1976, pension benefits paid have been adjusted annually to compensate for cost-of-living increases, as measured by the Consumer Price Index. The maximum pension receivable by persons over 65 who retire in 1987 is $6,500 yearly. If you retire at age 60, you get a little less for the rest of your life. If you retire after age 70, you get a little more.

TYPES OF COMPANY PENSION PLANS AND HOW TO DECIPHER THEM

There are two basic company plans: defined contribution, or money purchase plans, and defined benefit plans.

In a money purchase plan, the contributions to it on your behalf are invested by a money manager. When you retire, the money in your account is used to buy a pension. Clearly, how much income you get in retirement will depend greatly on how much money has been contributed, and how good a money manager has been investing the money.

In a defined benefit plan, your pension is based on a formula that evaluates your income and your years of service. Several formulas are used to determine what you will get on retirement. Your personnel officer will know what that is. The employer is legally bound to make up whatever money is necessary to give you your pension. When you read about an employer wanting to take a "surplus" out of a pension plan, it is always a defined benefit plan. It means that a good investment programme has resulted in more money in the plan than is required to satisfy the commitments to the employees.

There are variations in how your plan is calculated. A flat benefit plan, for example, is not related to your earnings, but depends on the number of years of service you have completed with your employers. The pension benefits, for instance, may be $10 a month for each year of service. If you leave after 15 years, you'll get $150 a month when you retire.

A career average plan gives you a pension based on your actual earnings over your working career. Your final pension will be based on, and be equal to, a percentage of each year's earnings.

Say your pension benefit is equivalent to two percent of your earnings each year. Your annual pension at retirement will be two percent of your average earnings times the number of years of service. For example, say your average earnings were $15,000 over 20 years of service. Your annual pension would be two percent × $15,000 = $300 × 20 years = $6,000 annually or $500 a month.

A specified period of years before retirement is used as the basis for calculating final average earnings pensions. It might be 1.5 percent of the average of your five highest years of earnings during the last 10 years before retirement.

Say your average earnings during your five highest years amounted to $20,000 and you completed 20 years of service. Your pension would be 1.5 percent × $20,000 = $300 × 20 years = $6,000 a year or $500 a month.

If you make contributions to your defined benefit plan, they are deductible from your taxable income. However, your and your employer's contribution is limited by a Revenue Canada ceiling on retirement income in RPPs. At present, the maximum pension allowed is $60,000 a year.

When you go to discuss your pension with your personnel officer, be sure to ask:

- if your pension is indexed to inflation;
- if your spouse or children will get anything when you die;
- if your pension offers death or disability benefits, or life insurance;
- if and when your pension is vested—that is, if and when you get your employer's contribution if you change jobs;

- whether you can take your pension plan contributions with you if you change jobs.

Let me say another little word about why you should at least consider saving for retirement. The CPP/QPP are not fully funded. If they were, your contributions would be invested until you claimed them in retirement.

The CPP/QPP are pay-as-you-go. That means that today's workers are paying for today's retirees' incomes. Fine today, not so fine tomorrow when the older population will outnumber the young. There is a real question as to how heavy a burden young workers and employers will shoulder. Remember, an employer-paid pension contribution is a payroll tax that raises the cost of employing someone. With that and the present trend to downsize, it is no wonder the unemployment rate does not go down. There is likely to be a lot of pressure from that huge older segment of the population to reap, in retirement, the benefits of what they sowed when they were in the labour force. What I'm saying is that no matter how it turns out, pensions, both public and company, are political pawns. If you count on only them to feed you when you're 64, good luck.

SPECIAL CONSIDERATIONS FOR WOMEN

There is no "good" age for reading about the pension situation for women in Canada. If you're young, single, or well educated, being poor when you're older seems pretty remote. If you're married and your husband is working, ditto. If you're older, it's probably irrelevant. In any case, since it's such a boring topic, we seem, as a nation, to have absorbed by osmosis the greatest myth of our age—that our government has a pension plan and Old Age Security (even the name gives credence to the myth) that will keep us comfortably till death.

Here is the reality:

- Almost half of all Canada's poor people are over 65.
- Fewer than one in three women in the work force has a pension plan at work.
- Many pension plans don't provide pension benefits for the widow if the husband dies before he retires.
- Fewer than two out of three private pension plans provide widow's benefits if the husband dies after retirement.
- Most of the plans that do provide benefits after the husband's death generally provide about half what the husband's entitlement would have been.

You may already have decided that none of these descriptions apply to you. Let me continue.

- The life expectancy of a woman today is 83.
- The average age at which women are widowed is 56.
- The average male dies within ten years after retirement.
- Half of all married women will be widowed by age 65.
- Half of all married women between the ages of 55 and 64 have no personal income of their own.
- Two out of three widows in Canada live below the poverty line (about $8000 at time of writing).
- Seven out of ten men who die do not leave a will.
- One in every three marriages ends in divorce.
- The average age of a divorcee is 35.
- There are 3 single women aged 45-65 for every man in the same age group.
- Divorced women aged 45-65 have a one in five chance of remarrying.

The pension system in Canada has been vastly oversold. Even for a man, the public pension system isn't wonderful. For women, it is just this side of disastrous.

First, women earn, on average, 66 cents for every $1 earned by a man. In other words, the average Canadian woman earns thirty-three percent less than the average Canadian man. The maximum pension benefit is out of reach for most working women.

Second, the benefits are averaged over lifetime earnings. Four out of five women drop out of the work force to have children. The length of time a woman stays out of the work force, earning nothing, has in the past been averaged into the amount she was earning while in the work force. Take the example of an average wage of $16,000. Say a woman spent 25 years in the work force, interspersed with 15 years at home raising children. Her benefit would not be 25% of $16,000 a year, or $4,000 a year; it would be 25% of $10,000 a year or $2,500, because the 15 years of earning zilch is averaged in when calculating her benefits. Quebec changed this provision of the QPP ten years ago, so that a working woman in Quebec does not have to average in the years during which she had children under seven years of age. The federal government has proposed legislative changes to follow suit.

Even more devastating, perhaps, is the fact that seven out of ten part-time workers in Canada are women. They almost by definition earn less, and therefore have less chance of receiving any significant amount from the public pension plans. In many cases, part-time workers are not even eligible to contribute to pension plans. Pension reform is supposed to take care of this in the future.

When it comes to private plans at work, things are no better. As we pointed out earlier, few women have pension plans at work. And since women tend to change jobs more often than men, they often lose the employer's contribution to their pension. So we are left with savings to fill the gap left by the government and the employer. Considering the fact that, on average, women make only 66 percent of what men make, saving is difficult although certainly not impossible. How difficult, though, is reflected in one of the first statistics we used: one half of all widowed or divorced women over 65 live in poverty; one in three single women do.

The trends in the world of Canadian women and pensions suggest tough times ahead for all of us who haven't won a million-dollar lottery, and maybe even for the lottery winner who isn't a good money manager.

PENSION REFORM: SOME HERE, SOME COMING

The changes to pension legislation that have been agreed upon will give us all a lot more flexibility. But because the reforms of 1986 and 1987 made pension rules more complicated, there is even more need for retirement planning.

The granddaddy of pension reform is the *Pension Benefit Standards Act*. It covers a million Canadians who work for the federal government, or who work for sectors such as banking and communications, which are federally regulated. The new act (new since January 1, 1987) is supposed to be the model for the provinces, which regulate private pension plans. It hasn't happened yet, but here's the rationale: The income tax changes in the May 1985 federal budget were intended to provide the same retirement savings opportunities for all Canadians. For example, people who do not belong to a pension plan can contribute $7,500 a year to their RRSP. Details are in Chapter 8 on tax planning.

We will have more choice about when to retire. Proposed changes mean we will have an early retirement option in company-sponsored plans, with reduced benefits, starting at age 55. The Quebec Pension Plan has long had an early retirement option, with 70% of full payment if you retire at age 60, 100% at age 65, and 130% at age 70. Since January 1, 1987, the CPP has had the same provisions.

These proposals are a clear indication that governments recognize not only the general need to move people out of the work force at an early age to make way for younger people, but also the fact that some unusally productive and energetic workers can and should be allowed to work beyond the normal retirement age of 65.

Eligibility changes now allow employees to join pension plans after just two years of employment. Part-time employees will also be able to join after two years, if they earn approximately $9000 a year or more. Most part-time workers earn much less, so they still won't qualify.

WORK PERFORMANCE, NOT AGE

Mandatory retirement ages may also be out because of provisions in the Charter of Rights and Freedoms. In 1986, Ottawa abolished mandatory retirement at age 65 for federal government employees, and is discussing how this is to be extended to employees who work in industries subject to federal regulation. This doesn't mean that 85-year-old pilots will be flying passengers in jumbo jets. Rather, mandatory retirement is likely to become based on work performance requirements rather than age.

Full vesting of pension benefits, which gives the employee the right to the employer's contributions, is to take place after two years of employment. Under present rules, many employees aren't assured the value of accumulated employer contributions until they've reached age 45 and have worked for ten years with the same employer. The present situation varies from province to province, but some pension plans already include more generous provisions.

MORE PORTABILITY OPTIONS

Improved portability for those who change jobs is to be provided by a number of options. Employees may leave accumulated benefits in the plan of their former employer, transfer them to the plan of their new employer (if the new employer has a pension plan and permits the transfer), or transfer the benefits to a locked-in RRSP.

Employer contributions will have to pay for at least half the pension plan benefits accumulated by an employee. In many cases, employee contributions now pay for most of the benefits for younger employees. Employers may escape this obligation, however, by committing themselves to indexing pension benefits to inflation as an alternative.

Survivor benefits are improving. A widow or widower of a pensioner is to receive no less than 60% of the full pension, and will continue to receive this even if he or she has re-married. If a plan member dies before retirement, the full value of the pension earned up to that date is to be transferred to a locked-in RRSP of the surviving spouse.

On marriage breakdowns, pension entitlements are to be split 50/50 between spouses, unless the courts or the spouses themselves decide otherwise.

Income-splitting of CPP retirement payments between you and your spouse, for tax purposes, has been allowed since January 1, 1987.

MEN WILL PAY MORE

Perceived sex discrimination in pension payments is to be abolished. Male and female workers who participate in the same plan, make the same contributions, and meet other identical circumstances as a group will now get the same monthly pensions. Ultimately, female pensioners can expect to collect more, since Canadian women live an average of at least five years longer than men. This means, of course, that on average men will pay more for a dollar of received pension benefits than women. And since it's been the other way around for so long, you can expect a few loud complaints.

WHO OWNS SURPLUS FUNDS?

The five-year rise in stock market prices and high interest rates have helped generate substantial surplus pension funds. There have been big hassles over who owns the surplus funds and we can expect more.

Labour unions oppose withdrawal of surplus pension funds, claiming that the money belongs to the employees. Employers say it's their money. Some pension consultants expect a massive switch by companies from defined benefit plans to money purchase plans. The hassle over withdrawal of surplus funds has been the trigger for such talk. But the propsect of having to pay for inflation indexing and the burden of administering defined benefit plans add to the possibility.

Whether employees would benefit or suffer from a switch to money purchase plans would depend on how much the plans earn on their investments, and for how many years of service the employee has participated in the pension plan.

The bottom line is that we must protect ourselves as best we can. If you're young, start saving immediately. Ditto, if you're single. If you're married, now's the time to do a complete financial evaluation to see how you and your spouse will fare in retirement, and what your own situation will be if you become widowed or divorced. If you don't do it yourself, start planning for an old age in poverty.

Now let me tell you a little about how to build your own nest egg.

REGISTERED RETIREMENT SAVINGS PLANS

Whether by luck or design, one of the most prescient insights of government was the recognition, as long ago as the mid-1950s, that Canadians would need all the help they could get in saving for retirement. In 1957, Ottawa created the RRSP—an empty box which, once registered as a retirement plan, can be used to hold almost any investment you choose to put into it.

An RRSP gives you an immediate tax deferral: you can invest up to 18% of your earned income to a maximum which is determined by your other tax sheltered investments, and the money so invested is deductible from your taxable income. (For 1987 only, you can invest up to 20% of earned income.) An RRSP also gives you a lot more money to invest. As long as you keep the money sheltered within the RRSP, any earnings are also tax deferred. In other words, you won't pay any tax on this money until you withdraw it.

Here's an example of returns on the same number of investment dollars from one of Canada's most respected authorities on RRSPs—Tom Delaney.

	Mr. Black (Non-RRSP)	*Mr. White* (RRSP)
Age	35	35
Tax bracket	40%	40%
Pre-tax amount available each year	$ 1,000	$ 1,000
Tax paid on above	$ 400	Nil
Net amount available for investment	$ 600	$ 1,000
Rate of return on investment	10%	10%
Balance after first year	$ 660	$ 1,100
Pre-tax amount available over 30-year period.	$ 30,000	$ 30,000
Net amount invested	$ 18,000	$ 30,000
Tax paid during 30 years	$ 34,048.49*	Nil
Net return on investment	$ 47,191	$150,943
Value of Retirement Fund: Principal and Interest	$ 77,191	$180,943

* Assume 40% tax payable on all "interest" in excess of $1,000 in any year.

If you are skeptical that you'll be able to invest in an RRSP for the next 30 years, here's one of Delaney's examples of how much tax you can save in one year.

	Non-RRSP	*RRSP*
Taxable income	$20,000	$20,000
RRSP Contribution (not maximum allowable)		$ 2,500
New taxable income		$17,500
Tax payable	$ 5,559	$ 4,714
Tax rebate or saving through RRSP ($5,559 – 4,714)		$ 845

The deadline for getting your 1987 money into a tax-sheltered retirement plan is March 1, 1988. Almost anything can go into an RRSP—you don't have to just buy one of the funds that are advertised. You can register money in a savings plan as an RRSP. You can register bonds or stock market shares, or mortgages on Canadian property. Even certain life insurance policies can be registered as RRSPs. And if you're unhappy about what other money managers have done with your money in the past and think you can do better yourself, you can administer your own retirement plan.

This is probably the most misunderstood fact about RRSPs. All Ottawa wanted to do in 1957 was encourage people to save for their own old age. The idea wasn't to tell them how to do it. You can register your own plan at any brokerage house or trust company, but if you go this route, you must shop around, because the trust company charge for registration varies considerably from company to company.

The second most misunderstood fact about RRSPs is whether or not they are insured. Financial institutions like banks and trust companies are members of the Canada Deposit Insurance Corporation. Deposits and *some* RRSPs issued by them are insured by the CDIC. But many banks and trust companies also issue RRSPs that are not covered by the CDIC. Similarly, insurance companies and mutual funds are not members of the CDIC—they are regulated by federal or provincial authorities, but losses are not insured under CDIC. Remember, there is no such thing as a stupid question—so ask.

There are now more than 300 RRSPs to choose from. The most important thing to realize when deciding which RRSP to buy is that they do not all do equally well in terms of providing investment income. Some managed plans consistently make 10, 15, even 25 percent a year. Others do considerably less well, managing a rate of return well under the rate of inflation. It's important to recognize these differences, because the amount you accumulate while you're contributing is the pool of capital you'll have to invest for your income in retirement. Here are some examples of what would have happened to an investment of $1200 a year during the period 1977–1986.

RRSP	*Annual Average Compound Rate of Return 1977–1986*
Growth Equity	21.9%
Canadian Security Growth	20.8
Xanadu	8.0
Domequity Growth	2.0

The first could have bought a guaranteed lifetime retirement income in 1987 of about $400 a month. The last could have bought a retirement income of about $130 a month.

Registered retirement savings plans come in several varieties—enough variety to satisfy just about any requirement. Since you can have as many RRSPs as you want, you should be able to manage your retirement money in a way that is entirely satisfactory to your investment objectives.

The basic plans include:

1. Equity funds;

2. Mortgage and bond funds;

3. Insurance company funds;

4. Guaranteed funds;

5. Special savings accounts;

6. Self-administered funds.

1. Equity Funds

Equity funds are usually investment or mutual funds. (The names are interchangeable. After a particularly traumatic scandal in the 1960s, the Canadian Mutual Funds Association changed its name to the Canadian Investment Funds Association. But the Americans stuck to the mutual fund designation.) Mutual funds are companies which have been set up to give small investors the opportunity to invest in a wide range of stocks, bonds, and/or mortgages which have been chosen by professional money managers. You buy shares (or units) in the mutual fund, and the mutual fund uses your money to buy shares in other companies listed on the Canadian, and American, or overseas stock exchanges.

2. Mortgage and Bond Funds

Mortgage and bond funds invest either in mortgages, bonds, or preferred shares. These funds are also called income funds. The big difference between these funds and equity funds is that equity funds are invested in common stocks which go up and down with the market, while income funds are based on interest rates and long-term debts which must be repaid.

These funds fluctuate inversely to interest rates. In other words, if your funds are locked into 10% mortgages when mortgage rates are at 18%, as they were in the early 1980s, the market value of the capital in your fund will go down until it reaches the equivalent of an 18% return on your money. You'll be able to sell your units in the fund only for that reduced value. It used to be that bond and mortgage funds were considered stable, conservative and safe. Not so today. These funds are often as volatile as equity funds.

3. Insurance Company Funds

Insurance funds are managed by insurance companies and can include either the cash surrender value of a life insurance policy you already own, or a single premium which you pay to them.

4. Guaranteed Funds

Guaranteed funds, issued by just about all banks, trust, and other deposit-taking institutions, guarantee the capital and the rate of interest you'll get. They're the equivalent of a term deposit.

5. Special Savings Accounts

Special savings accounts are exactly what they say they are—they guarantee your capital, but the interest rate will change with the times. Basically, what you're doing is registering a bank savings account as an RRSP.

6. Self-administered Funds

This is a do-it-yourself retirement plan. Investment houses will register your plan and you then have almost complete freedom to buy and sell stocks, bonds, mortgages, and so on.

HOW TO CHOOSE

At first blush, this wide variety may seem overwhelming. But if you follow these steps carefully, you can end up with an RRSP or a combination of RRSPs that will suit you.

Step 1: Examine your existing assets and, particularly your financial assets (guaranteed deposits, insurance, investments, etc.) Determine the proportion of your total financial assets each type represents, thus:

Guarantees (including Canada Savings Bonds)	____%
Equities (stocks and equity funds)	____%
Long-term bonds	____%
Cash value of insurance	____%
Other financial assets	____%
	100%

Step 2: Set your own goals and objectives. Go back to Chapter 2 on goals and priorities. Review your decisions.

Step 3: Examine all available investments of the type you have selected. If you need guarantees, because you have too high a proportion in equities, compare rates and terms.

If you require equities and know little about individual stocks, look at investment funds with a risk profile that suits your temperament. (See Chapter 17 on mutual funds, for more details). Compare rates of return, both long term and short term, looking for consistent, better-than-average performance.

If you know the markets well, consider self-directed RRSPs to hold specific stocks. But remember that if you hold stocks in your RRSP, you lose the tax exemption for capital gains. Money taken out of an RRSP, whether at retirement or earlier, is taxed as ordinary income. Here's a specific example.

Say you bought 100 shares of MacMillan Bloedel early in 1986 at $10 a share. In the spring of 1987, you decided to sell it at $28 a share. You have a capital gain of $1800. If you conducted this transaction outside your RRSP, you would declare on your 1987 tax return that you had made a capital gain which (I am assuming) fell within your allowable $100,000 capital gains exemption limit. However, if you bought the shares and sheltered them from taxes in an RRSP, you give up the right to a capital gains tax exemption. You've still made the capital gain, but when you take the money out of your RRSP, it will be taxed as income. And this is only fair. After all, you deducted from your taxable income the original $1000 you paid for the shares. And you have the profit from your good investment sheltered from taxes as long as it stays in your RRSP. Some advisors will tell you never to put shares in your RRSP because you lose the capital gains exemption. This is good advice if you have enough money to hold interest investments inside the RRSP and potential capital gains investments outside the RRSP. But there should be no hard and fast rules.

Long-term bonds, or an investment fund specializing in long-term bonds, can also be a good choice at particular times.

The single, most important thing to remember about an RRSP investment is to *regularly monitor and manage it*.

None of the available investments is ideal at all times because conditions change. Deposits in guarantees were excellent to own in 1981 and early 1982. Long-term bonds and mortgages appreciated in value tremendously from mid-1982 to mid-1983. The stock market almost doubled in value from mid-1982 to the end of 1983, and again in 1985-86. Guarantees were at half the rates paid in mid-1982.

WATCH TRENDS

You don't have to accept market changes and take your lumps while continuing to hold an investment that is adversely affected. One of the themes of this book is the importance of making independent decisions.

Read the business pages of newspapers and the weekly financial papers. Watch business broadcasts and listen to radio business reports. You'll soon become aware of interest rate and stock market trends. By paying attention to these trends, your awareness of conditions develops and allows you to make investment judgements comfortably.

STRATEGIC RETIREMENT EXERCISES

A few years ago, at a conference of the Canadian Institute of Chartered Accountants, Bill Crawford of Clarkson Gordon in Toronto enlightened us with a chronology of attitudes to providing for life after work.

Age	*Attitude*
20 – 30	— ignore
30 – 40	— cash poor, but thinking about it
40 – 50	— accumulation of assets
50 – 60	— defer excess income
60 – 65	— panic
65 – death	— minimize tax aspects
	— consider non-residency
	— consider heir's tax position

We still talk about retirement at age 65, but today, retirement age is really any age. By the time you get to be five or ten years from retirement, you should think of a couple of retirement exercises.

There will be a lot of adjustments and decisions to make, not all of them financial. For instance, without a work structure to govern your activities, you're going to have to make a lot of decisions on how to spend your new free time.

What options are open to you? Will you develop a skill or hobby you've always liked? Will you travel? Work part or full time? Go back to school? You'll also have to think about where you'll live. Will you stay in the same house, town, or country?

Though not overtly financial questions, the answers are contingent on how much money you'll have available at retirement. When you know this, you'll be able to judge whether you should be putting more retirement income aside. You'll also be able to see if your living standards will have to be altered, and to what degree.

HOW MUCH WILL YOU NEED?

The first step to discovering what you may need in retirement is to vow to be ruthlessly realistic in filling in the worksheets provided. You always need an emergency fund to deal with expenses that simply can't be foreseen. And you probably should aim for an inflation cushion". If you're planning to retire ten years from now, and there is no more than 5% inflation a year, you will need $1.63 to buy what you can buy today with $1. The following table shows you what you'll need in the future to buy today's $1 worth of goods.

If you retire this many years from now	*You'll need this much money to buy what $1 buys now*		
inflation rate	5%	10%	15%
10	1.63	2.59	4.05
15	2.08	4.18	8.14
20	2.65	6.73	16.37
25	3.39	10.83	32.92
30	4.32	17.45	66.22

WORKSHEET 1

Item	*Monthly Expenses* Now	After
Food — at home		
— restaurants		
Clothing — purchase		
— maintenance		
Transportation — car		
— licence		
— insurance		
— other		
— travel		
Housing — rent		
— mortgage		
— insurance		
— heat		
— electricity		
— phone		
— maintenance		
— taxes		
— furnishings		
Medical — prescriptions		
— dental		
Life insurance		
Savings		
Recreation		
Personal care		
Gifts		
Other		
TOTAL		

WORKSHEET 2

Estimated Monthly Income	
Private pension	
Canada/Quebec Pension Plan	
Old Age Security	
Other pension	
Deferred profit sharing	
Income from annuities	
Income from investment of life insurance cash value	
Dividend income	
Interest income	
Investment of capital from home sale	
Earnings from part-time job or self-employment	
Other income	
TOTAL	

The second step is to go through your monthly expenses now, before retirement, and estimate what your needs will be after retirement. Worksheet 1 may help get you started.

Then figure out how much you will have when you retire. That's what Worksheet 2 is for. Be sure to estimate conservatively.

Just completing these two worksheets will give you an idea of how much more retirement income you should be planning for now, to give you the kind of living standard you want in retirement.

The final step in the process: your cash flow position, calculated by simply subtracting your retirement EXPENSES from your INCOME.

Now's the time to think about these questions. To get an even more accurate picture of your retirement situation, you might want to live on your retirement income on a trial basis before the fact so that you can make the necessary adjustments.

Something else to remember is that you needn't make all these financial decisions in a vacuum. Involve your spouse as much as possible, since each one's needs will differ slightly and affect planning. For instance, in a two-career household, both members may retire at the same time. Or, one spouse may retire and adjust to the new lifestyle before the second spouse retires. The transition becomes smoother.

Take a look at your options for the accumulated assets in your RRSP. You have several choices. Whatever you do, you have to do it before you're 71. It's a good idea to be thinking about your options five to ten years before you turn 71, because you may have the opportunity to buy more retirement income in some years than in others. (Let me just remind you that in 1982, you could have bought $2000 a month for life with $100,000. Today, you can buy $1100.)

THE OPTIONS

Option 1: Take your money and run. You won't run far. The total you take out will be considered income in the year you take it out, and it will be taxed at your marginal tax rate.

Option 2: An Income for Life

A life annuity is just like being paid rent—you deposit the proceeds of your RRSP with a life insurance company, and they give you a monthly income for life.

Life annuities also have a few variations. You can have an annuity for yourself, with no guarantees of payout. It will simply pay until you die, even if you die a week after you buy it. If you don't like that idea, you can buy an annuity that will provide a payout for life, with a minimum guarantee of 5, 10, 15, or as many years as it takes to get from your age to 90, even if you die before then. The monthly income will go to your heirs.

You can buy a "joint and last survivor" annuity. This pays out for your life or your spouse's life, with or without a guarantee to age 90.

Option 3: Registered Retirement Income Funds

Registered retirement income funds are fairly new to the marketplace. They were introduced in the early 1980s as a means of protecting pensioners from the devastating effects of inflation. They offer protection by letting individual investors roll over investments in their RRSPs so they can continue to have control over their investment decisions.

The original restrictions on what you could invest in an RRIF, and how much you could take out each year, have now disappeared. You can manage your RRIF in the same manner as you manage your RRSP. You must withdraw a minimum amount each year, and you must withdraw it all by the time you turn 90. It is a welcome addition to the retirement products on the market because it provides more flexibility.

YOU PAYS YOUR MONEY AND YOU TAKES YOUR CHOICE

You can choose any combination of the above three options, including several different types of life annuity, term-certain annuities, and RRIFs. Life annuities are the only ones that will provide payment beyond age 90.

Specific provisions apply to RRSP and RRIF accounts passing to a spouse, and in some cases to children. They can reduce taxes payable on such amounts when you die.

Choosing the most suitable retirement options should not be left to the last minute. Under all the options, except for the RRIF, you may be locked in, which means that should you discover after you've bought a retirement plan that something else might have been suitable, you may have no recourse to change the plan. This is true despite the fact that in 1986, the federal government legalized the cashability of RRSP annuities. Many issuers of RRSP annuities have decided not to guarantee that they will be flexible. You still have to negotiate cashability with the issuer.

You can switch both your RRSP and your RRIF to a more attractive plan if you see one. Check on whether there are conversion fees. With the new regulations on RRIFs, you have plenty of choices that will make your golden years just that.

NEW REGISTERED RETIREMENT INCOME FUND (R.R.I.F.)

Lump Sum Investment: $100,000
Interest Rate: 10% Compounded Annually
Term Period: 19 Years
Payout based on a withdrawal of the interest only
until exceeded by the minimum fractional payout.

Dec. 31 of the year in which the buyer reaches age	*Market Value*	*Accumulated Value with Interest at 10%*	*Specific Fraction*	*R.R.I.F. Annual Payment (Interest Only) until exceeded by Fractional Payout*	*Balance Remaining After R.R.I.F. Payment*
72	100,000.00	110,000.00	(1/19th)	$10,000.00	$100,000.00
73	100,000.00	110,000.00	(1/18th)	10,000.00	100,000.00
74	100,000.00	110,000.00	(1/17th)	10,000.00	100,000.00
75	100,000.00	110,000.00	(1/16th)	10,000.00	100,000.00
76	100,000.00	110,000.00	(1/15th)	10,000.00	100,000.00
77	100,000.00	110,000.00	(1/14th)	10,000.00	100,000.00
78	100,000.00	110,000.00	(1/13th)	10,000.00	100,000.00
79	100,000.00	110,000.00	(1/12th)	10,000.00	100,000.00
80	100,000.00	110,000.00	(1/11th)	10,000.00	100,000.00
81	100,000.00	110,000.00	(1/10th)	11,000.00	99,000.00
82	99,000.00	108,900.00	(1/9th)	12,100.00	96,800.00
83	96,800.00	106,480.00	(1/8th)	13,310.00	93,170.00
84	93,170.00	102,487.00	(1/7th)	14,641.00	87,846.00
85	87,846.00	96,630.60	(1/6th)	16,105.10	80,525.50
86	80,525.50	88,578.05	(1/5th)	17,715.61	70,862.44
87	70,862.44	77,948.68	(1/4th)	19,487.17	58,461.51
88	58,461.51	64,307.66	(1/3rd)	21,435.89	42,871.77
89	42,871.77	47,158.95	(1/2)	23,579.47	23,579.47
90	23,579.47	25,937.42	(1/1)	25,937.42	

Total Payments from R.R.I.F. @ 10%: $265,311.66

Source: T. Delaney Inc., *Maturity Option Guide.*

NEW REGISTERED RETIREMENT INCOME FUND (R.R.I.F.)

Lump Sum Investment: $100,000
Interest Rate: 10% Compounded Annually
Term Period: 19 Years
Payout based on a $12,000 per annum withdrawal
until the funds have been depleted.

Dec. 31 of the year in which the buyer reaches age	*Market Value*	*Accumulated Value with Interest at 10%*	*Specific Fraction*	*R.R.I.F. Annual Payment ($12,000 annually) until the funds have been depleted*	*Balance Remaining After R.R.I.F. Payment*
72	100,000.00	110,000.00	(1/19th)	$12,000.00	$98,000.00
73	98,000.00	107,800.00	(1/18th)	12,000.00	95,800.00
74	95,800.00	105,380.00	(1/17th)	12,000.00	93,380.00
75	93,380.00	102,718.00	(1/16th)	12,000.00	90,718.00
76	90,718.00	99,789.80	(1/15th)	12,000.00	87,789.80
77	87,789.80	96,568.78	(1/14th)	12,000.00	84,568.78
78	84,568.78	93,025.66	(1/13th)	12,000.00	81,025.66
79	81,025.66	89,128.22	(1/12th)	12,000.00	77,128.22
80	77,128.22	84,841.05	(1/11th)	12,000.00	72,841.05
81	72,841.05	80,125.15	(1/10th)	12,000.00	68,125.15
82	68,125.15	74,937.67	(1/9th)	12,000.00	62,937.67
83	62,937.67	69,231.43	(1/8th)	12,000.00	57,231.43
84	57,231.43	62,954.58	(1/7th)	12,000.00	50,954.58
85	50,954.58	56,050.03	(1/6th)	12,000.00	44,050.03
86	44,050.03	48,455.04	(1/5th)	12,000.00	36,455.04
87	36,455.04	40,100.54	(1/4th)	12,000.00	28,100.54
88	28,100.54	30,910.59	(1/3rd)	12,000.00	18,910.59
89	18,910.59	20,801.65	(1/2)	12,000.00	8,801.65
90	8,801.65	9,681.82	(1/1)	9,681.82	

Total Payments from R.R.I.F. @ 10%: $225,681.82

Source: T. Delaney Inc., *Maturity Option Guide.*

CHAPTER 10

Estate Planning: Nobody Can Do It Better Than You

All men's gains are the fruits of venturing.

—Herodotus

No, you are not too young. And no, you do not have to be rich. You only have to be sane. Estate planning is nothing more than writing down what you want done with all the things you own after you die, and who you want to do the supervising. That means writing a will and naming an executor. Everybody has something, whether a bicycle, a record collection, or a few thousand dollars in the bank that they'd like to pass on to particular friends or relatives.

FIRST, THE WILL

A will has no legality as long as you are alive. That means you can write as many wills as you want, and change them regularly. A lot of fuss is made about how difficult and complicated it is to write a will. Maybe that's because standard wills are written in such awkward language (the lawyers who write tax laws must moonlight in will-drafting).

A will doesn't have to be incomprehensible. It is simply your set of instructions. It has to say who you are, where you live, and the date on which you've written the will. It has to say that it's the last set of instructions you've written. That's why all wills begin with "This is the last testament of me, ______" and so on.

There are several different kinds of wills: holograph, notarial, and English form. The following table shows which form of will is recognized in your province. If you move to another province, or overseas, check to be sure your will form is recognized in your new place of residence.

Holograph Will: Written entirely by hand, signed by the testator, and not witnessed by anyone. This style is acceptable in all provinces except British Columbia, Prince Edward Island, and Nova Scotia. It is convenient in that it can be written up in a hurry. Many people draw one up before they take a plane trip, for instance—just in case.

Notarial Will: Drawn up and witnessed by a notary. It's available only in Quebec. It does not have to be probated in Quebec, that is, it does not have to be presented before the courts to prove its authenticity. It is recognized in the rest of the country, but outside Quebec, it will have to be probated.

English Form Will: A standard format which is valid everywhere and is drawn up by a lawyer. This does have to be probated.

Forms of Wills Recognized

	Holograph	*Notarial**	*English*
British Columbia	no	yes	yes
Alberta	yes	yes	yes
Saskatchewan	yes	yes	yes
Manitoba	yes	yes	yes
Ontario	yes	yes	yes
Quebec	yes	yes	yes
New Brunswick	yes	yes	yes
Nova Scotia	no	yes	yes
P.E.I.	no	yes	yes
Newfoundland	yes	yes	yes
Northwest Territories	yes	yes	yes
Yukon Territory	yes	yes	yes

*Available in Quebec only

To decide which format is best for your needs, consult professional help. Sources include trust companies, a lawyer or notary, or an estate planner. Trust companies will give you advice for free. Lawyers or notaries will simply put your wishes into legal language and forewarn you of things you may not have thought of. You would do well to consult a professional even if you ultimately decide to write a holograph will.

There are some specific DOs and DON'Ts of will-writing which are worth checking:

DO include:

1. Where you, the testator (author) of the will, reside.
2. A declaration that the document is the last made, and is to supercede any others found.
3. Instructions to pay debts, taxes, medical expenses, and funeral expenses before the estate is distributed.
4. Who is to be appointed executor or executors.
5. Instructions for guardians of minors.
6. How you want the estate distributed. This is a key component of a will, and must include instructions for disposing of:
   a) your household goods and personal effects, car;
   b) your house and any other real estate you own;
   c) business interests;
   d) life insurance;
   e) special articles or bequests of money to family members, societies, funds, or institutions.

DON'T include:

Instructions on distributing possessions of minor value. This is because people often change their minds about who will get their antique radio or special rocking chair. Each change made to a will, no matter how small, requires that an entirely new will be drawn up. It's less time-consuming to write a memo about the instructions regarding your prized smaller items, and attach it to the will. In that way, if you do change your mind, you can rewrite the memo without having to churn out another entire document.

When you are drawing up the will, consider the effects inflation will have on the value of your estate. If you bequeath a life income to your spouse, and he or she becomes widowed years later, the amount is likely to be insufficient. You may want to make provisions for using capital from the estate to increase the income.

NEXT, THE EXECUTOR

This is a really big job, so you have to think carefully about who can do it. Here are the things an executor has to do.

Preliminary Tasks

1. Locate and review the will.

2. Meet with family and business associates.

3. Notify beneficiaries.

Assemble and Protect the Assets

1. Collect cash, bank accounts, business interests, personal effects, bonds, securities, real estate, collect rents if necessary, maintain properties, life insurance, annuities, pensions, bonds, miscellaneous assets.

2. Insure all property, protect business interests, collect valuables.

Prepare to Settle Accounts

1. Obtain probate (if an English form will).

2. Advertise for creditors.

3. File inventory of assets with tax department(s).

4. Settle asset values with tax departments and obtain releases.

Pay Expenses

1. Income tax to date of death.

2. Other taxes: municipal, school, etc.

3. Business debts.

4. Other expenses: legal fees, funeral expenses.

Account For Everything

1. Interim and final statement for beneficiaries.

Follow Instructions

1. Pay legacies.

2. Establish trusts.

3. Supervise investment.

4. Administer according to terms of will.

As you can see, the duties of the executor are not things to breeze through. Get other people involved in the process—your spouse, the lawyer handling your will, your accountant, your financial advisor.

Be clear on procedures. Your spouse should be aware of what's going on, especially if he or she is an executor. When choosing an executor, consider your spouse first, if you wish, but make sure he or she can handle all the responsibilities involved. Above all, get expert help on how to proceed. Here are a few special points to discuss with the person you consult:

1. If you're divorced and receiving or providing support payments, is there a provision for their continuation? If not, is it possible for the receiving ex-spouse to take out an insurance policy on the life of the provider?
2. If you live in Quebec, or if you married there, remember that the province has different laws affecting estate planning. Even if you don't live in Quebec, many provinces have recently enacted family laws that can overrule certain estate plans if a sufficiently large portion of the net family assets are not left to the spouse.
3. RRSPs, and other registered plans must be specially dealt with to avoid having them taxed in a lump sum at your death.
4. Special Instructions.

   Funeral
   Do you have any special instructions with regard to funeral arrangements, cremation, cemetary plot, and so on?

   Life Insurance How do you wish to dispose of your life insurance? To be paid directly to beneficiaries already named in policies or to be held in trust for beneficiaries?

   Business Interests Have you any instructions as to the carrying on, managing, or disposal of your business interests? In the event of sale is there any particular person or persons to whom your business should be offered?

   Guardian In the event that you and your spouse die while any of your children are minors, whom do you want to name as their guardian?

   Lawyer or Notary Do you have a lawyer or notary you would prefer to handle the legal matters in connection with the administration of your estate?

The following worksheet has been adapted from the Royal Trust's estate planning questionnaire. Much of the information should already be noted in your personal files (see Chapter 3).

ESTATE PLANNING WORKSHEET

GENERAL INFORMATION

Date ______________________

NAME: ______________________

ADDRESS: ______________________

____

TELEPHONE: ______________________

BUSINESS ADDRESS: ______________________

____

TELEPHONE: ______________________

Social Insurance Number: ______________________

STATUS: ☐ Single ☐ Married ☐ Separated*

☐ Divorced* ☐ Widow(er)

* Give date and details of agreement, if any.

DATE OF BIRTH ______________________

NAME OF SPOUSE: ______________________

Occupation: ______________ Date of Birth: ______________

CHILDREN: (name in full and, if married, name of spouse).

NAME	Born
______________	______________
______________	______________
______________	______________
______________	______________

DOMICILE: (Province, State, Country)

1. At time of marriage: ______________________
2. Place and date of marriage: ______________________
3. Present domicile: ______________________

MARRIAGE CONTRACT, if any:

1. Drawn up by: ______________________
2. Date of contract: ______________

WILL INSTRUCTIONS:

1. Funeral:
   (Monument, perpetual maintenance, and so on. Details of funeral arrangements can be left to spouse, children and/or executors).

2. Particular legacies:
   a) Disposition of clothing, jewellery, personal effects, household goods, furniture, both at home and office, automobiles, and so on.

   ____

   ____

   b) RRSP, DPSP, other pension plans.

   ____

   ____

   c) Residence(s): (The residence can be left outright to the spouse or the spouse can be given use of it with possibility of replacing it, subject or not to expenses).

   (i) Principal residence:

   ____

   (ii) Secondary residence:

   ____

   d) Bequests to children, relatives, friends or charitable organizations.

   ____

   ____

   ____

3. Life Insurance: (individual, group, permanent, term).

Companies	*Amount*	*Named beneficiary*

4. *RESIDUE:*
   - Can be left outright to surviving spouse or other beneficiary. May also be left in trust for spouse to receive income during his or her lifetime and capital, after his or her death, to children or others.

     a) Income: ______________________________

     b) Capital: ______________________________

     c) Encroachment on capital: ______________________________

   - If children are the capital beneficiaries upon cessation of the income trust:

     a) Proportion: ______________________________

     b) Age: ______________________________

     c) Income: ______________________________

     d) Encroachment on capital: ______________________________

   - If other than children are the capital beneficiaries upon cessation of income trust:

Share	*Name*	*Relationship*
____________	____________________	________________
____________	____________________	________________
____________	____________________	________________

- Provisions of remarriage. (Fiscal consequences)

  ____

- Appointment of Executor(s) and Trustee(s):
  (It is suggested that additional powers, other than those conferred by law, be stipulated in order to facilitate the administration, such as the power to retain investments, to invest and reinvest).

  ____

  ____

- Name of legal adviser whose services are to be retained for the preparation of the Will.

  ____

COMMENTS:

____

____

FINANCIAL DATA

ASSETS

LIQUID

Cash	$______
Term Deposits, G.I.C.s	$______
Bonds	$______
Stocks	$______
Mutual Funds	$______
Life insurance (less loans)	$______
RRSP	$______
RPP	$______
RRIF or annuity	$______
Real estate	$______
Personal effects and household goods	$______
Automobiles, boats, etc.	$______
Private loans, mortgages or notes	$______
Business interests	$______
Miscellaneous: ______	
______	$______
TOTAL ASSETS	$______

LIABILITIES

Bank loans	$______
Loans on stocks and bonds	$______
Notes and other debts	$______
Mortgages	$______
Others	$______
TOTAL LIABILITIES	$______
NET ESTATE	$______

CHAPTER 11

Strategies for the Unexpected

> Don't lay any certain plans for the future; it is like planting toads and expecting to raise toadstools.
>
> —Josh Billing

Back in the good old days—when I was growing up—we had some peculiar ideas. Among them: the expectation that we would have one job, or maybe two, during our working lifetimes; that we would marry for life and move into our own homes to raise our own children; that our children would grow up, get educated, get a job, move out, marry; and that everyone would live happily ever after.

The profile of the typical family only a generation ago allowed for a husband, who was the sole income earner and a wife, who stayed home and looked after the two-plus children. That family today is a small, although still significant, percentage of all Canadian families. But expectations and families have changed. Neither jobs nor marriages last forever. Mother and Father go out to work. Families are mended, blended or extended. Jobless adult children move back in with their parents. Retired parents move in with their middle-aged children. These familial rearrangements are so widespread that we have coined labels for them: DINKS (double income, no kids); SPOOKS (single parent, only one kid); and for the young adults whose careers got stopped just as they started, "the young and the rentless", and "baby boomerangs". Job termination has become so commonplace that the image of the silver-haired employee stepping up to receive a gold watch for forty years of dedicated service has given way to professional counsellors working out golden handshake packages, boards of directors devising golden parachutes for themselves in the eventuality of merger, takeover, or leveraged buyout leading to termination, and a new segment of the legal profession devoted to suing for wrongful dismissal.

As we proceed through the transition to a restructured economy, we cannot expect that none of these things will touch us.

"YOU'RE FIRED"

In the last decade, more than a million jobs have been eliminated as businesses all over Canada and the United States flatten their management curves and streamline themselves to meet new competitors. It's not over yet, and no company is immune. Some of the people who are let go drop out of the work force or retire; the vast majority go looking for another job, often with a very different view of what role that job should play in their lives.

KNOW THE OPTIONS

While you are working, take a bit of time to think about what your job means to you. If it's the centre of your life, if you depend on it not just for income, but for reinforcement of your self-image, maybe it's time to seek some of that support in other areas—perhaps with your family or in community organizations.

If you face involuntary separation—whether pink slip or golden handshake—the first thing you may have to decide is whether or not to accept a generic early retirement package. These are usually take-it-or-leave-it propositions and no one is singled out for dismissal. They are incentive packages which you accept or not. You will have only a limited time—30, 60 or maybe 90 days— in which to sign up.

Ask yourself whether you have an option to stay. Don't assume that if you don't sign up, the status quo prevails. In times like these, the status quo has no future.

Check out your financial needs and your life goals. Voluntary separation packages at work qualify as one of the big events that should trigger a re-evaluation of your priorities and objectives. Do the calculations of what you'd have if you accept the package. Termination consultants say if you're making $50,000 a year, you need 70 to 75% of that amount to continue living at the same level.

If you're planning to continue working, do you have enough resources to carry you till you find other work? If you're in your fifties, whether you plan on working or not, the package should include enhanced pension benefits.

ALL THIS AND TAXES TOO

When you lose your job, you may be too upset to think about all the material consequences. You may be even more upset later if you *don't* think about it, so it's worth making an effort to do so, no matter how hard it is.

Severance Payments

Depending on the circumstances, you may be offered a severance payment when you leave your job. Sometimes your employer will have to respect labour legislation that specifies how much you're entitled to. If you've been working at the same place for a long time, it's probably worth seeing a lawyer to make sure you get what you should.

In other circumstances, the severance payment will be largely negotiable, depending on a complex web of factors varying from how much you know about the company's business to your years of service and any gratitude or guilt your employer might feel towards you. In any case, being as cool as you can will probably be to your advantage. If you can't be cool, get help. This is one of those times when a good financial planner can make you aware of your options, and make a big difference in putting you on the right track.

For tax purposes, severance payments used to be entirely transferable to your RRSP. Since November 1981, the rules have changed, and you can only shelter $2,000 per year of service in your RRSP. The rules will change again in 1990 and in subsequent years, so this is something to look over carefully.

Pension contributions are entirely transferable to your RRSP, or to your new employer's pension fund, if you've already found another job.

Should you find yourself in a situation where you have to sue your employer to get more money, remember that your legal fees will not be tax deductible. If you get a settlement for wrongful dismissal, whether in or out of court, that money will be treated exactly like severence pay for tax purposes. Any other money obtained after a suit is brought is entirely taxable.

If your employer pays for a career consultant to help you find a new job, that is a deductible expense for the company. If you pay for it, it is not. In some cases, these expenses have been declared taxable benefits, but these rulings have also been successfully challenged. This is a grey area open to interpretation, but don't discount the possibility that you may have to pay taxes on this particular benefit.

Unemployment Insurance

Most people contribute to Unemployment Insurance when they are employed, and therefore are entitled to it when they lose their jobs. Should you end the year in which you received UI payments with extra revenue from either a new job or from a business, you may find that you have to reimburse some of the money. The ceiling changes every year, but it's clearly identified on your income tax form.

Your Benefits and Losing Them

To add to your troubles, it may be that you lose all your group insurance, medical insurance, disability insurance and any other benefits you're used to counting on the day you leave your job.

This is not a time when you need any more trouble. Make sure that the moment you know you'll be leaving your job, you obtain a full statement of your benefits, the conditions under which they expire, and whether or not you'll be given the option of prolonging any of them by prepaying them for a given period of time while you regroup and reorganize your life.

You may have to rethink your entire insurance portfolio. Many people are caught unawares when this happens. Don't let it happen to you.

Documents You Need to Have

You absolutely need your official separation certificate to obtain Unemployment Insurance benefits.

You'll also need a T4 from your employer, but it won't usually be issued until the end of the taxation year. If you don't have it by the end of February in the following year, follow up on it, because you'll need the slip to file your income tax return.

If it's not offered, ask for a complete statement of your pension account, benefits, stock purchase plan if you have one, and any other plans you have paid into or been a member of since joining the company. In this area, you may even have a pleasant surprise or two, since small amounts accumulate over the years.

Remember that there is far less stigma attached to losing a job today than there used to be. Everyone knows that the economy is being restructured, that companies are sometimes at the mercy of international economic forces beyond their control. Losing a job need never be a sign that you're incompetent or not worth employing.

If at all possible, ask your employer for a letter of recommendation that details your strengths, and maybe a weakness or two, (since no one will believe that you're perfect) to help you get a new job.

WHEN IT ISN'T YOUR CHOICE

Getting fired, or permanently laid off, is a kick in the psyche, no matter how balanced a life you lead. It hurts, and it makes you mad. Acknowledge those feelings, and don't let anyone belittle them. According to the stress experts, losing your job is right up there with death and divorce. If you have the opportunity, take advantage of counsellors. They may or may not find you a job, but their real value is to acknowledge your feelings, put them in perspective, assess your skills, set career goals. They'll also help in polishing job-search techniques, and in providing a support system.

STARTING OVER

You have three choices. You can look for another job, you can retire, you can go into business for yourself. Whatever you decide, it might help to budget closely for a while. Do a budget exercise, with fixed and discretionary expenses, as described in Chapter 2. If nothing else, it will relieve some anxiety. And remember the rule of thumb: one month of job hunting for every $10,000 of salary wanted. This doesn't mean that if you're leaving a $40,000-a-year job and you spend eight months looking that you'll get an $80,000-a-year job. But then again, these are turbulent times—maybe you will. If you have heavy debts, talk to your creditors about re-negotiating payments. Look over your borrowing potential—it's not the best time to borrow but if you sell assets to raise money to spend, you are vulnerable to never replacing the assets.

OPPORTUNITY KNOCKS

Sometimes a knock on the side of the head can be beneficial: losing your job may be the opportunity to start your own business. Tens of thousands of Canadians have done just that—small business and franchise growth in North America has been phenomenal. In fact, over the last ten years, self-employment has grown more than twice as fast as paid employment. Check out the possibility thoroughly—it takes commitment and multiple skills, from development plans to financial statements to raising capital to marketing prowess.

WILL YOU STILL FEED ME WHEN I'M 64?

More and more Canadians are living into their eighties and nineties, the ages when the risk of long-term illness increases. And more and more middle-aged Canadians are being asked to deal with their aging parents' finances.

It shouldn't be surprising to find that older Canadians do not have their financial affairs in order—neither have the majority of younger Canadians. People who are looking after their parents' investments need one overwhelming characteristic: tolerance. It's really easy, when confronted by a 75-year-old who wants to save for old age, to jump up and down in frustration.

The starting point is to review your parents' lifestyle needs to determine whether they have an income sufficient to provide them with the things they want. Go through the entire smart spending process with them: make sure, for example, that they have properly insured their possessions. You may find that their household insurance does not provide for replacement value. And check to make sure that they have proper medical or Blue Cross insurance, particularly if they travel south in the winter. And if they do travel south, remember there are senior citizen rates for travel and many other goods and services.

Check out your parents' income tax returns—many of us, not just the elderly, have trouble understanding tax returns. And many of us, not just the elderly, pay more tax than we legally have to. Check out whether their income is all earned from interest. If so, it might be advantageous to switch to dividend earning investments, which are taxed at a lower rate.

If necessary, you can have dividend or interest cheques, Old Age Security or other income deposited directly into their bank accounts. But if you do, you'll have to make sure to update bank books regularly.

Try to have wills reviewed and updated. Get a Power of Attorney for your parents in the event you have to look after all your parents' financial affairs. It's a good idea to do this in advance of any emergency. But under all circumstances, encourage your parents to look after their own affairs. It's good mental and physical exercise for them. Your role is to offer advice, and to remember that it's their money.

BREAKING UP IS HARD TO DO

Marriages are not made in heaven any more. A very high proportion of Canadian marriages end in divorce. So maybe splitting up is not that hard to do, but it's always traumatic. One thing that can make it less so is to know the financial aspects.

Marriage contracts have been common in Quebec for decades;

they are only becoming common in other provinces as the provinces pass family law reform legislation. If you are contemplating marriage, have a look at the legislation in your province which regulates the division of property and support rights both during and after marriage. If the legislation doesn't suit your circumstances, consider a formal marriage contract. In such a contract, you and your prospective spouse can agree on how your property and your debts will be divided on separation. Do this carefully, and be mindful of the fact that once the contract is signed, it cannot be changed or cancelled unilaterally. If you're planning to live with someone, you can have a cohabitation agreement written. If you're married with no marriage contract, and separated or divorcing, the family law legislation in your province will set out guidelines for property division. Family law legislation will also have guidelines for child support, even if you have agreed on a marriage contract.

Other things you should know relate to taxes. Alimony or maintenance payments are tax deductible for the payer, and income taxable for the recipient if they are clearly a periodic allowance for maintenance of the spouse and/or the children, if the spouses are living apart, and if the payments are made according to a written separation agreement or court order.

Only one parent can claim the equivalent-to-married exemption (soon to become a credit), so you and your spouse will have to agree on that, or the court will determine who may. If the children are under 14 and live with both parents during the year, both can claim child-care expenses.

The parent who gets the family allowance cheques also gets the child tax credit.

THE YOUNG AND THE RENTLESS

If your adult children move back in with you because life didn't work out quite the way it was supposed to, try to understand that it's not altogether their fault. I put it that way because there's a real tendency to be resentful—maybe because you were really enjoying having that extra room to lounge around in, maybe because *you* never went home again. In any case, what your kid needs is the same kind of TLC as a person who loses a job. Your youngster may not have access to company-paid professional counselling, but the same sequence of events and decisions applies—family support, re-evaluation of skills, choices to be made. The most important thing, with all these "it-can't-happen-to-me" events, is to remember that times have changed, and no one is immune. This kind of understanding won't make all the problems go away, but it will make you better prepared.

[illegible]

THE PEOPLE AND THE SERVICES

[illegible]

Part 3

Investment Strategies Through the Turbulent Nineties

CHAPTER 12

The Language and Strategy of Investing

Finally, the nitty-gritty of investing. But you know by now: you absolutely, positively need to understand the environment within which you have to invest your money, and you absolutely, positively have to have a personal plan. Without some understanding of the big world and the forces which are constantly moulding it, you are at its mercy. Recognition of this, embodied in your custom-made financial plan, will put you in control.

Despite all the seemingly different alternatives for investing your money—stock, shares, bonds, guaranteed certificates, debentures, options, futures, real estate, gold, antiques—the principle of investing becomes simple if you remember one fact:

THERE ARE ONLY TWO DISTINCT KINDS OF INVESTMENT

You can buy something and own it or you can lend your money out. That's it. All the alternatives listed above, plus any others you can think of, fall into one or the other of these two categories.

The first—buying and owning something—is called equity investment. Stocks, shares, mutual funds, real estate, real estate trusts, housing, gold, and collectibles all fall into the category of equity investment. That's what we're going to deal with in the next few chapters.

The second—lending your money out—is called debt investment. Bonds, guaranteed investment certificates, term deposits, whole life insurance, mortgages, and debentures fall into this category. We'll deal with them in later chapters. First, you may as well learn a few definitions.

Equity investment means owning a piece of the action. You put up your money to buy a piece or share of a car company or a bank, and you share in the fortunes of the organization. Or you buy a house or a piece of land. You get no guarantees of making a profit or even getting your money back.

If your investment does well, your share of the profit when you sell is called a capital gain. Depending on what kind of equity investment it is, the managers of the investment may decide to share some of the profits with you even if you don't sell. This sharing is called dividends.

If your investment does poorly, you stand to lose all your money. Only in specific circumstances can you lose more than your investment actually cost you.

The most important characteristics of equity investment are:

1. You own the investment; therefore, you have to manage it. If you don't manage it personally, you have a right to know how the investment is being managed by others.
2. You get no guarantees—not in terms of profits and not even in terms of getting your original capital back. All the more reason to want to know something about how much management your equity needs.
3. The potential for capital gains is infinite, and you share in those gains according to the proportion of your ownership.
4. Canadian tax laws treat income from equity investments more favourably than they treat the income from debt investments.

Debt investment is basically an I.O.U. You lend your money to someone. In return for foregoing the use of your own money, the borrower promises to pay you a fixed rate of return called interest. Interest will be paid on a regular basis during the time you can't use your own money. At a specifically stated future date, the borrower also promises to return your money to you.

There are three specific parts to a debt investment. There is a stated amount of *capital*, or *principal*, to be lent; there is a stated *rate of return*, or *interest*, to be paid at stated intervals; and there is a stated *maturity* date at which the borrower promises to repay your money.

The comparison of a debt investment with an equity investment is simple. Your invested money is guaranteed to be returned to you and you are guaranteed a rate of return. But the old gray mare just ain't what she used to be. Your invested money is "guaranteed" to be returned to you, as long as the borrower has assets when the debt is to be repaid. You are "guaranteed" a rate of return as long as the funds exist to pay you interest.

The most important characteristics of debt investment are:

1. You have lent money to someone. You'll want to ensure their past reliability regarding repayment.
2. You get guarantees as to the rate of return and the return of your borrowed funds. These guarantees depend entirely on the financial well-being of the borrower.
3. The potential for capital gain is zero, no matter how much the borrower makes with your money. His first obligation is to repay you plus interest, nothing more. There are, however, certain circumstances in which you can make a capital gain on debt investments. We'll look at them in Chapter 14.
4. The income from debt investment, that is, interest income, is taxed as though it were simply added to your earned income.

Strategic Tactic #1: Know Yourself

When you send your money out to work, what do you want it to do for you?

You have to know your own personal investment objectives. Basically, this means determining how far you lean to one side or other on a pendulum which has fear on one side, greed on the other. You have three choices; you can invest for:

- Income from your investments;
- Preservation of capital;
- Growth of capital.

There isn't a single investment we know of that will give you all three. So right off the bat, you're going to have to compromise. That's not hard to do, since there is an almost infinite number of investment options from which to choose.

Your objectives are dependent on your own personal circumstances; the checklist you must consider includes:

- Your age—the older you are the less you may be interested in high risk investment, which offers capital gains potential, but which also threatens capital losses.
- The number and age of people dependent on you.
- Your present net worth—how much you've already accumulated will determine to some degree how much you're willing to risk to accumulate more.
- Your present income.
- Your prospects for future income.

- The income you want in retirement.
- Your ability to supervise your investments. You'll have to decide how much time, interest and skill you have in managing your investments. Some investments take little time or knowledge (e.g., Canada Savings Bonds); others take considerable (stocks, "collectibles").
- Tax considerations. Some investments look a lot better on an "after-tax" basis; some kinds of investment income are more favourably treated by the tax act (e.g., dividends over interest) so you need to have some basic knowledge about: i) your own marginal tax rate; and ii) what the tax act allows you to do.
- Above all, your sleeping point. Some wag somewhere tells the story of the agitated investor who wailed to J.P. Morgan about how his investments kept him up at night. What should he do, he asked the great man. "Sell," Morgan answered, "down to the sleeping point." Pork belly futures may be fine for people, who can sleep through a hurricane; but forget it if you bite your nails every Thursday waiting for the bank rate to be announced.

Strategic Tactic #2: Review Your Options

You have to know what's available in the world of investments, in order to make as wise (and wide) decisions as possible. The main portfolio objectives are safety of principal, income and capital gains. But secondary considerations include having a market when you want to sell; how much management time the investment requires; how long your money may be locked in.

Once you have your investment priorities straight and have narrowed down your investment options, you must make decisions about how you're going to divide your money between investment alternatives. This is obviously a decision which should be clearer to you after you've worked your way through steps 1 and 2. It's also dependent upon how much money you have to invest. That doesn't mean you have to have a lot, but obviously your ability to diversify your holdings is reduced when your capital is relatively low. For example, if you're young, just starting out, and decide to buy a home, you may find your nest egg is tied up in the house (which, by the way, is fine, since you're building equity in the house while you accumulate more investment funds.)

There are obviously other ways of categorizing your investment possibilities besides the sleeping point criterion. On page 185, there's a general rating system I developed several years ago for the Royal Bank of Canada.

Strategic Tactic #3: Know What Not to Do

1. Don't start investing without a concrete investment plan. What do you want your money to do for you? Somewhere in the deep recesses of your mind you may know you're going to need some money for the kids' college or some money to live on after you stop working. Only if you set down specific goals can you estimate their costs. No one, of course, can be completely accurate about the cost, because hardly anything is stable and predictable any more. But we all know that interest rates tend to reflect the inflation rate. So, we can all figure out how much we have to invest at what interest rate in order to come up with any specific amount of money.
2. Don't think your investment plan is going to activate itself. Like New Year's resolutions, sitting down and making an investment plan is only the first step. You can even get to the point of knowing you will need $50,000 three years from now in order to put your two children through university. But if you don't start now to activate the plan by investing regularly, your children will be ready for university and you'll have to scramble for the fees.
3. Don't fail to keep records. Even if you don't want to manage your investments continually, you nevertheless need to review your financial position every year, or when big changes, either within the family or in the investment community, happen.
4. Don't take advice you don't understand, yet don't ignore the professional advice that's available to you. Think of your money management as a business. It's your money. You care about it more than anyone else in the world. You, therefore, are the chairman of the board of your own financial business. So mind your own business. That means appointing an advisory board of professionals—a lawyer, accountant, stockbroker, financial or estate planner, insurance broker, and real estate broker. You may not need them all, and they don't have to come together to advise you. But they are all available to you, some at no fee, some at a small consulting fee. Be sure you ask how much a consultation will cost before you go for one. There's no point in spending a lot of money if you don't have a lot of investable money. But even for free, you can get your questions answered. You can improve your own knowledge and financial skills, and can ask for many people's advice. Then make your own decisions. If you do have substantial assets, a group session with

your lawyer, accountant, and financial or tax planner will more often than not result in the more efficient use of your money, whether by lowering your tax bracket or by increasing your investment returns. If you don't have professional advisors, see Chapter 19.

5. Don't put all your eggs in one basket. Stephen Lewis, an American financial planner, put it best: "The national flower of the sensible investor is the hedge." Nobody knows the future—if we have hyperinflation, gold will do well; stocks and bonds will be disastrous. Merely high inflation will see commercial real estate doing as well as precious metals. A depression will make cash the best asset around, because it will be available to buy other assets at distress price levels.

If any one of us could predict the shape of tomorrow's economy with any degree of accuracy, not only could we make a fortune, we could start our own religion and confidently predict a following of millions. Failing that, economic survival will depend on hedging.

Strategic Tactic #4: Know the Risks

There are a lot of different possibilities against which we must protect ourselves. Among these are protecting our assets against the possibility of:

- inflation and deflation;
- the regular but unpredictable ups and downs of business activity commonly called boom and bust;
- market risk, which generally includes price swings in stocks, real estate, precious metals, bonds, and you name it;
- business risk, such as the unpredictable events which change the fortunes of specific corporations and even industries. Chrysler, Massey-Ferguson, General Public Utilities, the utility which owns Three Mile Island, and the Canadian oil industry all suffered specific mishaps which were generally unpredictable.
- interest rate risk—within the past five years, interest rates have gone from 22% to their present level. In the last ten years, they have gone from 10% to 22% to their present level.
- political risk, which really means being able to take into account government policy changes which may radically affect your investments. The Western Accord and the collapse of the OPEC cartel in 1985, the May federal budget of that year which eliminated RHOSPs and curtailed income-splitting, but gave us a lifetime exemption of $500,000 in capital gains, and the

tax reform proposals of 1987 which took away the $500,000 lifetime capital gains exemption are the most recent examples of why we must learn to hedge against politicians.

Strategic Tactic #5: Know the Alternatives

A Sample Strategy

If you're working:

20% cash
—bank accounts
—deferred annuities
—treasury bills
—guaranteed certificates

25-30% in stocks
—mutual funds, preferably growth funds
—growth stocks

15% in bonds
—corporate
—corporate or government bought at discount

25-30% in real estate
—home
—property for appreciation

5% precious metals, collectibles, speculative investments

If you're retired:

25% in cash
—bank accounts
—annuities
—treasury bills
—guaranteed certificates

25% in stocks
—mutual funds, preferably income funds
—blue chip stocks with good dividends

25% in bonds
—high grade corporate
—government, bought at discount

25% in real estate
—home
—income property

0-5% precious metals

The Fingernail Scale of Major Investment Choices

The State of Your Fingernails	*Type of Asset*	*Expected Rate of Return (1988) (before income taxes)*	*How Long You Have to Hold It to Get What You Expect*	*What You Stand to Lose*
Beautifully manicured	Savings accounts	6-7%	No specific investment period required.	No risk of losing what you put in. Deposits up to $60,000 guaranteed by an agency of the federal government. An almost sure loser even with today's inflation.
Evenly trimmed, but getting shorter	Term deposits; Guaranteed investment certificates; Canada Savings Bonds	7-10%	Money must be left on deposit for the entire term to take advantage of higher rate.	Early withdrawals impossible or subject to penalty. Rates geared to expected inflation.
A little ragged	Government or corporate bonds	8-11%	Investments must be made for the period until maturity of the bond (10-20 years) to be assured of the stated rate. Bonds may be sold at any time, however, in which case the net return depends on fluctuations in market price of the bonds.	Very little if held to maturity. Moderate fluctuations can be expected in realized return if bonds are sold prior to maturity. Rate geared to expected long-run inflation rate. This may differ from actual rate over the term to maturity of the bond.
Down to the quick	• Diversified portfolios of blue-chip common stocks • Real estate • Mutual funds • Precious metals • Collectibles	15-25%	No specific investment periods required and all may be sold at any time. The 20% average expected return assumes a fairly long investment period and can only be treated as a rough guide based on current conditions.	Moderate to substantial. In any one year the actual return could in fact be negative. Diversified portfolios have at times lost 25% or more of their actual value. Contrary to current opinion — a good inflation hedge.

Comparative Investment Alternatives by Investment Objectives

Investment	*Safety of Principal*	*Capital Gains Potential*	*Income*	*Marketability*	*Management Time Required*	*Cost*	*Tax Treatment*
Savings accounts	very high	none	steady	excellent	none	none	interest fully taxed
Canada Savings Bonds	very high	none	steady	excellent	little	none	interest fully taxed
Savings certificates	very high	none	steady	poor	none	none	interest fully taxed
Term deposits	very high	none	steady	moderate	none	none	interest fully taxed
Life insurance	very high	none	none	moderate	little	yes	interest
Government bonds	very high	fair to good	steady	good	moderate	none	int./cap. gain
Corporate bonds	high	fair to good	steady	good	moderate	none	int./cap. gain
Common stocks:							
"blue chip"	moderate to high	fair to good	moderate	good	significant	yes	dividends/cap. gain
"growth"	low to moderate	good	minimal	good	significant	yes	dividends/cap. gain
Preferred stocks	moderate	fair to good	good	good	moderate	yes	dividends/cap. gain
Mutual funds	low to moderate	fair to good	none	good	moderate	yes	dividends/cap. gain
Real estate							
own home	moderate	good	none	moderate	little	yes	no capital gains
other	variable	good	steady	moderate	significant	yes	capital gains
Mortgages	low to moderate	none	good to excellent	moderate	moderate	yes	interest
Commodities	low	good	none	good	significant	yes	capital gains
Currencies	low	good	none	good	significant	yes	capital gains
Collectibles	low	good	none	poor	significant	yes	capital gains

An Alternative Strategy

- Have money in the bank—perhaps literally, but certainly in highly liquid assets; enough money so that if things go badly, you'll have something to fall back on. My own preference is for the equivalent of four months of living expenses.
- Buy about $1000 worth of commodities in the form of bulk purchases of non-perishable items you will use up regularly. See Chapter 4.
- Pay off all your installment and charge accounts and credit card loans—that's a sure-fire double digit, tax-free rate of return. See Chapter 4.
- Open a tax sheltered registered retirement savings plan, which may or may not be invested in common shares.
- Consider buying a home, or equity in a home, which is still one of the best all-round, all-weather investments you can make. See Chapter 5.
- Buy term insurance if you have dependents, disability insurance even if you don't, because if you get sick, who's going to look after you? See Chapter 6.
- Streamline all your possessions' insurance by raising the deductible, that is, the amount of loss you're willing to assume, so that you have the lowest premium possible. See Chapter 7.

Once you've got all these things in place, or at least have considered them and made a clear decision to reject them as priorities, you can start looking at the stock market. And I do mean looking. If you're a novice, read the book first. One of the best ways of not succeeding in managing your money successfully is to act before you've finished planning.

CHAPTER 13

Owning a Piece of the Action: Stocks

> What concerns me is not the way things are, but rather the way people think things are.
>
> —Epictetus

There are some good reasons for considering investing at least some of your money in the stock market. The first is that over the long haul—in this case, the last sixty or seventy years—the average return on investments in common stocks has been at least double what you'd have made if you had invested money in short- or long-term bonds.

Certainly at the beginning of the 1980s, you'd have done better in bonds, just as during the seventies, you'd have been better off in gold. But smart money managers are never completely in one thing or the other. Stocks have a better performance rating over the long term, and they are preferred to bonds if you're looking for an inflation hedge. This doesn't mean that all common shares have kept up with the rate of inflation in the past or will do so in the future. However, unlike bonds, stocks have the potential for keeping up with inflation. And because stocks have the potential for capital gains, they are a tax preferred investment. Remember that the first $100,000 of all capital gains is tax exempt and only half of all capital gains above that are taxed, whereas *all* income derived from interest is taxed from dollar one.

On the other hand, in several European countries and Japan, disinflation has become deflation. Having a fixed income when prices are falling will make you relatively richer, just as having a fixed income when prices were rising made people poorer. Investing successfully means finding the stocks which have the greatest chance of yielding a high return, either by way of dividends, or by way of capital gains. That's what this chapter is about.

BUYING A PIECE OF THE ACTION

The basics of the stock market alternative are fairly straightforward. A stock is the same as a share. Both describe the process by which you become a part owner or shareholder in a corporation. You own shares in common with a bunch of other people—hence the name. You have an equity position that entitles you to share in the profits or losses of the company.

Here is a simple example of a corporate structure. Your hobby is making jam. You decide you want to expand your kitchen operation. You incorporate yourself with the name Butternut Farms Limited, and sell 19 shares to 19 of your friends at $50 a share. You keep one share and put $50 in the bank. The company is "capitalized" at $1000 (20 shareholders times $50 each) with 20 shareholders. The shares are called *common* shares, or *common* stock. If the company makes money, management (in this case, you) can decide to share the profits with shareholders in the form of a *dividend*.

Common stock is called common to distinguish it from *preferred* stock or shares. Preferred shares are shares that pay a dividend before any common shareholder can receive a dividend. Whereas the dividend of the common stock can go up if the company makes money, or down if it doesn't, the dividend of a preferred share is stated in advance and is fixed. The dividend of a preferred share is a bit like the interest rate on a bond in this respect, since interest is stated in advance and is a fixed rate of return.

Preferred shares are preferred only because their dividend must be paid before the dividend on a common share. However, they are not necessarily a better investment. Indeed, unless the preferred share is *convertible* into a common share, it doesn't have the same potential for appreciating in value if the company makes money. It does, however, get preferential treatment under Canadian tax law, and in cases of bankruptcy. The preferred shareholder is above the common shareholder on the list of people to be paid off.

HOW TO INVEST IN STOCKS

You need some money—not a lot. A hundred dollars can begin a stock market investment portfolio.

You need a stockbroker. That's because the stock market is organized into corporations called stock exchanges, where only members—investment dealers and brokers—can trade.

Opening an account with an investment dealer or stockbroker is even easier than getting a credit card. Basically, you just look in the yellow pages under "Investment Dealers" or "Brokers", pick one, phone for an appointment, go down, and open an account. The brokerage firm will want to know your name, address, phone number, age, social insurance number, a bank reference, and how you want your share registered.

WILL YOUR BROKER MAKE YOU JUST THAT?

You will eventually have to make a decision about what kind of relationship you want with your broker. Some people want a handholder—someone who will tell them what to buy, when to sell, and who will sympathize if they don't make money. The most important thing to know about your broker, and all brokers, is that they are commissioned salesmen—they make money when you trade. Whether you buy low and sell high, or buy high and sell low, your broker takes a commission on the purchase and sale. This fact does not mean that your broker, or account executive, as they like to be called, doesn't have your best interests at heart. He or she undoubtedly has. But it also means that the broker has a vested interest in getting you to trade. That's the only time he or she makes money.

Having put in this cautionary note, I must also tell you that a full-service broker is backed up by a wealth of research information that will be invaluable to you in making your own investment decisions, if you learn how to use it. If you can take responsibility for your own investment decisions, and don't want advice, research, or anything from your broker except access to trading, you can do your trades through a discount broker and pay a lot less in commissions.

YOU HAVE TO KNOW THE JUNGLE BEFORE YOU LOOK AT THE VINES

The stock market is a jungle. There are a lot of theories about how the jungle works. And there are a lot of gurus who make pronouncements regularly on what's going to happen in the jungle. Neither the theories nor the gurus are consistently reliable. That's obvious. If any of them were, there'd be no need for books like this. But that doesn't mean you should ignore either the theories or the gurus. The reason is that a lot of other people don't ignore them. In fact, so many people follow one or another of the theories or forecasters that their actions can move the market.

Some of you might remember when Joe Granville (a market guru who also dabbles in earthquake forecasting) said "Sell." So many people sold their shares that the stock market averages dropped a couple of dozen points, and the market lost several billion dollars of value. Yet six months later when he said "Sell" again, enough people disagreed that the market averages actually went up. Robert Prechter's every pronouncement moves the market today. The point really is that in order to make rational decisions, you have to know enough at least to ask intelligent questions.

HOW TO LOOK AT THE MARKET

There are literally tons of literature on how to look at the stock market. Stripped of the jargon and mystique, the professionals (who on average are no more successful in the market than anyone else) who study the market do so in two basic ways. One is called *fundamental* analysis. The other is called *technical* analysis.

Fundamental analysis means looking at the basic factors that might affect the fortunes of a company—its sales, earnings, assets, and dividend prospects—in addition to the general factors that may affect the company, the industry, and the economy itself.

For fundamental analysis, you have to have a better idea of what's happening both politically and economically than "Politicians lie" or "The economy is all screwed up." In Chapter 19 you'll learn how to read economic, business, and financial news.

Technical analysis is basically deciding what's going to happen in the market by interpreting charted patterns of the daily movements of particular stocks. Chartists have been around practically as long as there have been markets. In fact, one of the earliest technical theories was created by Charles Dow, founder of the *Wall Street Journal*, and after whom the Dow-Jones averages are named. (I still don't know who Jones was.)

If you are going to invest in the market, you have to be aware of two facts about technical analysis. First, it doesn't work consistently. Second, so many people follow charts that when the followers move in concert, they can also move the market. So you have to be aware of what the chartists are saying, if only to be able to explain to yourself why the market moved the way it did.

Again, I have to emphasize that I'm not advocating studying the market twitches hour by hour, or even day by day. Stock market investing, for me at least, is a long-term decision. Once you've done your homework and selected a stock, you're not going to sell it until you have a solid reason for doing so.

One more point about looking at the market. You will have noticed that the fundamental and technical appraoches are both graced with the word "analysis." Analysis is a scientific word. Scientific brings to mind logic, rational thought, and rational behaviour. However, the stock market is about as logical as your neighbourhood lunatic. Over the long run, the stock market moves within a more powerful world which controls it—like an economy that is clearly expanding or contracting, or an economy that is changing so rapidly that the impact of the changes is not clearly visible. In the short run, it is impossible to predict accurately because it can be so illogical and so hysterical.

The stock market can go for surprisingly long periods of time without reacting to all the seemingly obvious things there are to react to. Then it can go mad, either up or down, manic or depressive, about some trivial event. In many areas, and nowhere more clearly than in the stock market, successful money management requires an understanding of psychology, both normal and abnormal.

Eventually, the stock market responds and corresponds to reality. The really smart money manager can do very well indeed, even if it's small money, or even if the manager isn't an insider. In other words, you can do well in the stock market if you have a personality that allows you to:

- think for yourself;
- resist being one of the crowd;
- stick to an investment programme;
- learn from your mistakes.

So much for the overview. Now how do you decide if the stock market is for you? There aren't any foolproof ways, but there are a couple of tests you can take that will confirm the gut feeling you already have about your attitudes toward greed and fear, the two forces that rule all investment decisions. I suspect most people know in their hearts whether stock market investing is for them. But if you like quizzes, here's one that appeared in *Changing Times* way back in 1975.

Should You Be in the Stock Market?

There are no right answers or wrong answers, just choices that indicate different attitudes towards risk and reward. You'll find a discussion of what your answers mean at the end of the quiz.

1. A good reason for investing in common stocks is: (A) they offer a chance to get rich: (B) they offer a hedge against inflation; (C)everybody does it.

2. Owning a portfolio of common stocks would be: (A) fun; (B) nice, but the cause of a little worry; (C) foolish.

3 As a rule, you make decisions: (A) quickly, after grasping the essentials of the situation; (B) slowly, after point-by-point deliberation; (C) reluctantly.

4 Pick the word that best describes your conception of the stock market: (A) a game; (B) a speculation; (C) a gamble.

5 Based on the title alone, which of the following books about the stock market would you most like to read? (A) *Anyone Can Make a Million*; (B) *Your Battle for Stock Market Profits*; (C) *Fleecing the Lambs*.

6 What do you think is a reasonable rate of growth for a long-term investment? (A) 20% a year; (B) 8% to 10% a year; (C) haven't thought about it.

7 If someone gave you $1000 to invest, you'd probably buy: (A) gold; (B) 20 shares of Bell Telephone; (C) government savings bonds.

8. If you had to select a stock to invest in, you'd make your selection primarily on the basis of: (A) a tip from an investor friend; (B) your own investigation; (C) a broker's recommendation.

9 Assuming you own common stock in a company, you would: (A) check its price daily to see whether you should sell; (B) check regularly to see how the company is doing; (C) put the certificates away and forget them.

10. How would you describe your way of living? (A) stylish; (B) moderately conservative; (C) very conservative.

Maybe you've got the idea of the quiz by now. If you found yourself checking mostly A answers, then chances are you're a gambler by nature. Of course, some gamblers do okay in the stock market. Using options, short-selling, margin-buying and the like, some of them even strike it rich. And some of them go broke. It's all part of the game. Does that mean that gamblers aren't psychologically suited to the market? No. But trusting to luck is a poor approach to investing.

Did you check more C answers than anything else? Then maybe the stock market isn't your cup of tea. If you're perfectly happy with the sedate, but guaranteed, return to be earned from savings accounts, certificates and the like, so be it. You shouldn't buy common stocks if worrying about them is going to drive you crazy. On the other hand, you may feel you should do something more with your money or inflation will surely gobble it up. Read on.

If you chose mostly B answers, you probably have the attitude it takes to be a careful, feet-on-the ground buyer of common stocks. You want a bigger return on your money, you accept the idea of risk, and you're willing to take some trouble to keep it to a minimum.

Actually, B and C types have more in common than they might think. Neither wants to take big risks. Where they differ is in their definition of big. For the C group, an acceptable risk stops somewhere short of common stock ownership.

Now you've decided you want to know more. So where do you start?

Go back to your investment objectives. You have to decide whether you're interested in income or in growth. You may be interested in both.

IF YOU'RE INTERESTED IN INCOME

The first thing you look for are companies that have paid dividends for a large number of years. In particular, look for companies that have continued to pay dividends when times have been tough.

Second, look for companies that have a good record of earnings during both recessions and growth periods. Remember that blue chip or income-producing stock pays dividends, and dividends are treated more favourably under the tax law. This means that a dividend yield of several percentage points less than the going rate of interest on bonds and guaranteed certificates is equivalent on an after-tax basis.

IF YOU'RE INTERESTED IN GROWTH

People who are earning enough to satisfy all spending needs and who don't need investment income are prime candidates for growth stocks. They are generally younger, and have a sufficient number of earning years ahead of them that they can afford to take risks with at least part of their money.

A growth stock is generally associated with a company whose sales and earnings are growing faster than the market averages, and faster than the economy as a whole.

Characteristics of Proven Growth Companies:

1. Pay little or no dividends;

2. Maintain consistent sales and earnings increases;

3. Emerge as leaders in fast-growing industries.

Growth companies don't pay dividends, or if they do, they pay very low dividends. Basically, growth companies retain their earnings to plow back into the company for research, development, and expansion. It's important to look at how well a company has done with the money it hasn't paid you in dividends. The number you're looking for is the return on equity—the company's profits expressed as a percentage of all the money that shareholders have invested in the company.

If you look back at a successful growth company, you can see that sales and earnings almost always increased every year.

So, how do you find these companies? If you have a super broker, he or she will find some of them for you. But not all brokers are super, or even read the material their research departments churn out.

The only surefire way to be confident about your decision is to think it out yourself. This technique doesn't guarantee that you'll be a winner every time. It does guarantee that you will have gone through the decision-making process and reached a conclusion with which you are comfortable. To get started, turn your attention away from Bay Street, St. James Street, Wall Street, and Howe Street, and do what all investment counsellors and pension fund managers do—think about where the country is going, and what kind of goods and services it's going to need in the years ahead.

This is not the impossible task it may seem to be. Start thinking in broad terms about areas of the economy which are most likely to propser, or not prosper. Here are some random questions to help you start:

- Is the next decade or two likely to be more peaceful than the last couple of decades? If you think so, you may not want to invest heavily in defense industries.
- Is the pace of wage increases likely to escalate? If you think not, you may be more willing to invest in industries in which labour represents a large portion of total costs.
- Is government intervention in the economy likely to lessen? If you think so, you may be interested in looking at industries that are highly regulated, like telephone and electric utilities.
- How competitive with foreign producers are we likely to be? As you look at the industries prominent in the economy, you have to consider their involvement in foreign trade. One consideration is whether or not we can compete. The auto industry is an example of an industry that is having big problems competing. Another consideration is that even if we can compete, how likely is it that the countries to whom an industry sells its goods or services will continue to allow imports? What you're looking at here is how stable the country is, and how nationalistic its policies are likely to become. Remember: mines, factories, and banks can be nationalized; tariff and non-tariff arrangements can be changed.
- What is the significance of the fact that our population is aging? How will this affect the industries of the future? Remember that the war babies, born between 1946 and 1964, are in their early thirties; some of them have already reached the Big Forty. Ten years from now, they will be in their fifties. This group is overwhelmingly larger than any other age group in the population. In a very real sense, they shape a large chunk of the economy. They are in a big way responsible for the boom in elementary schools and toys in the late 1950s; for the boom in high schools and universities, clothing, records, movies, discos, VCRs, and unemployment in the 1960s, 1970s, and 1980s.
- Let your mind wander. Start making lists of questions. This is not something only the professionals can do. You know yourself that a lot of professionals haven't done wonderfully well in their investments lately, maybe because they haven't been doing their homework. The name of the game is to continually ask yourself what's new? What's happening? What does it mean? What should I do about it?

- Read your newspaper with two questions in mind: How will this affect the economy? How can I make use of this information? For example, say you, along with half the world, read a report about AIDS. Most people are appalled, sympathetic, concerned. Some people thought, "What can I do with the information?" They bought condom stock. Once you get your thinking into the investment mode, you may realize that the stock prices of drug companies might go up when a cure is found.

The secret of success in recognizing potential stock price changes is the ability to detect the often invisible relationship between two events. People and companies are not always in the business they say they are. Steel companies are in the automobile business. Airplane manufacturers are in the travel business. Tractor manufacturers look for better wheat sales.

There are lots of places to get investment perspectives and investment answers. This book is one of them, although I've listed many other places.

ADVICE FOR THE LONG TERM

1. Pay cash for stocks. You can buy on margin (by borrowing the money), but when you're just beginning, it's double jeopardy to have borrowed money (whether from your brother, your broker, or your banker) riding down with a declining investment.
2. Buy only quality stocks. This applies to all investments, really. You won't do yourself a favour buying 1000 $1 shares on the grounds that because they're cheap, the odds are greater that they'll go up faster.
3. Buy only one or two stocks. You are not a mutual fund. You will learn a lot more, and are likely to do a lot better, if you concentrate your time and efforts on a couple of stocks.
4. If you're going for the accumulation of wealth, you may end up deciding to buy a stock that pays a dividend. Make a decision right now that your dividends are to be reinvested. I remember once when I was on a fitness kick and couldn't psych myself up every day to jog. I was reading some uplifting article in which a regular jogger had gone from being a slob to being slim and sleek. How had he done it? One day he just got out of bed and said to himself, "I'm going to run every day from now on." Having made that decision, he said, "It was made for life. I didn't ever again have to ask myself 'Should I run today?' "

Do it with your dividends. Set up a special bank account, and deposit your dividends when you get them. At some point, you'll find something in which to invest them.

10 GOOD STOCK MARKET RULES

1. Before buying . . .think.
2. Deal only with reputable securities firms.
3. Beware of securities offered by phone by strangers.
4. Don't listen to high pressure sales talk.
5. Beware of promises of spectacular profits.
6. Be sure you understand the risks of loss.
7. Don't buy on tips and rumours.
8. Tell the salespeople to put it in writing.
9. If you don't understand the written information, ask someone who does.
10. Give at least as much consideration to buying securities as you would to buying other valuable property.

CHAPTER 14

Bonds and Bills: Making Interest Work for You

A billion here, a billion there . . .pretty soon it adds up to real money.

—Everett Dirksen

Just as there are good reasons to consider stocks for your portfolio, there are good reasons to consider holding bonds. Among the good reasons, bond holders have as close to a guarantee that their money will be returned as anyone who doesn't keep their money under the mattress. In addition, bond holders are guaranteed a regular income in the form of interest for as long as the bond has not matured (unless of course something terrible happens to the company). Even if something terrible happens to the company, bond holders stand at the head of the line when money is handed out. Besides all this good stuff, there are times when you can make a handsome capital gain on bonds.

A LITTLE DEFINITION MUSIC, PLEASE

A bond is a certificate of indebtedness, a sort of I.O.U. from the issuer. Issuers are governments of all sorts—federal, provincial, municipal—public utilities such as natural gas and hydro companies, and private corporations. These institutions float a bond issue, that is, they offer to sell you bonds because they want the money to finance some project dear to their hearts. In the case of private companies, the managers believe the project will make the company more profitable. Sometimes it does. Then the value of the corporate stock goes up. Even if the company doesn't become more profitable, the bond holder will be paid whatever is available first.

In the case of governments and utilities, they hope the project will make them more able to provide services to their constituents. Sometimes it does. Then the constituency becomes a more attractive place to live. But even if that doesn't happen, governments rarely go bankrupt. And even if they do, it's very, very rare that a bond holder will lose money.

By purchasing a bond, you agree to loan the institution a certain amount of money in return for receiving a stipulated rate of interest. That interest, or yield, is paid on specific dates over a certain time period, either within three years (a short-term bond), between 3 and 15 years (a medium-term bond), or over 15 years (a long-term bond).

Together with stocks, bonds fall under the category of securities. But there's a difference. When you own a stock, you own a part, or share, of that company. If the company grows, you can share that growth. Owning a bond simply means that you have loaned the particular institution, whether a corporation or government, a certain amount of money. You become the organization's creditor, not its part owner.

Unlike stocks, a bond requires the issuer to return the face value to the purchaser when it matures. However, once issued by the institution, bonds are traded in the bond market, and fluctuate in value much like stocks do. The reason for these fluctuations is simple: an integral part of a bond is the interest rate it bears. If interest rates change, that will affect the current value of any bond issued at a higher or lower interest rate.

Say, for example, a $1000 bond is issued with an interest rate of 10%. The bond holder will expect interest payments of $100 each year until the bond matures. Say now that interest rates fall to 9%. The 10% bond holder is holding a valuable commodity. Other people with $1000 can now get only $90 a year in interest. They would be willing to pay more than $1000 to own the 10% bond. The secondary market where bonds are traded will determine the going price for a 10% bond in a 9% environment.

On the other hand, say general interest rates rose to 11%. The 10% bond holder would own a commodity that was no longer worth $1000, because someone with $1000 could now buy someone else's bond and expect to receive $110 a year in interest. Despite the fact that institutional bonds fluctuate in value before maturity, they are worth their face value on the day they mature. It is this fact that provides the strategies for money-making bond market endeavors.

The bond market is often every bit as active as the stock market. Sometimes, as in the early 1980s, for example, it is more active, and very profitable. It was very profitable at that time because interest rates were extremely high—at the peak of the most recent interest rate cycle, corporate and government bonds were averaging 20% interest. The sudden onset of recession in late 1981 saw interest rates fall quite sharply, and they continue to fall to this day, with only intermittent increases. People holding or trading these high interest-bearing bonds saw the trading value of their certificates rise enormously. The value of a $1000 bond with an 18% interest rate, when general rates are 9%, could be as much as $2000. If that bond were sold in the market before maturity, the $1000 profit would be a capital gain, and therefore taxed at preferential rates.

Of course, interest rates are not the only factor determining the trading value of a bond. The financial structure of the institution, and the competence of the management team to use and manage its resources are of primary importance. The profitability of the corporation, the amount of capital it has, the mix of fixed and working capital to liquid assets, and its ability to raise new money are all factors which will determine not only the rating of a company or government, but its value in the bond market.

Bonds themselves have different characteristics. Some are convertible. This means the buyer has the right to convert the bond into the company's common stock, that is, those stocks with which there are voting rights, but not a guarantee of dividends. With convertible bonds, you get both a fixed rate of interest from the bond, as well as possible appreciation if the common stock price increases. Because of this option, the prices of convertible bonds are more subject to change than nonconvertible bonds.

Some bonds are redeemable. This means the company has the right to call in the bond before its maturity date. The issuer must pay bond holders a premium price if the bond is called in early. Bonds are usually called in when interest rates fall so significantly that the issuer can save money by floating new bonds at lower rates. By the mid-1980s, a significant number of the bonds that had been issued in the early 1980s were being "called".

Rating definitions of long-term bonds

The following are definitions of the general protective attributes of debt bearing any of these respective ratings. They are meant to be general in nature and do not constitute a comprehensive description of all the protective characteristics of each category.

Highest quality	**A++** This category encompasses bonds of outstanding quality. They possess the highest degree of protection of principal and interest. Companies with debt rated A++ are generally large national and/or multinational corporations whose products or services are essential to the Canadian economy. These companies are the acknowledged leaders in their respective industries and have clearly demonstrated their ability to best withstand adverse economic or trade conditions either national or international in scope. Characteristically, these companies have had a long and creditable history of superior debt protection, in which the quality of their assets and earnings has been constantly maintained or improved, with strong evidence that this will continue.
Very good quality	**A+** Bonds rated A+ are similar in characteristics to those rated A++ and can also be considered superior in quality. These companies have demonstrated a long and satisfactory history of growth with above-average protection of principal and interest on their debt securities. These bonds are generally rated lower in quality because the margin of assets or earnings protection may not be as large or as stable as those rated A++. In both these categories the nature and quality of the asset and earning coverages are more important than the numerical values of the ratios.
Good quality	**A** Bonds rated A are considered to be good quality securities and to have favourable long-term investment characteristics. The main feature that distinguishes them from the higher rated securities is that these companies are more susceptible to adverse trade or economic conditions and the protection is consequently lower than for the categories of A++ and A+. In all cases the A rated companies have maintained a history of adequate assets and earnings protection. There may be certain elements that may impair this protection sometime in the future. Confidence that the current overall financial position will be maintained or improved is slightly lower than for the securities rated above.

Source: The Canadian Bond Rating Service

TAX TREATMENT OF BONDS

The interest received on a bond is considered earned income, and therefore must be reported at tax time. You're taxed according to your particular tax bracket, as if the interest you have earned is part of your ordinary income.

CANADA SAVINGS BONDS ARE DIFFERENT

Autumn leaves and Canada Savings Bonds go together. Every November since 1946, when they replaced the wartime Victory Bonds, CSBs have been sold by the Government of Canada. Their unique characteristics, which make them different from other bonds, also make them so popular that the federal government can count on raising about twenty percent of the money it needs every year to run the country.

What makes CSBs different from other bonds is the fact that they are fully redeemable for cash at their full face value any time before their maturity date. (There are short periods when this isn't true.) They offer a guaranteed minimum yield, and are backed by the Canadian government.

The fact that the government will always give you your money back means that your Canada Savings Bonds are as close to cash as you can get. Because they are so liquid, that is, cashable, the government doesn't feel it has to offer you as high an interest rate as other institutions. The rates offered are usually comparable to those offered by trust companies and banks on their Guaranteed Investment Certificates or term deposits.

There are two types of CSBs: the regular interest, or R-bonds, in which the purchaser receives the interest in regular instalments; or the compound interest, or C-bond, in which the interest is reinvested, or compounded each year and paid out in one lump sum at the end of the loan term specified, or whenever the bond is cashed.

CSBs are available in $300, $500, $1,000, $5,000 and $10,000 denominations, while compound interest bonds are also available in minimal denominations of $100. You can cash your CSB in at any time, although each November the government revises interest rates paid on bonds issued since 1981. The changes reflct fluctuations in the prime rate, and help dissuade bond holders from cashing them in prematurely.

Canada Savings Bonds are available only to Canadians, and

are not transferable to another person. If you are a registered owner, you can sell them back to the Government of Canada, but to no one else.

Taxing a CSB can be a complicated exercise. Income from regular interest CSBs is paid directly to bond holders each year. Compound interest CSBs are a bit trickier. Though you earn interest continually, you receive it as income only when you cash in the bond. However, you must declare the interest at specified intervals—every one or three years, depending on the bond series—even though you haven't actually received the income.

TREASURY BILLS

Treasury bills are simply short-term obligations of a government. T-bills have maturities of one year or less. Auctions of 91-day, 182-day, and 364-day bills take place every week in Ottawa (other governments also issue T-bills, the most important being the United States Treasury). These auctions are watched closely by money market traders and analysts for signs of interest rate trends. Many floating rate and variable rate mortgages have interest rates tied to these bills.

The interest rate on Canadian T-bills is set in a sealed bidding process which takes place every Thursday morning, when they are auctioned off to the highest bidder. The banks and investment dealers that submit sealed bids try to estimate their interest rate as accurately as possible in order to win these highly desirable investments. There is a direct link between the value of the Canadian dollar and the interest rate which is paid on T-bills. The bank rate, at which the Bank of Canada will lend money to the chartered banks, is set on the basis of the T-bill rate, immediately after the auction on Thursdays.

The successful bidders in the Bank of Canada auction may hold some of the T-bills themselves, but they also sell to other interested corporations and individuals. In recent years, T-bills have become a popular investment for small investors, and investment houses have designed packages for people with as little as $5,000 to invest.

T-bills are sold at a discount from their face value. On their maturity date, you receive the full face value. The difference between what you paid and what you receive at maturity is the amount of interest you earned on your investment.

The interest earnings on your T-bills are taxable.

INTEREST RATE MOVEMENTS—WHICH ARE IMPORTANT?

Interest rates in Canada and around the world have exhibited great variability in the last decade. For many years, the Canadian government has maintained that Canadian interest rates cannot do otherwise than move in tandem with American rates. This is the basic policy pursued by the Bank of Canada, except when it widens or narrows the Canada-U.S. interest rate differential in an effort to maintain the external value of the Canadian dollar. To get even a toehold on an understanding of interest rate movements, we have to look at the behaviour of American interest rates.

MAXIMIZING YOUR REAL RETURN

In the summer, when local tomatoes come to market by the bushel, prices fall. In the winter, when supply dwindles, prices rise. Would that it were so simple when the commodity is money. Then central banks could keep a steady supply of money in the economy, and its price (the interest rate) would also be steady.

Watching the money supply was fashionable among U.S. monetary policy makers a dozen years ago when inflation was rampant. They decided the problem couldn't be solved until the "excess" money in the American economy was sopped up. The money supply—controlled by the Federal Reserve—went down. Interest rates—the price of money—rose. People and companies stopped borrowing and started paying back. The policy worked better than anyone expected. By 1981, the world economy was in a tailspin and lots of people, companies, banks and countries went bankrupt. So the policy was reversed: the money supply rose and interest rates fell.

The problem is that no one is sure that there is a one-to-one relationship between money supply and interest rates. In fact, most policy makers accept that there is some kind of relationship between the two, but acknowledge that other factors are important, too. Treasury bills and Treasury bonds are the "watched pot" of the future. Bills and bonds represent opposite ends of the yield curve or curve to maturity; bills are the short end, bonds the long end.

These interest rates have been caught in a whirlwind of volatility as the market tries to sort out the fundamental direction of the economy.

Here are the factors to consider when you look for an increase in interest rates:

- The huge American budget and trade deficits demand that the U.S. raise rates to entice foreigners to continue to invest in U.S. bonds and bills. To the extent that the U.S. doesn't solve its debt problems, foreigners' reluctance to hold more American securities will force American rates up.
- The world is now sensitized to rising interest rates. Any increase in rates fuels speculation that rates will return to 20%. Such fear stimulates demand for loans now and becomes a self-fulfilling prophesy.

Factors to consider when you look for a decrease in interest rates:

- The huge Third World debt and the sluggishness of significant parts of the industrialized world raise fears that the international banking system cannot withstand the strain of borrower defaults.
- The real cost of money, as measured by the spread between inflation and the long-term bond rate, is at record levels, suggesting that the trend of rates is still down.

For Canadians in the Canadian market, U.S. considerations have to be watched, as well as any deterioration or appreciation in the value of the Canadian dollar. Canadian interest rate policy has been to keep as wide a differential in interest rates as is necessary to keep the Canadian dollar at some particular level—apparently above 70¢ U.S.

In deciding on a strategy, it is useful to consider interest-bearing investments over equities if you can maximize your after-tax return. This is eminently possible when rates are high, or when rates are clearly falling. In particular, discounted bonds—that is, bonds selling below their face value, and stripped bonds (from which the interest coupon has been stripped away)—offer great scope for capital gains.

CHAPTER 15

The Fundamentals of Precious Metals

A question that sometimes drives me hazy:
Am I, or are the others, crazy?

—Albert Einstein

GOLD

Why would anyone want to convert hard-earned savings into gold? Technically, gold is not an investment. It pays no dividends, earns no interest, and costs money to store. Its price is extremely volatile; for example, in the last seven years, it has changed direction dozens of times, reaching a high of US $835 an ounce in January 1980, and a low of US $280 an ounce in February 1985.

Gold has never been officially accepted in North America as having any real value, let alone as being the ultimate store of value. On the contrary, both the Canadian and American governments are steadfast in their refusal to acknowledge the role gold has played throughout history, and for millions of people around the world.

Nevertheless, there are a number of prudent reasons for investing at least part of your savings in gold, including inflation, huge government deficits in Canada and the U.S., and Third World debt crises which threaten the stability of the western world's banking system. Did you know that despite our recent victory over inflation, the long-term value of the dollar has decreased to nine cents since 1900; that in 1940, you could buy 10 loaves of bread for a dollar; in 1960, four loaves; in 1970, only three? What part of a loaf will today's dollar buy?

Despite gold's volatility, it is still the only money that has withstood the test of being the ultimate refuge in an uncertain world. Holding gold is not unlike holding life insurance. If you don't die, all you have to show for the money you've paid in premiums is peace of mind that your dependents have been protected. In times of economic stability, all you have to show for the investment opportunities you've lost because your money has been tied up is a sense of well-being.

There are a number of ways to own gold.

Gold Bullion

Whether in the form of wafers or the familiar gold bars, bullion is considered the safest, simplest, and cheapest way of holding gold. Bullion is pure gold, designated ".999 fine" in Canada. It comes in a variety of weights, ranging from one-tenth of an ounce up to the standard trading unit, a 400-ounce bar.

All gold bars have a bar charge that covers manufacturing costs. The smaller the bar, the higher the bar charge. If possible, it makes sense to buy as large a unit as you can in order to reduce the bar charges. Some provinces in Canada charge sales tax, so be sure to research conditions in your province before purchasing bullion.

Current Sales Tax in Canadian Provinces

Province	*Bullion* %	*Coins* %
Alberta	—	—
British Columbia	—	4
Manitoba	—	5
New Brunswick	7	7
Newfoundland	11	11
Nova Scotia	7	7
Ontario	—	7
Prince Edward Island	—	—
Quebec	—	—
Saskatchewan	5	5
Northwest Territories	—	—
Yukon Territory	—	—

Bullion can be bought or ordered from some trust companies, banks, and private dealers. Some dealers charge a commission or transaction fee every time you buy or sell bullion. Try to find a dealer who does not apply this charge. Also, deal with a credible and well-known firm. Leading bullion dealers do business only with internationally recognized refiners. If you want to sell your gold, but find it hasn't been manufactured by a recognized refinery, you could be in for costly assay charges (analysis of the purity of the metal), or melting charges.

The advantages of holding bullion are that it's cheap (commissions are relatively low), highly liquid, and negotiable internationally. The main disadvantage is that since you own the physical gold, you will have to pay to store it. One thing you can do is use it as collateral for a loan. The financial institution will lend you the money at prime or a little over prime, and will store the gold for you.

Bullion Certificates

These are sold by many banks and gold dealers. The certificates give you proof of ownership of bullion, while an institution stores it for you. There is a commission charge on bullion certificates, as well as a small storage charge. Shop around before you buy certificates; you stand to save a lot by investigating the various commissions and storage fees institutions charge. Beware of certificate issuers who charge you manufacturing fees even if you don't take the gold.

Bullion certificates can be exchanged for gold itself (in which case you are taking delivery) any time you want. Furthermore, some institutions arrange for you to do so outside Canada. But taking delivery is not the point of bullion certificates. You don't really want the gold—you want its value and the ability to buy and sell it according to market conditions. A further disincentive regarding conversion is a Revenue Canada tax wrinkle that applies to all precious metals.

Say you buy a $3,000 certificate for 10 ounces of gold bullion at $300 an ounce. Later, you decide to take the real thing. Lucky you—the price has increased to $600 an ounce! But as far as Revenue Canada is concerned, they are lucky too. Your conversion is considered a disposition and repurchase of a commodity. Therefore, the taxman will tax your $3,000 profit as if it were a capital gain, even though you never sold the gold and, therefore, never earned a cent on the price increase.

The advantages of bullion certificates, then, include no storage risk, liquidity, and inexpensive price. The disadvantages include a possible liability if you convert to bullion at a higher price. Remember that in the last analysis, you are dealing in paper certificates, not the real thing.

Warehouse Receipts

Some responsible dealers in precious metals are trying to overcome certain delay problems with gold deposit certificates issued by banks and trust companies. In some institutions, the expression "on demand" does not always mean just that, and a certain amount of notice is required should you wish to exchange your certificates for bullion. Gold warehouse receipts, on the other hand, certify that a certain amount of gold, or silver, has been purchased by you, and is available to you or the bearer of the receipt on demand during any business day. The service is not widely available yet.

Bullion Accounts

Some foreign banks offer bank accounts made up not of dollars, but of gold. Just as if you were making a transaction with your bank account, you take your passbook to the bank and either deposit (buy) or withdraw (sell) gold as you like. As this format becomes more widely available, so do the number of alternative services. For instance, some institutions will buy and sell gold and other precious metals over the phone, costing you a bit more, but saving you a lot of time and inconvenience.

Beware of dealing with gold in this form internationally, however, as in some countries you can't get physical possession of the gold.

Bullion Coins

These are produced by a variety of countries, including Canada which, after South Africa and the Soviet Union, is the largest source of gold in the world. In the past, the most widely recognized and traded gold coins have been the South African Krugerrand and our own Maple Leaf coin produced by the Canadian Mint. This coin is solid gold, .999 pure, marked right on the coin. The Krugerrand's fineness is .9967. Bullion coins have a monetary, not numismatic (collector's), value, making them susceptible to market forces. Thus, their value fluctuates with the price of gold.

When you sell the coin, you rarely get back the amount you paid. The premium is inversely related to the unit of the coin. Thus, a quarter-ounce coin will have a higher premium than a one-ounce coin. Still another charge is the sales tax on bullion coins. Until recently, investors have had difficulty choosing between the Krugerrand and the Maple Leaf. However, with tensions in South Africa increasing, many Western investors have dumped the Krugerrand as a way of exerting economic sanctions on that country. This is perhaps the only example of political instability driving *down* the value of gold. The Maple Leaf, meanwhile, has been gaining in value and in popularity, as have the American Eagle and the Chinese Panda. Analysts speculate that international sanctions will have only a short-term effect on the value of the Krugerrand.

The advantages of gold coins include a relatively inexpensive price, liquidity, and ability to be negotiated internationally. On the downside, you must pay to store them, pay premiums and usually a sales tax as well.

Spread on Premiums of Popular Gold Coins

Coin/Country	*Purity*	*Buy premium %*	*Sell premium %*
1 oz. Maple Leaf/Canada	0.9999	2.5	3.5
0.1 oz. Maple Leaf/Canada	0.9999	7.0	12.0
100 Corona/Austria	0.9000	−2.0	0.0
1 oz. Panda/China	0.9990	5.0	9.0
50 Peso/Mexico	0.9000	−1.0	1.0
1 oz. Kruggerrand/ South Africa	0.9167	−2.0	0.0
1 oz. Eagle/U.S.A.	0.9167	2.5	3.5

Gold Mining Shares

This is where gold ownership gets a little more complicated. When you buy shares of a gold mining company, you are investing not only in gold, but in the management of the company. From the moment you buy the shares, until you sell them, you must follow not only gold trends, but the performance of the company. Make sure you know its production costs. Generally, the higher the production costs, the lower the ore grade. If the production cost per ounce turns out to be higher than the market price per ounce, it's time to find another company.

Find out the expected life of the mine. If it's only going to be around for a short time, there's not much point in making a long-term investment in it. While there's added research to be done when considering gold mine shares, there are also added benefits: you get dividend income, your stocks are highly liquid, and your investments can be eligible for tax shelters. With Canada a major source of gold, there are lots of Canadian gold mines operating in a stable political climate in which you can invest.

Gold Futures Contracts

These are highly speculative and difficult to trade successfully. Go this route only if you have nerves of steel, and money you can afford to lose on odds not much better than coin flipping. Gold contracts, usually for 100 ounces, are for future delivery at a date and price agreed upon by the buyer and the seller. They can be traded in commodity markets around the world, and are generally used for protection against unstable commodity and foreign currency prices, though they have practical value for industrial users of gold.

An advantage of futures contracts is that you can profit by selling them even if you don't own them. Say gold prices are falling. The futures market enables you to borrow someone else's gold, and arrange to sell it today for delivery at a set future date. If gold continues to fall in price, at the time you have to deliver your gold, you will be able to buy it at a cheaper price. The difference between what you originally sold the gold for, and the price at which you bought it, is your profit.

As well as the potential for profit, futures have the advantage of eliminating the need for storage.

GOLD JEWELLERY IS NOT NECESSARILY AN INVESTMENT

Gold jewellery is almost never an investment. But a lot of people think it might be, so there is some value to knowing what you are buying when you do buy, particularly around Christmas and Valentine's Day when gold jewellery sales flourish.

The important things to know when buying gold jewellery are the gram weight and the karats. Here are the facts:

- Twenty-four karat gold is pure: anything less than 24K is debased with a mixture of lesser metals and alloys.

24K	=	100% pure
18K	=	75% pure
14K	=	58.8% pure
10K	=	41.6% pure

- Most jewellery is 18K, 14K, or 10K
- Ten-karat gold is illegal, or non-existent, in Europe.

- One ounce of gold contains 31.1 grams.
- The usual markup for the artwork of jewellery is three times.
- Legitimate gold jewellery has a hallmark that will tell you its purity.

OTHER PRECIOUS METALS AND GLITTERY STUFF

Gold is not the only precious metal that is used as a hedge against inflation or deflation, market, business, or political risk. Platinum and palladium are the two most common alternative choices.

The biggest suppliers of platinum and palladium are the Soviet Union and South Africa—neither area a pool of tranquility. The fact that more than 8 out of every 10 ounces of platinum come from South Africa and 3 out of every 4 ounces of palladium from South Africa or the U.S.S.R. wouldn't matter much if nobody used the stuff. But the demand for both metals has been rising. Platinum and palladium are well known as the catalysts which reduce exhaust fumes in automobiles. But both metals are used in dozens of other applications, particularly in the electronics industries and in the manufacture of jet engines. Many petroleum refining processes use the platinum group of metals, as does the manufacture of agricultural fertilizers.

Clearly, money is to be made by the fast movers and agile analysts. And the same people from whom you buy your gold will direct you to the other precious metals. Just remember why you're buying it and how it fits into your investment plans. If it fills a particular requirement in your portfolio, go for it. If it doesn't, don't. As for the other glittery stuff, diamonds do fine when we're in the tangible assets cycle—they're not so wonderful when financial assets are making big bucks. Diamond investors have to keep their eyes on the political situation in South Africa, the monopoly power of the DeBeers cartel, and the "four Cs" of diamonds themselves—cut, colour, clarity and carat. Deal only with a reputable dealer and be sure to have the stone certified by an independent laboratory.

CHAPTER 16

Commodities and Collectibles

> If you bet on a horse, that's gambling. If you bet you can make Three Spades, that's entertainment. If you bet cotton will go up three points, that's business. See the difference?
>
> —Blackie Sherrode

If gold is the bedrock of financial security, then commodities, with their promises of huge trading profits, are the will-o'-the-wisps dancing seductively above it. Yes, it is possible to lose money in gold, if you really work at it, and it is also possible to make a bundle in commodities trading. But over the long term, gold is literally safer than money in the bank, whereas in the commodities game, 85% of the players are losers, while only 15% are winners—about the same odds as horse-racing or gambling. This fact doesn't have to keep you out of commodities. But you have to remember that commodity trading is a technique—a tool—to help you reach your financial goals.

Commodities are basic goods produced by primary producers. They are the raw materials consumed by secondary producers such as manufacturers. The most common examples of commodities include precious metals, like gold, silver, and platinum; other metals such as copper and nickel, produced by mine owners; agricultural goods such as wheat, corn, oats, soybeans, pork bellies (from which bacon is made), produced by farmers; and materials such as lumber and plywood, produced by sawmills.

There are three principal players involved in commodities markets: the producer, the consumer, and the commodities investor, or speculator. The attraction of commodities trading is the tremendous leverage that is possible. You don't put very much money down—5% to 10% of the purchase price is average. In addition, there is no interest charged on the balance as there is with stock margins. With this kind of leverage, a very small change in the price of the commodity has a great effect on your profit or loss.

If you purchased $10,000 worth of a stock from your broker, and put up the full $10,000, then a $1,000 move in the value of that stock would increase or decrease your investment by 10%. If you margined the stock at 50%, and thus put up only $5,000, then the $1,000 gain or loss would be 20%. That's leverage. But if you put up only $500 for a $10,000 purchase, as with the commodities market, then a $1,000 move up would show a 200% gain, while a movement downward would lose you *double* your money. That's really leverage!

You don't actually buy the commodities, and though you have the right, you are not obligated to take delivery of them. You are trading *contracts* to buy or sell the commodities in the future. What you are assuming is that at some point in a specific period in the future, the price of the commodity will have changed. If you feel it will be higher then than it is now, you contract to buy; if you feel it will be lower, you contract to sell.

How do you contract to sell something you don't own? When you make the contract, you are not required to deliver until the future date specified. That gives you plenty of time to get the commodity. In practice, you will never have to, since your plan is to offset that contract before delivery is required. Offsetting is a procedure by which your contract to deliver a commodity is cancelled. You do this by selling what you have bought, or by buying what you have sold. When you are in a "long" position, that is, you own a contract to *buy* a commodity, you offset this by obtaining another contract to *sell* the same commodity. If you start out by buying someone else's contract to sell it, you are in a "short" position and must buy a contract, to offset your position.

There are a number of commodity futures exchanges which operate in a similar manner to stock exchanges. There is the Chicago Board of Trade, which deals chiefly in grains, plywood, broilers (chickens), and silver; the Comex in New York, dealing only in metals; the Chicago Mercantile, which handles eggs, pork bellies, cattle, and lumber; the London Terminal Market, dealing in cocoa and sugar; and the London Metal Exchange for copper and silver. There are several others, including the Winnipeg Commodity Exchange which handles, among other things, canola and gold. These exchanges regulate the contracted amounts so that they are the same for all traders. This eliminates opportunities for big-time speculators to edge out the little guys. It also makes offsetting possible. The exchanges record and report the price during each day of trading. Unlike stocks, commodity futures prices are allowed to move only so far each day. This is to prevent trading activity from causing massive price moves. Once the price of a commodity future has moved to its permissible daily limit, no trading can take place outside that limit. It can still take place within the limit, however, and the next day it can move to a new limit. This regulates the futures market, but if spot prices—that is, the price at which the commodity is being bought and sold in the present—are extremely volatile, you may not be able to buy or sell your futures contract until the limited price movements catch up to the spot prices.

Consumers and producers of commodities are also active traders. Chocolate manufacturers, for example, trade in cocoa bean futures as a hedge against changes in the world price of cocoa, though they seldom take delivery. Nor are they as much interested in making money on the trade as they are in maintaining a uniform price for cocoa beans for manufacturing purposes. Thus, if world prices go up, and they hold a futures contract at a lower price, they can sell that contract, take their profit, and apply it to their operations back at the plant.

Producers hedge as well. The cocoa bean producer might be unsure of what his beans will bring on the market a year from now, and he would like to be assured of a reasonable price. So, he sells a contract at a price that will provide him with a profit, and insures him against a drop in world prices. Then he watches the market carefully, and hedges where he can.

How do you compete against these insiders? They may know chocolate, but like you, they don't know which way the price is going. All any of you can do is make an informed guess. Say a manufacturer calculates that to make his profit six months from now he needs to be able to buy cocoa at that time for 30 cents a pound. He will buy a contract to take delivery at that price on a specific date.

But the effect of that transaction is to establish the two sides of an argument. The buyer says that in six months time cocoa will be worth 30 cents a pound or higher. The seller says it will be worth 30 cents or lower. It will certainly be one or the other, and that's where the speculator enters the picture. He backs one or the other by placing what is, in effect, a side bet with another speculator.

Some people feel that since they do not produce anything, speculators must make their money on the misfortunes of those who do produce. Others feel that speculators are essential to trading, since they will often take risks that others won't. Suppose a farmer wants to sell his eggs for future delivery, and needs to make 40 cents a dozen to cover his costs and make a profit. He may find that none of the users around will pay him more than 35 cents. He would be losing money, and obviously wouldn't sell. Enter the speculator. He is betting that sooner or later a user will have to give in to the farmer's required price. He buys the eggs now at the 40-cent price, in the hope that when the users give in, the price will be 40 cents or higher. In that way, speculators serve a useful function in the market place.

Another theory says that speculators tend to drive prices up or down out of all proportion to reality. For example, in the above case, the speculators may drive the price up to 50 cents. The farmer will see that the speculators are way off base, and rush in to sell, thereby getting more than he could otherwise expect. Other farmers will see what is happening and rush in too. This action will tend to drive prices down. Of course, the ideal theory holds that if all buyers and sellers are fully knowledgeable, the market will always find its proper level. But since people are never fully knowledgeable, especially about the future, the market sometimes does get out of whack with reality. Therein lies the challenge of commodity trading.

So, how does an amateur who knows little or nothing about a particular industry get involved in commodities trading? Very carefully.

In order to trade successfully in the commodities market, you must know when the price of a commodity is going to move up or down, and that's not easy. The best available knowledge about a commodity and its market is essential. Your broker might help. Watching what other traders are doing will give some indications as well. For example, if the further you look into the future, the progressively lower the price of a commodity gets, then the market, strangely enough, is tending to rise. Conversely, if the furthest futures price is progressively higher than the closest price, the market is tending to fall. These indicators are more clearly seen when a market is about to change from being a discounted (lower future price) to a premium (higher future price) market.

Qualifying as a bona fide trader depends on the amount of money you have, and the tolerance threshold of your broker. Most houses won't touch you unless you have a net worth of $50,000 or more. But you can find brokers who will make transactions for you, even if you don't have more than $2,000 to trade. The best rule of thumb to follow is *never* put up more than you can afford to lose.

The cost of the commodity you wish to trade depends on the commodity, and on the exchange's policy that is in effect at that time. A contract for 5,000 bushels of wheat, or 40,000 pounds of cattle, costs about $1,500. A contract for 25,000 pounds of copper costs $1,300. The amount of money you stand to make also depends on the contract. A two cent per bushel move upward in wheat will make you $100—more than enough to cover the $65 commission. A one-cent-a-pound rise in copper amounts to $250, again more than enough to cover the $80 commission.

Like all highly-leveraged transactions, commodity trading is risky for speculators. But that's also why there are generous rewards. Commodities should be avoided unless the rest of your investment portfolio is in good shape, and you are prepared to lose everything you put into commodities. It is purely and simply highly-leveraged risk taking.

CURRENCIES

Currency trading has become very big business in the 1980s, as financial assets produce bigger gains than tangible assets. As with commodity trading, there are three principal players—central banks, which have a stake in maintaining a value for their currency; institutions, either financial or real (such as manufacturers) who need foreign exchange; and investors or speculators. The purpose of currency speculation—which is all us little guys might do—is to take advantage of changes in currency values between countries. (Should you feel slighted by my concentrating on an audience of little guys, let me remind you that to open a futures account, most investment houses will require you to make an initial deposit of $5,000 to $10,000, and to complete a net worth statement which shows a minimum liquid asset balance of $50,000.

The way the currency futures market is set up, you can put up a relatively small amount of money to "control" a relatively large amount. This leverage allows you to make (or lose) big sums on small changes in currency values.

Take the Canadian dollar (please!) The strength or weakness of the Canadian dollar is strongly influenced by how much money Canada owes its major trading partner, the U.S.; how much higher (or lower) our inflation rate is than theirs; how much higher our interest rates are; how much political dissension there is in the country; how realistic the Japanese think it is that they can get access to the U.S. market through Canada, and so on.

Suppose you decide in July that the Canadian dollar is destined to be 85¢ U.S. You put down $2,500 U.S., and get one contract of $100,000 Canadian, to be delivered the following March. Basically, you've paid $75,600 U.S. for the $100,000 Canadian. Say the dollar begins to rise, and reaches 80¢ US. If it's not yet March, you can sell (or deliver) your contract. You'd get $80,000 U.S. But you only paid $75,600, so your profit is $4,400. All you put up is $2,500, so you've made almost 200% on your money in less than 8 months.

As you can see, the leverage is enormous. One problem: leverage can break you if the market moves against you. But maybe you think the Canadian dollar will go down. After all, our inflation rate is higher than that of the U.S., and every December, when U.S. subsidiary companies in Canada have to send dividends to the States, they turn in a lot of Canadian dollars to get U.S. dollars. Well, you can speculate on that move, too. You can sell a Canadian dollar contract any day before your contract date—in this case, March. Say you sold it in July when the Canadian dollar was worth 75.5¢ US. If the dollar does in fact go down, say to 70¢ U.S. before March, you can buy one contract to cover your sold contract, for which you will pay only $70,000 U.S. Your profit—as always with the Canadian dollar—is $1,000 per penny move. And don't forget, all you've put up is $2,500.

Should *you* be in the commodities or currency futures market? If you're already in the market, you probably don't need advice (or won't take it anyway). If, however, you're just getting into it, I'd caution you to do a bit of reading and "trading on paper" before you start. One daunting thing about futures trading is that you can be right and still lose money. The single biggest problem the small investor has (aside from calling the right shots) is being undercapitalized. In other words, you can make the right move—by buying a currency or a commodity that ultimately goes up—but lose money by being caught in a whipsaw action that sees the currency or commodity go down when you don't have additional capital to cover your (temporary) loss. Whatever amount of money you want to put in, be sure you have twice as much in reserve.

The best things to read are general business papers like the *Wall Street Journal*, which will tell you about fundamental economic and political pressures in various countries, plus one or two books on currency trading, which you can find in your local library. In addition, spend some time at your broker's office going through the charts and literature that are widely available.

Finally, after you've been in the game for a while, do a quick figuring of how much you're making an hour—take all the money you've made, subtract your losses, commissions, and taxes, and divide by the number of hours you've worked and worried about your position.

That bottom line will tell you better than anything or anyone else whether futures trading is for you.

COLLECTIBLES

Back in the good old days of the 1970s, hard-money and collectibles investors laughed, cavorted and jigged all the way to the bank—which quite commonly was in downtown Hong Kong, or in some backwoods farmland in the wilds north of Battleford. While the Dow-Jones, Standard and Poor's and the TSE indexes began the 1980s up barely fifty percent over the beginning of the 1970s—a compound rate of just over four percent—gold gained 1,000 percent, silver averaged a compound rate of twenty percent, diamonds increased by fifteen percent each and every year, and collectibles, whether stamps, paintings, coins, chinoiseries, antiques, Persian carpets or comic books, all managed to outpace the rate of inflation for the decade.

So much for the 1970s.

By the early 1980s, the hard-heads weren't quite so playful. Gold hit bottom in 1985, dropping to one-third of its 1980 value, silver was down from a high of $50 U.S. an ounce to one-tenth that value, diamonds were down by 50%, and the bottom had simply fallen out of the collectibles markets.

Today, the non-traditional investor is back in business. The fact is, non-traditional investing has always been an alternate route to financial independence, but as with more traditional routes, nothing happens in a vacuum. The first observation is that non-traditional investments—gold, silver, diamonds, currencies and collectibles—are no longer non-traditional. Fifteen or twenty years ago, a respectable portfolio consisted of just three kinds of assets—stocks, bonds, and real estate. Thus, in 1970, an investor who bought into the non-traditionals was going against the conventional wisdom; if the analysis was correct, that investor made a lot of money. Harry Browne, who made his fortune in the Seventies, writing best-sellers such as *How You Can Profit from the Coming Devaluation*, hit the nail on the head in describing the change in the investment climate : "We non-traditional investors are no longer different . . .what we understand today is now common knowledge and it's time to be suspicious." If you remember back 15 or 20 years ago, people who advocated borrowing to the hilt and paying back with cheaper dollars were going against the mainstream—and they made fortunes. If you kept on doing that in the early Eighties, however, you got clobbered.

Now that hard money and tangible assets are moving into the mainstream of investment portfolios, investors need to do the same kind of homework they have always had to do when buying any asset—look for present and potential value.

There is no end to the range of things that qualify as collectibles, but they do share certain characteristics, including rarity, demand, popularity, craftsmanship, antiquity, aesthetic beauty, and tastefulness, as well as educational or historic value. Some such items, in a rough order of popularity and profitability are rare coins, stamps, oil paintings, antique furniture, cars, and rugs.

The collectors' market is capricious, however. One year an item may be worth thousands; the next, it could be worthless. Usually, it is next to impossible to predict what will become a collector's item. Who was to know that the Mickey Mouse watches of the 1940s would later be prized by collectors, but that other items from the same era would not?

It could be argued that the stock market is just as unpredictable, but before you buy stock, there are at least a few ways of evaluating a corporation's performance. With the exception of coins and jewellery, perhaps, whose value is determined to some degree by the price of the metal or gemstones they contain, often the only criterion for judging the value of collectibles is personal taste—emotional appeal. And, as gold expert Peter Cavelti put it in his book, *Gold, Silver and Strategic Metals*, "One of the first things professional traders learn is that investment considerations and emotions don't mix well."

We are not completely without data, however. Financial advisors are increasingly recommending to their wealthier clients that they put as much as 20% of their funds into art, antiquities, and other tangible holdings. One survey of comparative yields of tangibles showed that Chinese ceramics headed the list with a ten-year compound rate of return of 19.2% per year. Next in line were high-grade American stamps, producing 15.4%; then paintings by old masters, yielding 13%; as well as non-gold U.S. coins producing 13%, all for a period of ten years. There has been a stunning increase in art prices recently as investors who have made big profits in the stock market over the last three or four years have put some of those profits into tangibles. Lately, the

Japanese, the world's biggest creditors, have been bidding up prices, not just of old masters, but of baseball players as well.

There are some basics if you want to get into collectibles. First, stick to *the* rule for any investment: the best buyer is a well-informed buyer. Gather as much information in your particular area of interest as possible. Try to become an expert, (experts tell us it takes two to three years to become a high-class *amateur*).

Read. If there is a developed market for the objects you are collecting, such as coins, there's likely to be a number of publications, or even an association of kindred souls. Such groups can be a mine of information and advice. Attend auctions, and browse in antique shops. Be warned: if such painstaking research is alien to your temperament, consider another form of investment. Especially in the collectibles field, ignorance is the surest way to put a hole in your wallet.

Buy only from reputable dealers and auctioneers. The collectibles market is fraught with fakes and flawed merchandise. If you're just starting out, minimize your risks by buying or specializing in collectibles of known worth or with a history of regular price appreciation. Be a disciplined shopper. Buy only what you want to specialize in. Buy only collectibles in excellent condition, and buy the best you can afford. For coin collectors, numismatic gradings are available to help you determine the quality of what you are buying.

Make sure you're guaranteed the authenticity of a collectible against a full cash refund. Don't be intimidated. You're entitled to the genuine article, so insist. Get used to holding most items in your collection for a long time. Getting rich quick is not the name of this game. Even my friend Peter had to wait for the rest of the world to catch up to his appreciation of Emily Carr and Eskimo carvings. For him, it was worth the wait.

Beware of jewellery made of precious metals as an investment. In the long run, these items are less valuable than you might think, since precious metals are usually alloyed to a certain fineness before becoming jewellery. The cost of this is passed on, as are a number of taxes, excises, wholesale and retail charges before the item is sold. In effect, it becomes worth somewhat less than the material of which it is made. When you try to resell it, it will probably be worth less than you paid.

Check out the tax regulations of your particular collectible. When you sell, the profit you make is taxable as a capital gain.

Keep abreast of financial trends which can affect collectibles. For example, a bullish stock market means more cash for investors, and a greater chance that they'll be interested in collectibles, having already taken care of the basics. This now becomes the peak season for you. Conversely, when the stock market is sluggish, display your collectibles in a conspicuous place, and enjoy.

Summing up the collectibles market, two conclusions stand out. First, the market is never dead for long or manic forever. Second, the market is changing fundamentally. Of greatest significance is the fact that many pre-1970 "non-traditional" investments such as gold and antiques have moved into the mainstream beside the old traditionals such as stocks and bonds. This could mean two things: first, the market for gold will become bigger, broader and more dependable. Second, a new category of "non-traditionals," with stratospheric potential for gain, will emerge. Those who stand to make the most are those whose trend-following techniques direct them to the next wave of "non-traditional" investments. Strategic materials, anyone? Wheat? Clean compressed air?

CHAPTER 17

Pooling the Risk: Mutual, or Investment, Funds

The prudent way is also the easy way.

—Paul Samuelson

One way to invest in almost any market without doing so much of the work is to buy mutual funds. (Just about everyone calls them mutual funds but in Canada, the name was officially changed to investment funds in the early 1960s because of a world-wide scandal that tainted the word "mutual" for a lot of people. The Investment Funds Institute of Canada is the association that represents most of the mutual funds in this country, and they would be happier if you would call mutual funds "investment funds."

A mutual fund is a pool of money. It is also a company which has been incorporated for the purpose of investing in securities. Mutual funds raise capital in the same way as other companies: they sell shares, called units, to anyone who wants them. The difference between a mutual fund and say, a mining company, or a shoe manufacturer, lies in what the managers do with the money they raise. A mining company goes out and buys drills and bulldozers. A shoe manufacturer hires employees, and buys raw materials. The mutual fund manager takes the money and buys a diversified group of stocks, bonds, or other assets in the hope of making income or a capital gain, or both.

Mutual, or investment, funds are easier to research than stocks, bonds or mortgages, because there are only a few hundred of the former, and several thousand of the latter.

The most important thing to know about mutual funds is that the price of a mutual fund's units is always specifically related to its net asset value. (You know net asset value—that's the total assets of a company less its liabilities. It's the same concept as net worth when you figure out what you're worth.) The reason a mutual fund's unit price has a definite relationship to its net asset value is that all mutual funds, when they take your money, promise to buy back your shares on demand at the net asset value on that day.

You can look up the net asset value of mutual funds in the financial section of your local newspaper, after the stock quotations. What's listed is not the price per share, as in the stock price quotes, but the net asset value per share (NAVPS). There are no highs or lows for the day, and no bid or ask prices.

There are other differences between mutual funds and stock prices. Remember that when you buy common shares, you buy them "in the market" from someone who already owns them. Only infrequently do you buy shares directly from the company that issues them. Mutual fund shares are always bought directly from the company, out of its treasury, and they are always sold back to the company.

As a result of this difference, the number of shares outstanding and the amount of money available for investment are always changing. That's another big difference from buying shares in a producing or service company where the number of shares outstanding is fixed. Just for the record, most mutual funds are called *open-end* funds because they endlessly sell shares from their treasury. This distinguishes them from *closed-end* funds which are also pools of money, but don't continuously sell more shares. They are a relatively small part of the world of investment alternatives.

What you get by putting your money into mutual funds is diversification and professional money management.

Buying professional money management doesn't invalidate the whole concept of this book, which is that you should "do it yourself." Doing it yourself means making a conscious, rational decision. If you decide you have neither the time nor the temperament to manage your own investments, you are smart to buy professional help. If you're just starting out, and don't have enough money to spread around to minimize the risk of loss, you are smart to pool your resources with others, and buy that diversification.

Even if you decide on mutual funds, you still have three things to do.

1. You have to decide what your objectives are for the money you want to put into a mutual fund.
2. You have to decide on the mutual fund.
3. You have to know how much the investment is going to cost compared to what it might pay.

There are dozens of mutual funds from which to choose. Your financial objectives will narrow down the choice. Check back to Chapter 2 and Chapter 12 to review your financial objectives. A mutual fund must state its financial goals in its prospectus. You'll want to look more closely only at the funds which meet your goals.

In Chapter 9, when we were looking at RRSP alternatives, we classified funds by the type of asset they held. Here we'll catergorize them slightly differently:

Growth funds: The main goal of a strictly growth fund is to make your money grow. You would not be interested in getting any income from such a fund, and would not be excessively bothered by moderate volatility.

"Balanced" funds: If you are somewhat more conservative, you may want growth, but with some income. In this case, you'd be looking for a fund that specializes in high-quality stocks which also carry a dividend. Sometimes, they buy bonds as well. The considerations for this kind of investment are: your assets, tax bracket, and temperament. You may not need the income, but if you feel uncomfortable with the fluctuations that inevitably come with high growth funds, you're better off with a more stable mutual fund.

Income funds: These are mutual funds whose objective is to provide you with a stable income. These funds look for solid blue chip stocks that have a long history of paying, and even increasing, dividends, and whose share price is relatively stable. As well, they invest the pooled money at their disposal in debt-type securities. This means that your money is lent to institutions like governments and corporations.

Step one, then, is to find a fund that matches your own investment objectives. You can ask your broker to give you a preliminary rundown of funds, or you can get basic information from the Investment Funds Institute of Canada.

Step two is to decide on a fund. The best advice here is as elsewhere—look at the performance record. You're going to want to look at the record over a fair number of years. You want to know how the fund performs when markets are good, and when they're bad. The *Financial Post* and the *Financial Times* both publish a performance rating for several dozen mutual funds monthly. Several ratings books come out each year as well, usually around January, to coincide with the advertising push for RRSP money. Many mutual funds are eligible to be put into an RRSP.

Look at the performance record rather than the advertising. Often, much too much is made of the advantages of getting professional money management. It's not all that hard to find a mutual fund whose professional money manager has lost money year in, year out, or managed to make it at a rate considerably less than you could get if you left your money in a non-chequable savings account. On the other hand, it's not all that hard to find a mutual fund whose money manager has been astute enough to make 15 and 20 (and more) percent year in, year out.

Step three is to find out how much getting into or out of the mutual fund of your choice is going to cost you.

Mutual funds are divided into "load" and "no load" funds. A load is a charge you have to pay for the privilege of having a professional money manager invest your money. It's a sales commission, an acquisition fee, a premium. It can range up to nine percent of your investment. Sometimes, the load is levied when you buy the fund. Sometimes, there's no charge when you buy, but there's "rear-end load" when you sell. Be sure to ask. Be sure to ask whether, in addition to the load, there's a management fee.

No-load funds are sold mainly by banks and trust companies. They have management fees. Find out how much they are.

Whether or not a mutual fund carries a load should not be the primary consideration when you make your decision to buy. Performance over time, according to your investment objectives, should be. You're a lot better off in a load mutual fund that consistently makes 20 percent a year than you are in a no-load fund that consistently makes six percent a year.

If you decide the mutual fund idea appeals to you, make sure you look at a few funds' prospectuses. The prospectus will tell you what the fund's investment objectives are, how much money is in its investment pool; what its dividend or payout policy is; what is in its portfolio, that is, what stocks or bonds, or other things, it has bought.

Another thing you'll want to know is whether you can transfer your units to another fund if you aren't happy with the performance of the fund you've bought, or if your investment objectives change. If you buy a mutual fund that is one of a family of funds—

some management companies manage five or six funds with different objectives—you may be able to switch with no fee, or with a very small fee. Be careful when you buy, because switching can involve some very heavy costs which, of course, reduce your net return.

INVESTMENT CLUBS

Every time I give a workshop on effective money management, the question that pops up most frequently is "What about investment clubs?"

An investment club is nothing more than a miniature mutual fund. It is a group of people who either work together, or know each other socially, who decide to pool their money to invest on a regular basis. There are thousands of investment clubs in Canada and the United States, and although there are no official track records as to how these clubs do, random samplings suggest that a great many of them, without the benefit of a professional money manager, consistently outperform both the market averages, and many of the publicly traded mutual funds.

You cannot get into an ongoing investment club unless you know of one that has a vacancy. It's just as easy to rally a group of friends, neighbours, or work associates, and start your own. If you limit your investment each month to an amount small enough that losing it won't bankrupt you, but large enough that you are prepared to work at making it work for you, it's one of the best ways of becoming a successful investor.

Rule Number 1 Keep your investment club small. A dozen people is manageable. Don't forget that all the phoning and organizing is voluntary. Remember also that your group has to be compatible. Compatiblity varies inversely with the number of people involved.

Rule Number 2 Sit down with the prospective group, and set out a list of objectives. Are you going to limit your investment to stocks, or are you going to look into other investment possibilities, ranging from bonds to term deposits to gold to other tangibles? How much would you like your investment to grow? Some clubs have achieved compound annual growth rates of 20 or 30 percent by sticking to growth and speculative stocks. How much risk is the group prepared to take? Obviously, all you can do at this stage is set the parameters for your group. But it's a good idea for everyone to know that you are (or aren't) going to buy highly speculative penny stocks, or sit safely on bank term deposits.

Rule Number 3 Decide at the outset how much you are going to invest, how often you're going to invest it, and whether or not you are going to begin with a larger initial deposit. Most investment clubs are set up as learning experiences. The amount you invest will depend on the overall affluence of the group. You can decide on $10, $20, $30, or $50 a month. The more you invest, the faster the pool of money will grow. The important thing is that the amount of money be significant to each member, but not so much that a setback in the market causes people to panic. The other important thing is that the money be invested regularly, no matter whether market conditions are good or bad.

Rule Number 4 Make it clear at the outset that investing is a long-term commitment. Nothing destroys an investment club faster than a member who decides to pull out three months after joining. When you have a small pool of money fully invested, it is difficult to both make it grow and return it to a withdrawing member. Many clubs rule that a member must give several months' notice before withdrawing.

Rule Number 5 Have a constitution. Draw up a written statement of your investment philosophy; how much each member is expected to contribute each month, both in dollars and in information; and the procedure for getting into and out of the club.

Rule Number 6 Plan to have professionals address your club on a regular basis. If you are a knowledgeable business group, you may have professionals among you who can give you the fundamentals of investing. If you aren't, tap the investment community—bankers, brokers, economists—for speakers. Also make it clear to each member that they have to contribute specific knowledge each meeting—"hot tips" don't qualify.
A sample investment club constitution follows. You can contact the Canadian Association of Investment Clubs through A.D.H. Smith, First Canadian Place, P.O. Box 122, Suite 3700, Toronto M5X 1E9.

Sample Articles of Agreement for an Investment Club

Name:	This Club shall be known as the ____________ Investment Club.
Purpose:	The purpose of this Club shall be to make money for its members.

Officers: The officers of this Club shall be a President, Vice-President, and Secretary-Treasurer elected from among members of the Club.

Officers shall be elected at the January meeting, take office the day of election, and serve for one year or until new officers are elected. Upon the occurrence of a vacancy, an interim election shall be held to fill the vacancy for the balance of the Club year.

It shall be the duty of the President to preside at meetings, to appoint committees, and to oversee all Club activities.

The Vice-President shall assume the duties of the President when he or she is absent or temporarily unable to serve.

The Secretary-Treasurer shall keep a record of Club business and report on previous meetings. He or she shall also collect and disburse funds, maintain a set of books covering the club's financial operations, assets, and members' shares, and prepare a quarterly statement of liquidating value.

The signatures of any two of these three officers shall be required on all cheques drawn against the Club's account and on all orders to release securities.

Membership: Membership shall be limited to ______________.

No member may transfer his or her membership. He or she may resign at any time and shares shall be liquidated in accordance with the procedure laid down in a subsequent article of this agreement.

A new member may be admitted only after a unanimous vote of approval by the membership. New members must agree to be bound by all the terms and provisions set out herein.

Procedure: Meetings—Meetings shall be held quarterly at a time and place determined by the membership.

The January meeting shall be designated as the Annual Meeting.

Special meetings may be called by the officers upon notice to the membership.

The quorum necessary to conduct business shall consist of a simple majority of the shares in the Club. Proxy votes, given in writing, will be considered in determining a quorum.

Operation—Investments shall be received from members at the rate of ______dollars per month per member.

A quarterly statement of liquidating value effective the first business day of each quarter shall be prepared for each meeting.

The value of a share in the Club will be determined by dividing the liquidating value by the total number of shares held by all members of the Club.

The number of shares purchased by the monthly individual contribution is determined by dividing that amount by the share value as arrived at above.

Any member wishing to resign may withdraw his or her shares after sixty days' notice. The liquidating value of a withdrawal is determined by the share value at the date of withdrawal, less any commission charges incurred to secure the cash.

If a member should be delinquent in respect of investments for three consecutive months, membership will be automatically terminated, and refund shall be made on the same basis as in the case of a member resigning.

Amendments—These articles may be amended by a two-thirds vote of the total shares of the Club.

Other—No member of the Club shall be personally liable, as a partner or otherwise, under this agreement.

No purchase shall be made at any time on margin.

The assets of the Club shall never be pledged as security or collateral for any loan.

Adopted: ______________________________ *Investment Club*

Members:

CHAPTER 18

Real Estate and Being on the Other End of a Mortgage

If I had just put $2 million into that deal, I'd be a rich man today.

—Andrew Tobias

Real estate is a multitude of things, ranging from win-win to lose-lose propositions, and everything in between. During the boom years, it was hard to lose on a principal residence, because values generally went up in a straight line, and proceeds were tax-free.

Recent developments are a sharp reminder that caution is always the watchword—and even that, sometimes, can't help.

The people who grabbed luxurious Calgary bungalows during the high-interest rate period of the early 1980s surely never thought they'd leave the keys with the banker and walk away from their investment when oil prices collapsed.

A house in a good Halifax neighbourhood with small but steady growth in value has turned out to be a better investment in the 1980s than a house in one of the resource towns where prices were climbing fast at the start of the decade. Workers in Sept-Iles, Quebec, had the highest average wage in the country less than ten years ago . . .the housing market there collapsed with iron ore production on the North Shore.

In the spring of 1987, there was a buying panic in Toronto with coffee-table auctions pushing purchases over the asking price, as people were afraid to be left out (of what?). The same kind of fever gripped the market in 1981, when people thought they should grab a house with an 18% mortgage or they'd have to pay 30%.

Nothing is simple in real estate, and it's probably illusory to think it ever was. If you're thinking of investing in real estate, the primary rule is to look carefully at your own personal situation: your abilities, your tolerance level for risk, your cash flow, and your staying power if the unexpected happens.

LOCATION, LOCATION, LOCATION

Hardly original, but there you are. You can do everything else right when you buy a property—it can be properly zoned, it can be attractive and well-maintained, it can have everything possible going for it—but if it's in the wrong location, you'll never make a maximum return on it.

Location can mean different things according to the type of property. A good residential location isn't necessarily a great commercial location. It's important that residential properties be close to parks, schools, and shopping; commercial properties need to be close to business services.

This chapter will look at the different factors involved in choosing the right properties, administering them well, and selling them at the right time.

LOVE HAS NOTHING TO DO WITH IT

Like almost any other kind of investment, real estate may not be for you. Here are some of the things you need to know about yourself in order to decide:

- Are you willing to tie up a lump sum for several years? Sometimes it's hard to sell property in a hurry, so you should be prepared for the possibility that you won't be able to take out your down payment, and that you may have to put in extra money for carrying costs, sudden maintenance requirements, tax increases, whatever.
- Unless you want to be part of a larger consortium of investors with hired managers, you should be prepared to devote time and attention to your property, or to monitoring the performance of your managers. In either case, it's hard to watch over properties that are thousands of miles away. If you can't supervise it yourself, maybe you don't want to be involved at all.
- Can you face the prospect of tenants phoning you about a dripping faucet at two in the morning? What will you do if you suddenly find yourself with three empty apartments? Are you

any good at the administrative and interpersonal skills you'll need to attract good tenants, keep the building in good repair, and keep accurate records?

- How's your sleep record? Will you stay awake in terror if you are afraid your properties' values have plummeted, or if a sudden problem requires a large injection of cash? Over the long run, returns on real estate can be very high. But you may have to work hard to get there.

Only you can answer these questions. Only you can decide how much time and effort you are willing to invest along with your hard-earned dollars.

WERE YOU MEANT TO BE A BIT PLAYER?

The real estate market is increasingly dominated by large developers, and by consortiums owned by many small investors with professional management. Small investors acting alone can still make a lot of money, as long as they know what they're doing—that's a big caveat.

Rent controls, capital gains taxes, zoning, the impact of foreign money seeking stable investments and willing to take a low return, government restrictions on land use—these are some of the factors that can affect the investor's return on investment considerably. The small investors who do well usually rely on proven values, or develop antennae for the *next* unfashionable area slated for gentrification or development, and ride the trend to profit.

Look around at the market in your area. Decide what kind of money you want to invest, and what kind of property you want to buy. Before you make any commitments, have a firm idea of what financing is available, how you can carry the costs, how long you want your involvement to be, whether or not you want to have one or more partners, how much responsibility you can take on, whether you want to see older properties which may need renovations, or whether you want to stick to newer ones.

If you already know all these things, get to know a really competent broker who is prepared to invest some time in educating you at the outset with the philosophy that if you do well, you'll keep doing business with him or her as you increase your sophistication, your capital, and your appetite for the market. Remember that brokers are paid on commission for transactions, so the quicker you get in and out of deals, even if they're small, the more attractive that makes you as a client to the broker.

GET TO KNOW THE LANGUAGE IF YOU WANT TO HAVE A GOOD TIME

This is a good life principle, but it's especially true in the arcane world of real estate, where gossip, rumour, and personal connections often play a big role in knowing when and what is happening where. For example, how are prices set? Who is the best source of funds, advice, and professional help? How do you budget for expenses?

Land is the starting point in real estate. They aren't making it any more, so the supply is fixed and, theoretically, it should always be a safe investment. Tell that to the homeowners at Love Canal.

There are a number of things to know about land. If it's raw, or undeveloped, what is the time frame in which you want to see it developed? It's not worth much unless it can be used for something—even if that something is preserving a rare species of bird.

The uses of land also determine its value: downtown land with a high-density zoning in a perfect location for a major office tower is obviously worth much more than the ring of lots around the garbage dump.

Even if you're buying real estate strictly as an investment, you should always make sure you've seen the property in person. You can't smell a funny odour in a picture.

While, in general, a limited supply of anything desirable should mean that prices will always go up, with land there can be anomalies. When overall prices are falling, as commodity prices have in the last few years, land prices may follow, at least in the geographic areas where the economy is weakest. If you bought an excellent piece of real estate in 1929, you had to hold on to it until the 1940s to see it reach its purchase price again. Slumps in the market are most likely to happen when people desperately need to sell. Can you face a situation like that if it arises?

I know I'm always telling people to shop around, but in real estate, the market is so competitive that it really is worth investigating thoroughly and negotiating when you find what you want. Maybe I'm anti-social, but when the herd gets going, I feel more inclined to wait out the panic than to risk getting trampled.

LEVERAGING ISN'T JUST FOR IVAN BOESKY

If you're one of those people who always want to pay cash, real estate isn't where you'll make the most money. First of all, prices are high enough that not many of us have the money in loose change. Second, investing only what you have limits your growth potential enormously. If you invested $50,000 cash in a $50,000 property, and property values went up 15% a year, after five years your property would be worth about $100,000. Your equity would have increased by $50,000.

But if you took that same $50,000 and put it down on a $200,000 property (assuming that income from the property will cover the cost of borrowing), your property would be worth $400,000 in five years at 15% growth per year. This would increase your equity by $200,000—a much better return on your original outlay.

Lenders usually cast a friendly eye on income properties, so that you can often obtain a higher percentage of the value as a mortgage—often as much as 90%. Make sure your projections leave you a little room to cover the costs out of income. If you can't get a return on the property that is more than your borrowing costs, you should make sure you can either increase revenues by raising rents, or that the increased value of the property will pay your bills and still make you a profit when you decide to sell the property.

YOU THOUGHT THEY'D LIKE A MARBLE WHIRLPOOL THAT TOOK UP THE WHOLE GUEST ROOM . . .

Once you own a property, spending money is like falling off a log. There is no end to the improvements that can be made, but there is an end to your pocketbook.

Look at proposed improvements in the harsh cold light of day. Do they truly add proportionately to the property's value? Some improvements may be dictated by law, or by basic health and safety considerations. Others may be purely personal whim, and you may find yourself out of a lot of money if you proceed with them. Make sure your expenses will pay for themselves.

NOW THAT'S A HEADACHE!

Did you ever wonder why promoters offer all-expenses paid junkets to Las Vegas and other places where there are nice unbuilt condos for sale?

Purchasing properties sight unseen is the best headache recipe I know. When the party's over, you may find yourself stuck with a much bigger tab than you bargained for.

If you do want a pre-building price on something, be prepared to do a thorough investigative job on the builders and any other firms involved. Demand to see previously completed work, and to talk to clients who have dealt with them. Don't hand somebody your life savings because he or she brought you down to Florida for the weekend.

WHEN TO IGNORE THE LAWYER/PRODUCTIVITY INDEX

A recent study showed that the countries with the fewest lawyers, like Japan, were the most productive, and that the ones with the most lawyers, the United States and Canada, were the least productive.

Sometimes, if you are willing to work hard and spend the time doing your own research and coordination, you can save a lot of money doing things yourself. Other times, the amount you save up front can cost you a fortune further down the line.

Real estate agents, architects, engineers, contractors, lawyers, accountants, and other professionals can be mighty useful when you need them. You may, for example, save a few thousand dollars by not using an agent to sell your property. On the other hand, a good agent who knows the market well can save you both time and money, whether you're buying or selling.

Figure out how much money you're trying to save, what can go wrong, and whether it's worth doing without the services of a professional. Don't skimp on things like keeping good records and making sure titles are in order. When you do use professionals, be prepared to pay attention to the quality of the service you are getting.

Do *not*, I repeat *not*, try to save money by not retaining a competent lawyer (or notary in Quebec) to complete the transaction for you. Title searches, vital to your interests, may be an endless source of trouble if not well done. Your offer to purchase, if it doesn't specifically state your legal rights, doesn't protect you. Even if your lawyer reviews it, make sure everyone understands what you want.

STAYING ON TOP OF THE TRENDS

The real estate market is like the stock market . . .the people who notice a trend first are in a position to capitalize on it, and they are usually the ones who make the most money.

The big deals are almost always done by developers, but they have to put them together first. If you can buy up a block of houses about to be rezoned for high-rise development, for example, you'll be in a position to sell to the developer.

Advance knowledge of zoning changes, planned developments, and social trends can give a real estate investor a significant edge in making the right choices—and in avoiding the wrong ones.

Be aware of such things as plans for new roads or services, buildings to be constructed nearby, and plans for nearby vacant land. Existing property values can be greatly affected by these things. A lovely family home that suddenly finds a high-rise next to it loses value. A dingy shack that sits on land needed for a major development can be worth a lot more.

Look around the neighbourhood for telltale signs of investment, or other signs such as frequent arson. Check city hall registers to see if there have been a lot of transactions in the area recently, and if the names are familiar.

If you are thinking of buying an income property, what is its competition in attracting tenants? Are there several other buildings offering similar attractions and lower rents in the area? Is a new high-rise with a health club opening up down the street? Is the neighbourhood grocery store about to shut down? You can't be too knowledgeable about the context of your investment.

IF IT HAD TIRES TO KICK . . .

The physical appearance of a building can tell you a lot, but then again, a fast spit and polish can hide a lot too. Attractiveness sufficient to be competitive in the area is important. But such elementary things as heating, plumbing, and electrical systems are just as important. They are big ticket items if they have to be replaced. If you aren't qualified to judge the state of the building, investing in a good inspection may prevent you from making a money-losing investment.

Bad systems in the building may also affect operating costs above and beyond repairs. For example, a badly designed heating and cooling system may mean that people leave their windows open a lot, or that they add electric heaters that create a fire hazard.

If your utility costs or taxes go up, or if you have vacancies, your investment can quickly become unprofitable. You should know how much of an increase in costs you can bear before you reach that stage.

If you're investing in an unbuilt property, don't base your

projections on rent schedules that are unsupported by factual material. What is the rental market in the area? What kind of vacancy rate is being projected? What kind of tenant turnover?

If you're looking at an existing building, and you detect problems, who's to blame for them? Is the building in a bad location, or has it been badly maintained or managed? Can you turn it around? How is the credit standing of the tenants? Is it in an area where one vulnerable employer is providing most of the income?

YOU WANT WHAT???

Is the asking price reasonable? The seller won't tell you. The most significant information you can find is available through real estate agents who have access to computerized accounts of actual recent selling prices and levels of activity in the area.

In several Canadian cities, market survey companies provide reports on sales and prices in given areas. If you subscribe to such a service, you'll be able to monitor the market on an ongoing basis.

Remember that not every comparison is absolutely fair, but you can still get a good idea of how the asking price of the property you're interested in compares with the market in the area.

Another approach is to calculate the replacement cost of the property. How much would it cost you to buy equivalent land and build an equivalent building on it? If there is a big difference between replacement cost and market value, take a careful look at the reasons why. You should never use the replacement cost calculations on their own.

The want ads for income properties often cite a price/income ratio as a key variable in the sales pitch. While it makes good sense to evaluate the price of a property in light of the income it generates, it is also important to do this within a framework consisting of the investment climate, inflation, supply and demand, interest rates, rent controls, taxes, and the market and cost factors already mentioned.

Look at your financing options, and consider the potential of refinancing. You may be able to get a better deal that outweighs the penalties. Don't forget that a small rise or decrease in interest rates can have a major impact on your cash flow, and hence your ability to keep your property.

You should also know that refinancing income properties may have unforeseen tax consequences, so you should look for a competent tax advisor before proceeding with it.

HOW TO BORROW WITHOUT LOSING YOUR SHIRT

We've already agreed that you won't be making any big time real estate deals unless you borrow. How long will you be making payments? How flexible is the lender? Can you renegotiate your financing? What fees will you have to pay?

Some lenders will charge closing costs for negotiating and arranging a loan. If money is scarce, the lender may require a carrot to induce him or her to make the loan. This is often called "points," as in percentages. Points can be reduced or eliminated as the size of your down payment is increased.

You will have to purchase fire and liability insurance on any developed property. The lender will probably make you buy life insurance so that your loan will be paid off if you die. Many lenders require you to deposit a portion of your property taxes every month. Try to avoid this arrangement, because you don't get interest on this tax money kept in an escrow account.

Recently, life insurance companies and other lenders have begun issuing equity participation loans. This means they lend you money at below market rates in exchange for a stake in future profits, or in the sale of the property.

FROM SCARBOROUGH TO BAGHDAD . . .

You can almost always do better than the asking price when you're trying to buy a property. Only in the most severely overheated markets do properties go for more than the asking price—and even then, there are no doubt skillful professionals fanning the flames.

Haggling is part of the real estate game; most people expect to have to negotiate. However, there are ways and then there are ways . . .the buyer is almost always in the driver's seat. The vendor has to wait until the right offer comes along. The buyer almost always has another option.

This doesn't mean that buyers should resort to cheap tricks such as sending three friends to offer ridiculously low amounts for a property so that the vendor's price will come down radically. (The last person I knew who did that took possession of a property with not a light bulb or a fixture anywhere, and $5,000 worth of landscaping uprooted.)

If you can take a respectful approach that leaves the vendor some self-respect, you'll probably do better. Often, you can leave a few days of thinking time for both parties, when mutual give-and-take still leaves a large gap between asking price and offer to purchase.

If you find yourself in a situation where you are caught up in bidding fever and become either desperate to buy or desperate to sell, all bids are off. If you're looking at the property strictly as an investment, rule number one is to stay calm, cool, and collected.

After you've made the right investment at the right price, and all your conditions have been met, then you can break out the champagne.

CHAPTER 19

How to Read the Financial Pages (and other interesting exotica)

A little knowledge is not a dangerous thing to the one who does not mistake it for a great deal.

—William Allen White

WHAT IS THE STOCK EXCHANGE?

The stock exchange is really a couple of hundred organized auction houses around the world. What is auctioned is not Victoriana, but shares of companies. There are five in Canada, the Toronto Stock Exchange being the largest, both in terms of the number of shares that are traded, and in terms of the value of the shares. The others, in order of value of shares traded, are Montreal, Vancouver, Alberta, and Winnipeg.

Exchanges are private organizations. People have to buy memberships, called "seats", on the exchange. A seat allows the owner to trade shares in any securities listed on the exchange.

The founders of the stock exchange control all aspects of trading and membership. They decide what qualifications people need to become members, and they decide what requirements companies have to meet to be listed. The conditions and requirements are designed to protect investors. Generally speaking, most members are corporations like investment houses, and members of the exhange are recognized as authorized traders on all other exchanges. The exchanges also set commission rates for buying and selling stocks. Any exchange you want to do business with will tell you its rates. What they won't tell you is that you can do business with discount brokers who will charge you as much as 70 or 80% less than full service brokers.

Reading the financial pages of a newspaper is no mean feat, especially since there is no standardized form for setting up stock, bond, and commodity futures quotations. But read them you must. We're going to reproduce the *Financial Post* format on the grounds that it is all-inclusive, and if you master it, you'll have no trouble deciphering your local paper's financial page.

HOW TO READ THE POST'S TABLES

Stock prices less than $5 are shown in cents.

Earnings are basic earnings per share before extraordinary items.

To make it easier for readers to relate earnings figures to the stock quotation, The Post has developed a system of presenting price, dividend and earnings data. Here are some examples of earnings figures and how to interpret them.

	Earnings per share			
	Latest interim or fiscal period		Prior or latest fiscal period	
1.	'83 Dec	.81	'82 Dec	1.21
2.	'84 Jan	u1.12	'83 Jan	u1.10
3.	Mar 3m	d1.05	'82 Dec	3.61
4.	Dec 26w	.34	'83 Jun	.92
5.	'83 Dec	x10.79	'82 Dec	x7.72

Example 1. Earnings for year ended Dec/83 were 81¢ per share; for the year ended Dec/82 $1.21 per share.

Example 2. Earnings for the year ended Jan/84 were US$1.12 per share; for the year ended Jan/83 US$1.10 per share.

Example 3. Losses for the three-month period ended Mar/83 were $1.05 per share; earnings for the year ended Dec/82 were $3.61 per share.

Example 4. Earnings for the 26-week period ended Dec/83 were 34¢ per share; for the year ended Jun/83 92¢ per share.

Example 5. Earnings for the year ended Dec/83 were 10.79 times the preferred dividend requirement; for the year ended Dec/82 7.72 times the preferred dividend requirement.

Letter code

- a After participation
- b Before participation
- d Deficit
- E Exact number of shares
- L Date of transaction
- p Latest 12-month cumulative dividends, including extras
- □ Restricted voting shares
- r Dividend in arrears
- s Shareholders' interest in statutory earnings
- t Tax deferred dividends
- x Times dividend earned
- u U.S. funds
- v Variable rate pfd.
- y Stock dividend equivalent to cash payment shown
- z Less than board lot
- ■ New figure
- # Categorized as a development issue by the Vancouver Stock Exchange.
- ‡ Not exempt from reporting material changes to Toronto Stock Exchange.

Exchange on which largest volume took place in the week:

- C Alberta Stock Exchange
- M Montreal Stock Exchange
- T Toronto Stock Exchange
- V Vancouver Stock Exchange
- W Winnipeg Stock Exchange

Where there have been no transactions during the week covered the word "nil" is shown under sales.

Twelve-month cumulative earnings before extraordinary items are used to calculate the price/earnings (P/E) ratios.

When there are no interim figures, the figures shown are for the two latest fiscal years. When there are interim figures, latest interim earnings figures are shown in the left hand margin, and the latest fiscal year in the right hand column.

Dividends and earnings reported in U.S. dollars are adjusted to Cdn. funds using the current exchange rate for the calculation of P/E ratios and indicated Yield.

The Financial Post cannot accept any responsibility for quotations.

STOCK PRICES Pages 20-27

Your guide for week ending July 31.
An exclusive single record of final weekly quotations of all five Canadian Stock Exchanges: Montreal, Toronto, Winnipeg, Alberta and Vancouver.

Compiled by *The Financial Post* **Information Service**

INDUSTRIAL, SENIOR MINING AND OIL STOCKS

①		②	③	④		⑤	⑥	⑦	⑧	⑨	⑩		⑪		
Range 53 Week High $	Low $	Company	Indic. Div. Rate $	Week Ended July 31 High $	Low $	Close or Latest $	Net Chge.	Sales 100s		Ind. Yld. %	P/E ratio latest 12 Mos.	latest interim or fiscal period	Earnings per Share $	prior or latest fiscal period	$
225	136	ABC Technologies	....	179	165	167	−8	386	V	...	...	......	.....	......	.....
425	240	ACDS Graphic System.....	....	295	240	240	−55	144	M	...	...	......	.....	......	.....
$5¼	300	ACSI Group....................	....	370	360	360	unch.	54	M	...	27.7	'85 Jun	.13	'84 Jun	.09
$5⅜	325	ADS Associates	....	395	370	370	−25	26	M	...	...	......	.....	......	.....
$19⅛	10	A.G.F. Mgmt. B pf.	.36	$17⅝	15⅝	17½	+1⅞	1618	T	2.1	18.4	May 6m	.58	'86 Nov	.75
$10	5½	A.H.A Automotive ‡	....	$6¼	6	6	−¼	120	T	...	15.4	Mar 3m	.12	'86 Dec	.43
$10½	7	A.I.L. Alta Inv. A	p.20	L	Jun 11/87	10½	..... .	nil		1.9	...	......	.....	......	.....
$15½	9	AMCA International	up.25	$12¾	12¼	12⅝	−⅛	623	T	2.6	...	Jun 6m	du.73	'86 Dec	du2.76
$25⅝	22⅜	Do. 8.84% pf.	2.21	$24⅝	24⅜	24⅜	−⅛	128	T	9.1	...	'86 Dec	.....	'85 Dec	.....
$25½	22⅜	Do. 9.25% pf.	2.31¼	$25	24⅝	24⅝	−¼	61	T	9.4	...	'86 Dec	.....	'85 Dec	.....
$27⅛	19	Do. 9.50% pf.	2.37½	$25⅛	24¼	25	+⅝	31.1	T	9.5	...	'86 Dec	.....	'85 Dec	.....
194	100	AME Limited.....................	.05	180	180	180	unch.	30	M	2.8	13.9	Mar 3m	.02	'86 Dec	.11
245	45	APP Applied Polymer# ...	....	98	70	80	−5	45	V	...	...	......	.....	......	.....
$5¾	425	ARC International	....	$5⅝	5⅜	5⅝	+⅜	271	T	...	31.3	Jan 9m	.11	'86 Apr	.12
$13⅜	7½	◻ATCO Ltd. Class I..........	.20	$13⅛	12¾	13	−⅛	3002	T	1.5	14.3	'87 Mar	.91	'86 Mar	.57
$13⅜	7½	Do. Class II...................	.20	$13¼	12¾	12¾	−¼	18	T	1.6	14.0	'87 Mar	.91	'86 Mar	.57
220	170	Abalone Res. #	....	185	178	185	unch.	30	V	...	...	......	.....	......	.....
140	50	Abbey Woods Dev. #	....	100	100	100	−5	40	V	...	...	......	.....	......	.....
→ $43	21	Abitibi-Price	.60	$35¼	32⅝	34½	+1¼	2409	T	1.7	21.7	Jun 6m	.78	'86 Dec	1.50
$50	46	Do. 7.50% A pfd..........	3.75	$46½	46⅜	46½	unch.	5	T	8.1	...	'86 Dec	x12.66	'85 Dec	x10.77
$15½	375	Do. wts.	....	$11	10	11	+¾	962	T	...	...	......	.....	......	.....
390	175	Absorptive Tech. #	....	300	275	295	−5	133	V	...	...	......	.....	......	.....
300	50	Access ATM Network ‡...	....	75	70	70	−10	93	T	...	...	Dec 3m	d.41	'86 Sep	d1.06
124	47	Access Technology #	....	85	80	85	unch.	422	V	...	10.6	'85 Oct	.08	'84 Oct	.50
$8⅛	225	Accugraph Corp. A ‡	....	400	385	400	unch.	145	T	...	...	Nov 3m	d.02	'86 Aug	d.17
$5¾	350	Acier Leroux Inc.............	....	425	425	425	unch.	8	M	...	8.7	Apr 6m	.15	'86 Oct	.45
$21	16	Acklands........................	.60	$18	17½	17½	−½	155	T	3.4	33.7	May 6m	.34	'86 Nov	.59
355	200	AcuVision Systems #	....	285	255	260	unch.	1089	V	...	...	......	.....	......	.....
60	22	Ad Com Marketing #	....	30	22	25	−5	450	V	...	...	......	.....	......	.....

1. These two figures tell the highest and lowest price that one share of Abitibi Price sold for between this day and this day one year ago.
2. The name of the stock—often abbreviated. This one is Abitibi Price.

3. The dividend that Abitibi Price is paying is $0.60 a share.

4. These two figures tell the highest and lowest price that one share of Abitibi Price sold for during the week. Your local daily paper will give daily highs and lows.

5. When the market closed on this day, one share of Abitibi Price was selling for $34.50.

6. This figure represents change in the price per share from the closing price of the week before.

7. This tells us how many hundreds of shares traded on this day. Abitibi Price trading volume was 240,900 shares.

8. The *Financial Post* lists the final weekly quotations of all five Canadian stock exchanges: Toronto, Montreal, Winnipeg, Alberta, and Vancouver. T is for Toronto.

9. This figure gives the yield, or return, as a percentage, that is the $0.60 dividend as a percentage of the $34.50 share price.

10. The P/E Ratio is the Price Earnings Ratio: the price of one share of Abitibi Price stock divided by earnings per share for a 12-month period. Usually, the lower the P/E ratio, the greater the chance the share price will rise.

11. These four columns are designed to help readers relate earnings figures to the stock quotations. In this case, the earnings for the 6-month period ending June 1987 were $0.78 per share. For the year ending December 1986, earnings were $1.50 per share.

Should you ever have occasion to go to the visitor's gallery of a stock exchange, or to take a tour offered at all the major exhcanges, . . . you will want to know exactly what it is that goes by on the electronic ticker.

Decoding Ticker Tape Symobols

Stock Symbol

BCE	BCE	BCE		BCE
253675	25003675	23675	3675	3625B
25 shares traded at $36.75	2,500 shares traded at $36.75	200 shares traded at 36.75	100 shares traded at $36.75	Quote $36.25 bid

Here is an example of the New York Stock Exchange listings, taken from the *Globe and Mail's* Report on Business.

NEW YORK QUOTATIONS FOR SEPTEMBER 10, 1987

① ② ③ ④ ⑤ ⑥ ⑦

Stock		PE Rat	Sales 100s	High	Low	Close	Net Chg
ADT	.92	29	1400	51½	51⅜	51⅜	
AM Intl			669	7¾	7¼	7¾	+ ½
AM Int pf	2		29	27⅞	27⅝	27⅝	+ ¼
AMR		12	4220	58⅝	57¼	57⅜	- ¼
ASA	2a		1529	66½	64⅞	64⅞	- ⅜
AbtLab	1	24	5065	61¼	59¾	60¾	+ ⅝
Abitibi g			55	25⅜	24¾	24¾	- ⅝
AcmeC	.40	13	652	12⅞	12	12¼	- ½
AdaEx	3.42e		109	21¾	21⅛	21¾	+ ⅝
AMD			7753	21¼	20⅜	21⅛	+ 1
AMD pf	3		653	52¾	52¼	52¾	+ ¾
Adobe			688	9½	9	9⅜	+ ⅛
Advest	.12a	9	124	12	11½	11⅝	- ⅛
→ AetnLf	2.76	9	6821	60⅞	60¼	60¼	- ⅛
Aileen			48	3⅜	3⅛	3⅛	- ⅛
AirPrd	1	21	2691	48¾	47⅞	48⅝	+ ⅞
AirbFrt	.60	11	74	26⅛	26	26	+ ⅛
AlskAir	.16	14	1629	21⅝	21¼	21½	
Alberto	.24	20	92	24¼	23⅜	23¾	- ¼
AlbCulA	.24	17	57	21	20	20¾	+ 1
Alcan s	.60	20	12930	34	32¾	33¾	+ 1¾
AlcoS s		18	337	26⅝	26¼	26⅝	+ ¼
AlexAlx	1	22	458	25¼	24¾	25	
AllegCp			25	90	90	90	
AlgInt			906	15½	14⅜	15¼	+ 1
AllgPw	2.92	10	643	37⅞	37½	37¾	+ ¼
Allegis	1	32	3752	97¼	96⅝	96⅝	- ⅛
AllenG	.56		136	16½	16	16¼	+ ¼
AldSgnl	1.80	14	2767	45⅛	44⅜	44⅜	+ ⅛
ALLTL	s1.36	18	888	33	31⅝	32⅝	+ 1⅜
CnsFrt	.90	17	1100	37⅞	37¼	37¼	- ½
ConsNG	1.50	20	712	42⅞	42⅜	42⅜	- ⅛
Cnrail n	.25e	14	4391	35¼	34⅝	35¼	+ ⅞
Contel	2	12	1696	36⅜	35¾	36⅛	+ ¼
CntlCp	2.60	9	2742	44½	43¾	44	+ ¼
Contlll	.08e		1127	5¼	5⅛	5⅛	- ⅛
CtData			1291	34½	33⅞	34	+ ½
Cooper	1.68	21	1366	66½	64¾	66¼	+ ⅝
CoprTr	.44	14	142	37⅝	37¼	37¼	- ⅛
Copwld			93	10⅜	10⅛	10¼	+ ⅛
Coreln	.64	26	50	16¾	16½	16½	
CornGl	1.40	20	1270	70½	69⅝	70½	+ ¾
Crane s	.90	12	499	30⅝	29⅞	30⅜	+ ⅛
CrayRs		24	5018	97¾	93½	94¼	- 2⅜
CrmpK s	.68	116	40	25½	25¼	25½	+ ⅛
CrwnCk		16	78	126	125⅜	125½	- ⅛
Culinet			1213	13⅜	12⅞	13⅜	+ ½
CumEn	2.20		1006	81¾	80⅛	80¼	- ¾
DPL	2.08	8	304	25⅜	24⅞	25¼	+ ¼
DamonC	.20		136	23⅜	23	23⅛	+ ¼
DanaCp	1.44	26	559	50	49¾	49⅞	+ ⅛
DataGn			1159	31¼	30¾	31	+ ⅛
Datapt			596	8⅜	8⅛	8⅛	
Deere	.25		6076	36	35⅝	35⅝	- ⅛
DelmP	s1.41	10	263	19¼	18⅞	19¼	+ ¼
DeltaAr	1.20	9	1903	54½	53¾	53⅞	+ ⅛
Deltona		46	25	5½	5½	5½	+ ⅛
DensMf	1.24	15	101	33½	32⅝	33½	+ ⅞
DeSoto	1.40	18	25	40⅛	40	40	+ ¼
DetEd	1.68	5	4138	15⅜	15⅛	15⅛	- ⅛

1. The name of the stock—often abbreviated. This one is Aetna Life Insurance Co.
2. The dividend that Aetna is paying is $2.76 per share. It should legitimately have its own heading.
3. The P.E. Rat is the Price Earnings Ratio: the price of one share of Aetna stock divided by earnings per share for a 12-month period. In this example, it is 9.
4. This tells us how many hundreds of shares traded on this day. Aetna's trading volume was 682,100 shares.
5. These two figures tell the highest and lowest price that one share of Aetna sold for on this day.
6. When the market closed on this day, one share of Aetna was selling for $60.25.
7. This figure represents change in the price per share from the closing price of the day before: − 1/8 means 12.5 cents lower.

WHAT IS THE UNLISTED OR OVER THE COUNTER MARKET?

Publicly owned companies which cannot, or do not want to, meet the requirements of any exchanges are traded as unlisted or "over-the-counter." The unlisted market doesn't have a physical place in the stock exchange. It trades on the telephone among account executives who make a market, that is, facilitate the buying and selling of unlisted stocks. Traders are linked by an automated quotation computer system called COCATS—the Canadian Over-the-Counter Automated Trading System. In the U.S., the American system is called NASDAQ—National Association of Securities Dealer Automated Quotations.

Here are two examples of such listings: the first of the Canadian unlisted market, as found in the *Financial Post;* the second of the NASDAQ listings, from the *New York Times.*

UNLISTEDS

Quotations provided by the Canadian Over-the-Counter Automated Trading System

Weekly trading summary of selected unlisteds at July 30, 1987

①	②	③	④
Name	**Volume**	**Close**	**Change over week**
		$	$
Action Traders ...	5,400	3.80	−.15
Amertek	50,890	4.45	+.35
Andover Tel.	7,500	0.75	+.05
Arjon Gold Mines	12,000	0.14	+.01
Augdome Corp. .	27,100	0.32	−.08
Balfour Channel .	10,000	0.40	unch.
Belleterre Quebec	27,400	1.30	+.25
Bijou Res. Corp	—	0.25	—
Biron Bay Res. ..	77,764	1.65	+.55
Blackstone Expl.	—	0.10	—
Border Chemical	400	3.25	unch.
Boston Bay Mines ...	—	7.00	—
Britoil PLC	252,800	6.83	+.38
Century Energy ..	10,000	0.80	−.20
Chelsea Creek Res	1,200	0.30	−.30
Clark Pharm. ..	174,400	1.60	+.20
Corp. Properties .	2,000	3.50	−.50
Easynet Data ...	50,500	0.28	+.03
Garrison Creek ...	3,000	0.50	−.05
Goderich Elevators ..	200	26.50	unch.
Golden Hope Mines	4,000	2.80	+.15
Gotaas-Larsen Ship. ..	—	41.75	—
Guardsman Res.	—	0.30	—
H O Financial Cl A ...	—	6.75	—
Hubert Lake Un.	—	0.13	—
Intrex Real Est. .	235,500	0.18	−.05
Jingellic Minerals	—	1.15	—
Kaolin of Can.	—	0.06	—

1. The name of the company.

2. The number of shares traded during the week.

3. The price at which the shares closed.

4. The change in share price during the week.

Nasdaq National Market

① 52-Week High	Low	② Stock	③ Div	④ Sales 100s	⑤ High	Low	Last	⑥ Chg.
3 3/4	1 7/8	Dtaslh		11	2 3/8	2 3/8	2 3/8	...
4 1/2	1 13/16	Datvsn		108	2	1 7/8	1 7/8	− 1/8
9	6 1/2	Datron		3u	9 1/8	9 1/8	9 1/8	+ 3/8
6 3/4	4 1/4	Datum		5	5 1/4	5 1/4	5 1/4	...
35 3/4	28 1/2	Dauphn	1.20	194	35	34 3/4	35	...
13 1/8	10 1/2	Davox		36	11 1/4	11	11	...
8 3/8	4 3/8	Dawson		40	7 3/8	7 1/4	7 3/8	...
37	5 1/8	Daxor		73	11 1/4	10 3/4	11 1/4	...
14 7/8	8 7/8	Daysln		563	9 3/4	9 1/2	9 1/2	− 1/8
21 7/8	10 7/8	DebSh s	.20	572	19 1/4	18 7/8	19 1/4	+ 1/4
3 5/8	2 1/8	Decom		235	2 5/8	2 3/8	2 5/8	+ 1/16
10 3/4	3 3/4	Decor	.01r	5	5 1/4	4 3/4	5 1/4	...
19 1/2	14 3/4	DeerfSv		4	18 3/4	18 1/4	18 3/4	...
9 1/2	3 3/8	DefnPr		146	3 7/8	3 3/8	3 3/8	− 3/8
26 7/8	14 3/4	Dekalb	.32e	561	25 3/4	25 1/2	25 1/2	− 1/4
24 1/4	12 1/2	DelaOts	.04e	4	19	19	19	+ 1
27 3/4	14 3/4	Delchm	.28	6	21 3/4	21 1/2	21 1/2	− 1/4
7 1/2	5 5/8	Delpinf		10	6 1/4	6 1/8	6 1/8	− 1/8
1 5/16	3/8	DeltaDt		10	1/2	1/2	1/2	...
3 3/4	1 3/8	CCA		37	1 13/16	1 3/4	1 3/4	− 1/16
45 1/4	32 3/4	CCB s	1.24	6	38 1/4	38 1/4	38 1/4	− 3/4
12 1/4	6 1/4	C COR		11	10	9 1/2	9 1/2	...
14 3/4	8 1/2	CCC		87	10	9 3/4	9 7/8	...
24 1/2	15 3/4	CCNB	.40a	20	24 1/2	23 3/4	23 3/4	...
19 1/4	14 1/4	CCX Nt		6	19	18 1/2	18 1/2	...
24 3/4	12 1/4	CDC		101	20 1/4	20 1/8	20 1/8	− 1/4
6 3/8	1 1/16	CEL		60	1 1/4	1 1/8	1 1/8	− 1/8
15 1/4	8 1/2	CEM		46	13 1/2	13	13	− 1/4
7	3	CFI St		22	6 1/2	6 1/4	6 1/4	...
25 1/2	13 3/4	CFS		8	17 1/2	17	17 1/2	+ 1
4 3/16	2 3/8	CIS Tch		132	2 3/4	2 5/8	2 3/4	+ 1/8
24 1/4	11 1/2	CJI		3	12 1/4	12 1/4	12 1/4	− 1 3/8
13	11 7/8	CK FSv		20	13	12 1/4	12 1/4	− 3/8
32 1/2	13 5/8	CML		38	30 1/8	29 7/8	29 7/8	...
11 11/16	4 3/8	CMS E s		51	6 3/4	6 1/4	6 1/4	− 5/8
25 3/8	20 7/8	CNB	.08b	2	24 1/2	24 1/2	24 1/2	− 1/4
27 3/4	15 3/8	CPI s	.16	2418	23 1/2	23	23 1/4	...
5 1/2	2 9/16	CPT		160	2 7/8d	2 1/2	2 3/4	+ 3/16
8 1/2	4 1/2	CR PL		1	4 1/2	4 1/2	4 1/2	...
4	1 1/4	CSC Ind		1	3 1/4	3 1/4	3 1/4	...

1. The highest and lowest price at which the stock has traded during the latest 52-week period.
2. The name of the company—in this case, Daxor, an organization that collects and freezes blood for individuals.
3. The dividend, if any.
4. The volume of sales in hundreds.
5. The highest, lowest, and closing price of the day.
6. The change in the closing price on this day from yesterday.

The over-the-counter market is not for beginners. Yes, it's perfectly legitimate, but its fundamental difference from the stock exchanges we've just described is enough to keep all but the most experienced investors away. In the over-the-counter market, dealers set the price—you have no way of knowing whether the price reflects supply and demand, or something else. Also, since the stocks traded in the over-the-counter market are not listed on a stock exchange, you have to do some digging to find the financial condition of the company. Being listed in an exchange doesn't, of course, guarantee that the company won't go bankrupt. But at least you have some reassurance that minimum standards have been met.

HOW A TRADE IS EXECUTED

After you open an account with a broker, you may buy and sell shares simply by phoning in your order. The stock market is one of the few industries which is conducted on the strength of your word. Here's a typical trade. You phone your broker and place an order to buy 100 shares of Bell Canada. You can at this point state a particular price at which you want it purchased, or you can instruct your broker to buy the stock "at the market." Your broker writes out the order, and phones or wires it down to his company's trader, who sits by the telephone on the periphery of the trading floor of one of the major stock exchanges in Canada. All orders are time stamped when they are received, and again when they are executed or filled. The trader passes the message on to the floor trader who moves to the area of the exchange floor where Bell Canada is traded. The floor trader will look at the bid and ask prices for Bell, shown either on a trading post or quotation board, depending on which stock exchange it's being traded at.

The stock market is a double auction: all bids and offers for shares are screamed out to attract attention. Another floor trader, who may have a client wanting to sell Bell stock, will listen to the bid price, and if he decides it's the best price he can get, he will indicate to the buying floor trader that he's willing to sell at that price.

The selling trader will write up the transaction in triplicate—one for himself, one for the buying trader, and one which gets time-stamped and typed into a computer terminal for electronic transmission to every brokerage office in Canada and the U.S. where Bell is traded.

The floor trader, meanwhile, will notify the company trader, who in turn will phone or wire the information to your broker, who will then tell you.

An official confirmation will be mailed to you, indicating the day by which you must settle your account. Settling your account means paying for shares you've bought.

Let's clear up a common misconception. First, common stock is issued by the company whose name it carries. This is one important way companies raise the money they need for the things they want to do. But unless you're buying new issue, anything you buy in the stock market will not come from the company. It is paid to the person who last owned the stock you bought.

Now, this doesn't mean that companies aren't interested in the price of their own stock after it's been issued. They are interested, for a variety of reasons. One reason is that they may want to raise more money by issuing more shares, and they'll want to get the best price they can.

Another reason is that many companies offer their employees shares in the company by way of extra compensation. That compensation won't be too attractive if share prices are consistently falling.

A third reason is that in these days of mergers and supermergers, companies often use their own shares to pay for another company. Once again, it's important for share prices to be rising.

BONDS

Bond prices are traded in the bond market just as stocks are exchanged in the stock market. Many people aren't aware of this fact because they are most familiar with Canada Savings Bonds, which are always worth their face value, and therefore cannot fluctuate in price. CSBs are not, strictly speaking, bonds for that very reason. Other government and corporate bonds do, in fact, fluctuate in price. The price changes reflect interest rate trends, and the ability of the bond issuer to meet its financial obligations. Bond quotations are usually categorized as government, provincial, and corporate. Provincial bonds include the issues of provincial utilities such as Alberta Government Telephone and Nova Scotia Power.

These listing examples are from the *Financial Post*.

Government bonds

July 31 1987	① Int. rate %	② Maturity date	③ Bid $	④ Yield %
Canada	13.500	Sep 1 87	100.35	9.00
Canada	9.750	Sep 6 87	100.05	9.00
Canada	13.000	Oct 15 87	100.75	9.05
Canada	12.000	Nov 15 87	100.75	9.20
Canada	11.000	Dec 15 87	100.55	9.45
Canada	10.250	Feb 1 88	100.25	9.75
Canada	11.750	Feb 1 88	100.95	9.75
Canada	9.750	Mar 6 88	99.95	9.80
Canada	10.500	Mar 15 88	100.40	9.85
Canada	10.750	Oct 15 88	100.95	9.90
Canada	10.000	Nov 16 88	100.15	9.85
Canada	9.750	Dec 15 88	99.00	10.55
Canada	11.000	Feb 15 89	101.45	9.95

Provincial bonds

July 31 1987	Int. rate %	Maturity date	Bid $	Yield %
Alberta Govt Tel	11.500	May 31 03	101.80	11.25
Alberta Mun Fin	12.250	Dec 15 02	106.85	11.30
Alberta	7.875	Oct 15 91	93.15	9.90
B C Hydro	10.000	Oct 15 00	94.75	10.75
B C Hydro	13.500	Jan 15 11	117.05	11.40
British Columbia	11.500	Aug 23 88	101.55	9.95
British Columbia	10.750	Feb 6 90	101.55	10.05
British Columbia	12.000	Oct 20 93	106.45	10.55
British Columbia	11.000	Jun 20 95	102.10	10.60
Manitoba	11.750	Mar 15 93	105.20	10.50
Manitoba	11.500	May 15 95	106.30	10.30
Manitoba	10.000	Dec 5 99	95.90	10.60
New Brunswick Elec	11.750	Feb 8 93	104.95	10.55
New Brunswick Elec	10.375	May 15 95	99.05	10.55
New Brunswick Elec	7.875	Nov 15 96	85.20	10.40
New Brunswick Elec	10.000	Mar 1 00	94.55	10.80
New Brunswick	11.500	Oct 19 88	101.65	10.00
New Brunswick	9.500	Mar 2 90	98.45	10.20
New Brunswick	9.875	Jul 17 98	95.35	10.60

Corporate bonds

July 31 1987	Int. .ate %	Maturity date	Bid $	Yield %
B C Telephone	11.350	Nov 15 05	100.30	11.31
Bell Canada	11.625	May 2 90	103.25	10.24
Bell Canada	12.650	Nov 15 03	108.75	11.45
Bell Canada	11.000	Oct 15 04	99.75	11.03
Bell Canada	9.850	Oct 15 05	92.50	10.80
Bow Valley Res CV	11.000	Mar 1 01	50.00	.00
C I L Inc	12.375	Dec 15 93	108.20	10.57
C I L Inc	14.500	Apr 15 96	108.15	12.91
Canadian Utilities	12.000	Jul 15 00	106.75	11.01
Canterra Energy CV	8.500	Jun 15 00	83.00	11.00
Consumers Gas	13.250	Mar 15 93	110.40	10.74
Dofasco Inc	13.500	Nov 1 00	108.00	12.26
Finning Tractor CV	11.500	Jun 24 01	120.00	8.95
Gaz Metro	11.500	Nov 15 05	100.50	11.43
Genstar Corp	11.750	Jun 1 95	100.50	11.65
Imperial Oil	12.000	Mar 31 93	106.55	10.44
Interprovincial Pip	12.700	Nov 15 04	110.50	11.30
Ivaco Inc CV	9.500	Apr 15 10	106.00	8.88
Maclean Hunter CV	8.250	May 1 04	222.00	.00
Maritime Tel & Tel	10.950	Dec 15 05	98.00	11.21
Nova Corp	12.000	Dec 17 90	103.25	10.82

1. The interest rate at which the bond was issued.
2. The date at which the bond matures. (Note that some bonds are extendable beyond the maturity date.)
3. The bid price is the price people are prepared to pay to buy the bond. Note that bonds are denominated in thousands, but are quoted in hundreds.
4. The yield to maturity. If you buy a $1000 bond that has a 15% interest rate, and redeem it at maturity for $1,000, your yield is 15%. If, however, you buy a $1,000 bond with a 13-1/2% interest rate, you would have had to pay $1,003 for it last February 27. Its yield to maturity on September 1, 1987 was 9%.

MUTUAL FUNDS

Mutual funds

For week ending July 30

① Funds	Net asset value per share ($)	Change over week ($)
PRICE QUOTATIONS	②	③
Institute members		
20/20 Group Financial		
Cdn. Conv. Deb.	10.06	−0.03
Cdn. Conv. Pfd.	10.98	+0.05
Sunset	13.16	+0.02
A.M.D.		
Amer. Blue Chip	12.45	+0.25
Cdn. Blue Chip	12.64	+0.12
Dividend	9.89	−0.02
Fixed Income	9.88	−0.01
Resources Can.	14.35	+0.38
Option Equity	4.57	+0.09
Preferred Income	10.28	unch.
Special	5.51	+0.11
AIC Advantage	12.46	+0.32
All Canadian		
Compound	17.98	+0.22
Dividend	14.06	+0.18
Nat. Resources	7.27	+0.19
Revenue Growth	3.62	+0.01
Univest	7.57	+0.16
Allied Capital Mgmt.		
Canadian	6.34	+0.09
Dividend	4.93	−0.05
Income	5.49	−0.03
International	7.92	+0.04
International ($US)	5.93	−0.03
Assoc. Inv.	7.73	+0.05
Bolton Tremblay Group		
Canada Cumul.	17.78	+0.32
International	9.11	+0.27
Pfd. Income	10.99	+0.02

1. The name of the fund. Many companies sponsor more than one fund. They are grouped under the sponsor's name.
2. Mutual fund quotations do not list the "price" of the share. Each share of a mutual fund is in fact a fraction of the entire holdings of the fund. When you sell your shares back to the company, the money you will get will be the market value of the underlying securities, divided by the number of shares outstanding. This is the Net Asset Value Per Share.
3. The change in the net asset value per share from the day before.

OPTIONS

Stock options are the right to buy or sell shares of a company's stock for a specific price within a specified time period. The options market is similar to the stock market, except here, you simply buy or sell the option to buy or sell the stock. The following format comes from *The New York Times.*

Chicago Board Options Exchange

① Option & NY Close	② Strike Price	③ Calls-Last Sep	Oct	Nov	④ Puts-Last Sep	Oct	Nov
MayDS	45	r	2 1/2	3 1/4	r	r	r
45 3/4	50	3/16	5/8	1 3/8	r	r	r
Mc Don	50	5 1/2	r	7	r	5/8	7/8
55 5/8	55	1 3/8	2 5/8	4	3/4	r	2 3/4
55 5/8	60	1/8	3/4	2 1/8	5	r	5 1/2
55 5/8	65	1/16	r	1	r	r	r
McDn o	46 5/8	9 1/8	s	r	r	s	r

1. The name of the company, in this case, McDonald's (as in hamburgers); the closing price of the stock itself on the New York Exchange.

2. The price at which the owner of the option has the right to buy or sell the stock. It is called the strike price. Notice that options are traded at four different strike prices. The range, from $50 to $65, is an estimate of where the stock might be selling in the next few months.
3. A call option is the right to buy the stock at the strike price any time until the third Friday of the specified month.
4. A put is the right to sell the stock at the strike price. The letter ‘s’ means that no option was offered. The letter ‘r’ means that the option wasn’t traded that day.

FUTURES/COMMODITIES

Financial futures are contracts to deliver, at a specified time and price, some financial instrument. Canadian dollars are traded on the International Money Market (IMM) in a standard contract of $100,000. Contracts have delivery dates of March, June, September, and December. These examples are from *The New York Times.*

Financial Futures

Financial

①			②	③		④	⑤
—Season— High	Low		High	Low	Close	Chg.	Open Interest
CANADIAN DOLLAR (IMM)							
100,000 dollars; $ per Canadian dollar							
.7673	.6950	Sep	.7582	.7546	.7555	—49	9,586
.7667	.6960	Dec	.7550	.7517	.7522	—52	14,079
.7655	.7052	Mar	.7512	.7480	.7489	—55	1,380
.7650	.7325	Jun	.7494	.7455	.7456	—58	129

1. The highest and lowest price of a contract to be delivered in each of the contract months.
2. The highest and lowest price for each delivery contract on the trading day.
3. The last price at which contracts were written on that trading day.
4. The highest and lowest trading price of the contract.
5. Open interest is the number of contracts that have been written. There are, for example, 9,586 contracts outstanding for $100,000 Canadian for September delivery. That represents a cash investment of more than $19 million (19,096 X $2,000 initial margin requirement), and a trading value of almost $1 billion.

Commodity Futures

A commodity futures contract is an agreement by which a buyer and seller agree to trade a specific amount of a commodity at some specific future date.

①			②		③	④	⑤
—Contract—							Open
High	Low		High	Low	Settle	Chg.	Int
LUMBER (CME)							
130,000 bd. ft.; $ per 1,000 bd.ft.							
219.70	159.50	Sep	207.00	204.00	206.70	+2.90	1,164
202.50	156.70	Nov	192.90	187.80	192.40	+4.50	3,586
194.20	156.00	Jan	185.30	180.90	184.40	+3.20	1,071
188.80	156.00	Mar	180.00	176.00	179.50	+3.10	715
184.50	164.50	May	176.50	172.40	176.30	+2.60	296
179.40	165.30	Jul	175.60	172.30	174.40	+2.10	170
178.00	165.50	Sep	172.60	170.10	173.40	+2.00	66
Est. sales 1,925. Tue.'s sales 1,865.							
Tue.'s open int 7,068, off 107.							

1. The highest and lowest trading price of a contract to be delivered in January, March and May.
2. The highest and lowest price for each contract on the trading day.
3. The last price at which contracts were written on that trading day.
4. The change in the closing price since the day before.
5. Open interest is the number of contracts which have been written. There are a total of 2,082 contracts outstanding each for 130,000 board feet of lumber for delivery between January and May. That represents a cash investment of more than $4 million (2,082 x $2,000 initial margin requirement) and a trading value of almost $40 billion.

FOREIGN EXCHANGE

Currencies are quoted because they are traded in increasing volumes to pay for imports and exports of countries around the world. This is the *Financial Post's* listing.

1. The name of the currency.
2. The number of $U.S. per unit of currency ($1 Canadian = .7564 $U.S.)
3. The number of units of currency per $U.S. ($1 U.S. = $1.32 Canadian.)

FOREIGN EXCHANGE

Friday, September 4, 1987

The New York foreign exchange selling rates below apply to trading among banks in amounts of $1 million and more, as quoted at 3 p.m. Eastern time by Bankers Trust Co. Retail transactions provide fewer units of foreign currency per dollar.

①	②		③	
	U.S. $ equiv.		Currency per U.S. $	
Country	Fri.	Thurs.	Fri.	Thurs.
Argentina (Austral) ...	.4554	.4554	2.196	2.196
Australia (Dollar)	.7238	.7228	1.3816	1.3835
Austria (Schilling)	.07924	.07943	12.62	12.59
Belgium (Franc)				
Commercial rate	[illegible]	.02685	37.31	37.25
Financial rate	.02665	.02670	37.52	37.46
Brazil (Cruzado)	.02067	.02066	48.39	48.39
Britain (Pound)	1.6540	1.6570	.6046	.6035
30-Day Forward	1.6504	1.6535	.6059	.6048
90-Day Forward	1.6427	1.6461	.6087	.6075
180-Day Forward	1.6343	1.6376	.6119	.6106
Canada (Dollar)	.7616	.7608	1.3130	1.3144
30-Day Forward	.7606	.7597	1.3148	1.3163
90-Day Forward	.7583	.7574	1.3187	1.3203
180-Day Forward	.7550	.7539	1.3245	1.3264
Chile (Official rate) ...	.004495	.004495	222.49	222.49
China (Yuan)	.2687	.2687	3.722	3.722
Colombia (Peso)	.004002	.004002	249.90	249.90
Denmark (Krone)	.1445	.1448	6.9200	6.9075
Ecuador (Sucre)				
Official rate	.004963	.004963	201.50	201.50
Floating rate	.005797	.005797	172.50	172.50
Finland (Markka)	.2294	.2288	4.3600	4.3700
France (Franc)	.1664	.1667	6.0100	6.0000
30-Day Forward	.1663	.1666	6.0125	6.0027
90-Day Forward	.1661	.1664	6.0205	6.0105
180-Day Forward	.1656	.1658	6.0390	6.0300
Greece (Drachma)	.007315	.007299	136.70	137.00
Hong Kong (Dollar) ...	.1282	.1282	7.7990	7.8020
India (Rupee)	.07692	.07692	13.00	13.00
Indonesia (Rupiah)	.0006105	.0006105	1638.00	1638.00
Ireland (Punt)	1.4830	1.4790	.6743	.6761
Israel (Shekel)	.6223	.6223	1.607	1.607
Italy (Lira)	.000792	.0007704	1300.00	1298.00
Japan (Yen)	.007052	.007090	141.80	141.05
30-Day Forward	.007072	.007110	141.41	140.65
90-Day Forward	.007111	.007150	140.63	139.86
180-Day Forward	.007177	.007113	139.33	138.64
Jordan (Dinar)	2.9070	2.9070	.344	.344
Kuwait (Dinar)	3.551	3.551	.2816	.2816
Lebanon (Pound)	.003731	.003731	268.00	268.00
Malaysia (Ringgit)	.3986	.3986	2.5085	2.5087

HOW TO READ AN ANNUAL REPORT

Most people who buy stocks don't read the annual reports of the companies in which they have invested. That's mostly because annual reports are often boring and self-serving. But companies are getting smarter about communicating with their shareholders, and maybe the improvements in readability, plus the massive demonstrable evidence that you can't take anyone else's word for it will encourage more people to crack the covers.

All annual reports have to have four financial statements. You should look at them, as well as the president's report to the shareholders (that's you).

Financial statement #1 is the balance sheet. It's the same as your net worth statement. On the left (in Canada) is what the company owns. On the right, what the company owes, plus the shareholders' interest in the company. "Assets equals liabilities plus shareholders' equity." This means if the company owns more than it owes, you have something of value.

Financial statement #2 is the earnings statement. It might be called the profit-and-loss statement or the revenue and expenditure statement. It tells you how much was taken in and how much was spent. If the first is bigger than the second, the company made a profit. If the second is bigger than the first, it didn't.

Financial statement #3 is the retained earnings statement. These are the profits earned over the years that you haven't received as dividends. They belong to you, but your directors have decided to reinvest them in the business.

Financial statement #4 is the changes in financial position statement. It may be called Source and Application of Funds, or Source and Disposition of Funds, but it is basically a link between the company's balance sheet for two consecutive years. It tells you how the company got money during the year and how it used the money.

The president's report to shareholders will tell you the highlights of the past year, and the outlook for the current year, including expansion and contraction plans, management and product changes.

You can get a really good guide to reading financial statements. The Canadian Securities Institute (with offices in Toronto, Vancouver, Calgary and Montreal) puts one out, as do several investment houses. All you have to do is ask.

MAKING ECONOMICS MAKE SENSE

This is not an oxymoron. Economic data can make sense, and from time to time, you want reassurance of that fact. You can get some satisfaction out of the trade papers, which won't sort out what's important, but which certainly will keep you in touch with the world of business, finance and the politics thereof. One of the best all-around sources:

The Economist
P.O. Box 904
Farmingdale, New York

Canadian print sources include:

The Globe and Mail, Report on Business (daily)
Canadian Newspapers Company Limited
444 Front Street West
Toronto, Ontario
M5V 2S9

Financial Post (weekly)
Maclean Hunter Limited
777 Bay Street
Toronto, Ontario
M5W 1A7

Financial Times (weekly)
Southam Inc.
920 Young Street
Suite 500
Toronto, Ontario
M4W 3L5

Canadian Business (monthly)
CB Media Limited
70 The Esplanade
2nd Floor
Toronto, Ontario
M5E 1R2

Your Money (monthly)
CB Media Limited
56 The Esplanade
2nd Floor
Toronto, Ontario
M5E 1A7

The Canadian Money Saver
P.O. Box 370
Bath, Ontario
K0H 1G0

American print sources include:

The Wall Street Journal (daily)
200 Burnett Road
Chicopee, Massachusetts 01021

Barron's (weekly)
200 Burnett Road
Chicopee, Massachusetts 01021

U.S. News and World Report (weekly)
McGraw-Hill Inc.
1221 Avenue of the Americas
New York, N.Y. 10020

There are a couple of radio and TV shows that concentrate on money matters. TV Ontario has "Moneysworth", Global TV in Ontario has a weekly programme, "EveryBody's Business", CBC has a weekly programme, "Venture." "Wall Street Week" and "Nightly Business Report" are American public broadcasting system productions. All cover personal finance as well as current financial news.

Among the annual crop of business material, the Economic Council of Canada (Ottawa), the C.D. Howe Research Institute (Toronto), and the Department of Finance (Ottawa) all put out eminently readable, *short* books on the state of the world economy and Canada's place in it. Specific reference books that I like include *The Delaney Report on RRSP's*, by Tom Delaney (Toronto: McGraw Hill Ryerson) and the *Dictionary of Finance and Investment Terms*, by John Dowes and Jordan E. Goodman (Barrons Educational Services Inc.).

Give it a try for six months. If you like it, you'll then be ready for more depth and breadth and you'll feel comfortable with the weird ways of this particular world.

CHAPTER 20

Your Place in the New Economy

> Keep strong if possible. In any case, keep cool. Have unlimited patience. Never corner an opponent, and always assist him to save his face. Put yourself in his shoes—so as to see things through his eyes. Avoid self-righteousness like the devil—nothing is so self-blinding.
>
> —B.H. Liddell Hart

It's a doggy-dog world out there, according to the young friend of a friend of a friend. It's also, as we said when we started, a world of tremendous change—most significantly, change from a world firmly based on the discovery, processing and distribution of natural resources to one in which jobs and wealth are increasingly the product of discovering, processing, and distributing information and knowledge.

But there are lots of other changes you have to take into account if you're going to perfect your good money management practices. And you're going to have to take account of them yourself because nobody is going to take you by the arm and whisper in your ear that the world has changed. That's one of the first big lessons of transitional times: you can't take the background environment in which you're going to do your spending and saving and investing and borrowing for granted. You can't take for granted stable prices, or easy trade relations, or predictable tax laws.

If you can't take for granted all the things we used to take for granted, then you also can't make as much use of mass analysis and mass advice. Remember what we said right at the beginning of this book—you care about your money more than anyone else in the world. Other people can help you acquire the skills and knowledge you need to make informed decisions, but *you* have to take responsibility for making the final decision.

So let's look again at some of the big structural changes that are becoming increasingly visible—so you can think about how these changes may affect your own job, and the prospects for the next generation.

First, the place of natural resources in the world economy. Never before in the history of the world has a collapse in raw material prices *not* resulted in a global depression within a year or two. That's what the business cycle was all about. Yet raw material prices collapsed almost ten years ago and the depression has been confined to pockets in the industrialized world. It begins to appear that whereas the health of the natural resources sector used to be central to the health of the industrial sector, now it's only marginal. And we can see, in the employment numbers in all the primary industries, that in fact, those industries are no longer big employers. Agriculture, for example, even up to the Second World War, used to employ one out of every three Canadians. Today, fewer than one out of 25 works the land. The same is true in mining, fishing and logging.

Even with falling employment and historically low prices, output is rising. It's rising in the primary products sector, and it's rising in the manufacturing sector. This is a critical change from the past, and a good indication of how information is being built into production processes—information that used to be supplied by people.

A lot has been written about how technological change means de-industrialization; and how we will all end up either serving hamburgers at McDonald's or practicing our digital dexterity on a computer keyboard. But technological change is not creating less industry—the world is producing more goods than ever before. However, it's doing it with fewer people and with less raw material. A good example of this is the communications business. Formerly, a ton of copper wire was needed to transmit a certain number of telephone messages; now it takes only 100 pounds of fibreglass cable. We need to use only five percent as much energy to produce the fibreglass as we needed to produce the copper wire.

Another example can be found in the forest products industry. Instead of people sizing up a log to decide whether it should be cut into two-by-fours or one-by-sixes, a computerized sawing machine can scan the internal structure of the log, spot the knots, review the orders on hand in the saw mill, factor in the various spot prices for lumber, almost instantaneously decide how the log should be cut, and cut it. Such a mill in British Columbia gets ten percent more lumber out of each log, and uses twenty percent fewer people to do it. This formerly labour-intensive industry has been transformed into a knowledge-intensive one.

These kinds of changes have enormous implications for government policies (they now have to choose between whether to have policies which favour production or which favour employment; historically the same policy served both purposes) and for individual decisions—what new education do we need? Where should we live? In what should we invest?

There's another big change we should keep in the backs of our minds. That is the tremendous growth in the trade in money as opposed to the trade in goods and services. Money was invented so that traders wouldn't have to schlepp bags of whatever they produced around every time they wanted something someone else made. Trade in goods (and their invisible twin, services) has always been the focus of the real world; money was the facilitator—the symbol economy. But since the early 1970s, when the world shifted from fixed to floating exchange rates, the thing people are trading more than anything else is money. According to Peter Drucker in *Frontiers of Management*, foreign exchange transactions are twelve times bigger than global trade in goods and services, and the London-Euro currency market, in which the world's financial institutions borrow from and lend to each other, turns over $75 trillion a year, which is at least 25 times the value of trade in goods and services.

No one really knows—let me rephrase that—no one I know really knows why capital flows have taken on a life of their own. But more and more people understand that the *fact* affects our personal financial well-being. Thirld World countries have built up debt that no amount of economic growth will enable them to repay. Since most of this debt is owed to Canadian, American, and European banks, we are paying more for our mortgages and our banking services so that these institutions can build up their loan loss reserves and eventually write off the debts. And as investors, we are getting smaller dividends than if it all hadn't happened.

The United States has gone from being the world's biggest investor in other people's countries (weren't multinationals an American invention?) to being the world's biggest host to foreign direct investment. Canadians have poured $35 billion into the U.S. in the last ten years to set up subsidiaries there. The American budget deficit and trade deficit have turned the U.S.A. from the world's premier creditor to the world's biggest debtor. And that fact affects us personally, too. The U.S. administration used high interest rates, not just to get rid of inflation, but to attract all that capital so it could run a budget deficit. Successive Canadian governments use high interest rates to hold up the value of the Canadian dollar. (Today's interest rates may not be high by 1980 standards, but they are still higher than in other politically stable countries). Much of the protectionist sentiment in the U.S.A. stems from its inability or unwillingness to deal with its own domestic problems. Yet it affects our own personal financial decisions. Although we can identify things that are different from the way they have been for decades and even generations, no one has yet come up with a definitive statement on what it all means and where it will all end. It is not clear whether exchange rates will stabilize; whether the American trade and budget deficit will decline on schedule; whether the Japanese trade surplus will also decline; whether there will be enough economic growth in the world that the Third World will repay some of its debt and the world's financial institutions will gracefully and without incident write off the rest.

Nor is it clear whether at some point foreigners will stop lending to the United States; whether the ensuing American dollar devaluation will create runaway inflation or deflation; whether the commodity-producing countries will default massively on their debts, thereby triggering a banking crisis.

What is much clearer is that all this mucky stuff—the relationships we don't quite understand—means that unpredictability is the only certainty for the forseeable future. The next step is to figure out how you can move toward financial security.

What I've tried to do throughout this book is provide you with a framework within which to make your own decisions. Just to recap, think of personal money management in four specific areas: cash management, which includes budgetting, saving and spending; debt management, which requires decisions about how much you borrow, and how big a mortgage to carry; risk management, which involves all insurance decisions, as well as estate planning; and investment management, wherein you decide what to do with your savings. It is clear that decisions in one area may affect decisions in other areas—something to keep in mind at all times.

Although I am all for personal responsibility, this does not mean you have to do everything yourself. Investment counsellors, financial advisors, mutual funds are all perfectly legitimate helpers. Remember that you are the chairman of your own personal financial business—get advice when you feel you need it—just don't follow it blindly, without evaluation.

FINAL WORDS OF CAUTION

- Never, ever, buy an investment you don't understand. If you're a beginner, forget the hype about buying on margin, leveraging with options, shorting anything, or speculating in commodities or currencies. You will make more money if your investments *don't* provide the excitement in your life.
- Never, ever, buy an investment with which you're not comfortable.
- Never, ever, buy an investment on a hot tip, unless it's the third time the tipster has come round, and the first two times he was right. And even then, consider it carefully.
- Never, ever, buy an investment that doesn't have a purpose in your portfolio.
- Diversify your holdings, but not so much that you can't supervise them. If you're going to do it all yourself, a dozen different holdings seems barely manageable. If you have decided on a portfolio that includes assets other than securities, consider mutual funds for diversification. If you have a lot of money, and managing it isn't your full time job, consider using an investment counsellor, who at the very least will keep track, do the paper work, and brief you regularly.
- Review your investment objectives once a year or if something big happens in your life (marriage, death, etc.) or in the world.
- Be of good cheer and keep in mind that you're embarking on a difficult task. You're running an obstacle course that includes being patient, not selling until you have something better to do with your money, and cutting your losses short. No one is right all the time—not you, not the host of well-meaning professionals who have only your best interest at heart—and their own commissions, sales fees, service charges and premiums. You will get no real sympathy when you worry aloud about your investments.
- Never abdicate the overall responsibility for your own financial well-being. Remember at all times—the gods will help you, but only if you take a good helping for yourself.

Index

Credits

Every reasonable effort has been made to find copyright holders of excerpted material. The publishers would be pleased to have any errors or omissions brought to their attention.

Excerpt from Economic Council Report on p. 8 from the Economic Council of Canada. Budget checklist on p. 64-67 from the Royal Bank. Reprinted with permission. Information used for Rental and Home Ownership Costs chart on p. 79 from Statistics Canada, Prices and Price Index Division. Home-Buying Checklist on p. 80 reprinted with permission from *Changing Times* magazine, © 1981 Kiplinger Washington Editors, Inc., Nov. 1981. This reprint is not to be altered in any way, except with permission from *Changing Times*. Deductions and Tax Credits chart on p. 126-127 reprinted with permission from *Touche Ross: Your Guide to Canadian Personal Tax Reform* by Mary Turner, Prentice-Hall Canada, Inc., Scarborough, 1987. RRSP charts on p. 146-147 and p. 156-157 from *The Delaney Report on RRSPs – 1987*, by Tom Delaney, McGraw-Hill Ryerson, Toronto, 1987. Reprinted with permission from the author. Estate Planning Questionnaire on p. 163-166 adapted from the Royal Trust Company's Will Planning worksheet. Material used with permission. Comparative Investment Alternatives Table on p. 183 from *Your Money Matters*, reprinted with permission from the Royal Bank. "Should You Be In the Stock Market?" reprinted with permission from *Changing Times Magazine*, © 1975 Kiplinger Washington Editors, Inc., June 1975. This reprint is not to be altered in any way, except with permission from *Changing Times*. Bond chart on p. 201 reprinted with permission from the Canadian Bond Rating Service. Stock quotations on p. 243-244, 250-251, 252, 255 reprinted with permission from the *Financial Post*. Listing from the Report on Business p. 246 reprinted with permission from the *Globe and Mail*. Listings on p. 248, 252, 254 reprinted with permission from the *New York Times*.